ABCs *of* Cultural -*Isms*

Bible Truth or Grave Consequences

ABCs *of* Cultural -*Isms*

Bible Truth or Grave Consequences

DEBRA RAE

Packaged by WinePress Publishing, PO Box 428, Enumclaw, WA 98022. The views expressed or implied in this work do not necessarily reflect those of WinePress Publishing. Ultimate design, content, and editorial accuracy of this work are the responsibilities of the author.

Cover by Ragont Design

Unless otherwise noted, all Scriptures are taken from the King James Version of the Holy Bible.

Rotherham, Joseph Bryant. 1981. *The Emphasized Bible*. Grand Rapids: Kregel Publication.

ISBN 1-57921-483-5
Library of Congress Catalog Card Number: 2002107779

Dedication

This work is dedicated to the Lord Jesus and His justified followers everywhere who, despite having fallen, never fail to dust off and pull themselves up again (Prov. 24:16). It is likewise dedicated to my loving husband, whom God has used in no small measure to grant me the desires of my heart (Ps. 37:4).

Contents

CHAPTER 1

THE SIN FACTOR

> . . . Unto Him [Jesus Christ] that loved us, and washed us from our sins *(hamartia)* in His own blood . . . (Rev. 1:5).

Every Christian has a testimony. Mine started in Sunday school with the simple refrain: "Into my heart, into my heart, come into my heart, Lord Jesus." This I sang as a guileless second grader with hands neatly folded and eyes tightly closed. In that instant of time, while yet seated on my little wooden bench, I opened wide my heart and, as a result, fixed the course of my entire life.

Through the years, I have been blessed immeasurably by the kiss of God. Nevertheless, I remain but a sinner, saved by grace. Granted, in today's culture of tolerance, "sin" may well be considered an archaic term. Seldom is it spoken except, perhaps, with tongue in cheek. In reality, sin packs a wallop that exceeds most human expectations. I know by experience that it never fails to reap what it sows. In the end, sin earns the disagreeable wages of death. For these reasons, I realize my need to take heed (Gal. 6:7–8; Rom. 6:23).

In order to sidestep sin, I have undertaken study of its attributes. An especially pernicious Greek word for sin, *poneros*, characterizes

Satan, whose sin knows no bounds. Not content to face his inevitable fate alone, the devil actively recruits as many as he can to accompany him en route to perdition. While active evil in no way characterizes my failings as a born-again Christian, *poneros* is not the only word for sin. The New Testament describes sin in a number of relevant ways—for example, stumbling, albeit unwittingly, while negotiating one's path or even straying from that path altogether.

When the apostle Paul wrote, "If after the manner of men, I have fought with beasts at Ephesus," he addressed the primary amusement among Romans of the early Christian era. In so doing, Paul referenced yet another Greek word for sin. You see, in ancient times, thrill seekers required criminals, but particularly Christians, to entertain huge, jeering crowds by fighting wild beasts (1 Cor. 15:32).

Visualize with me, if you will, an ancient arena: *With javelin in hand, the contestant faces his antagonist—a beast poised to maim and kill. Throngs cheer as the sixty-five-foot run ensues. Almost as if in slow motion, the spear-thrower balances rhythm of his legs with back-and-forth motion of the javelin. A split-second distraction; then, suddenly, the release—a mere snap of the wrist executed with explosive effort. Taunting onlookers roar, "HAMARTIA!" The mark is missed with grave consequences following.*

And so it is with sin. Sin misses the mark, overtaking its defenseless prey as assuredly as holiday season weight fluctuation—but with far graver consequences.

Hamartia is one of many Greek words for sin. Simply put, it means to miss the mark with grave consequences following.

The Mark: God's Word

To miss the mark presupposes a well-defined, fully accessible target. Even today, the mark for which believers rightly aim remains the "more sure Word." The traditional (and I believe correct) Bible position is that of verbal plenary, which maintains that in its original language, the written Word is fully "God-breathed" to the slightest stroke of the smallest alphabet letter. As such, it is profitable for doctrine, reproof, correction, and instruction in righteousness (Matt. 5:18; 2 Tim. 3:16).

According to the founder of Harvard's graduate school of law—by laws of evidence, as presentable in a court of law, the Bible clearly seems to be inspired. Nevertheless, for years, skeptics discredited the Old Testament for lacking secular collaboration regarding existence of the Hittites. In time, sound archaeological evidence silenced doubters with confirmation of the Bible's historical accuracy regarding this once mighty empire.

Of three hundred prophecies surrounding the birth, death, and resurrection of Christ, all were fulfilled precisely despite impossible odds of only one chance in ten to the ninetieth power. God's living Word made flesh, Jesus Christ is the Christian's supremely worthy role model. God's Word serves as the plumb line for truth and justifiably so. Validating authenticity of the New Testament alone are nearly eight thousand manuscripts and fragments thereof.

While God's Word ("made flesh" and written) is the Christian's worthy focus, postmodernists fail to designate any bulls-eye whatsoever. To them, truth is relative and varies per individual and circumstance. In contrast, Paul admonishes believers to hone in on the so-called mark. How? By proving what is good, acceptable, and perfect in God's sight (Rom. 12:2). Unfortunately, even the best meaning evangelical Christians miss this mark by embracing tenets contrived by the world's celebrated thinkers, not the least of which include Hegel, Feuerback, Darwin, Marx, and Freud.

George Frederick Hegel (1820s)
Hamartia: Nix Right or Wrong

While God's law in itself cannot save, it nonetheless leads the lost to Christ. According to Galatians 3:24, the law serves as a schoolmaster, or "child conductor." As a trusted escort, the law faithfully wards off bad company, thus insuring safety in the child's timely transport from one destination (lost) to the next (saved, Gal. 2:16; 1 Tim. 1:8).

Furthermore, the law is for the lawless. Upon first attending school, children do not know the rules; they are lawless. To provide protection, order, safety, efficiency, and comfort to all, master teachers enforce appropriate rules. In time, their well-trained students function within the spirit of that law and, as a result, require no posted directives (1 Tim. 1:9).

In similar fashion, the perfect law of liberty follows the spirit of law, not solely its letter. When God's law becomes engrafted on hearts of practicing believers, their liberty is defined not by freedom *from* law but rather by freedom *in* law. You see, Christ came to *magnify* the moral law; to *honor* civil, natural, health/dietary laws; and to *fulfill* ceremonial laws (James 1:25; Matt. 5:17; 1 Pet. 2:13; Gal. 3:3).

Though the law is limited, it nonetheless has value. Notwithstanding, in the 1820s, George Frederick Hegel undermined the certainty of fixed rights or wrongs. This will-worshipping German philosopher portrayed the Ten Commandments as being arbitrary. Hegel determined his "truth," not by God's immutable law, but rather by democratic consensus (Rom. 3:20; Gal. 3:21).

Simply put, Hegelian conflict resolution is group consensus under peer pressure. Commonly used in business and education, collaborative partnerships align with today's trendy New Age mindset. Even believers fail to escape the deadly trap of moral relativism spawned by "group think." For example, broad-minded Christians often fall for Satan's provocative question, "Hath God said?" Regarding alternative lifestyles, divorce, and anything-goes ecumenicism, many unwisely, even if naively, weigh in the "yes, buts" heavier than solid scriptural text (Gen. 3:1).

Beliefs, as these, spring from Hegel's morally-iffy contribution to postmodern thought. They spell *hamartia*.

Ludwig Feuerback (1830s)
Hamartia: God is Make-Believe

The first verse of the first book of the Bible tells it all: "In the beginning, *God*." The Father is a *spirit*, Jesus is a quickening *spirit*, and the Holy *Spirit* empowers for service. When Moses, Saul, and those who tarried in Jerusalem encountered this selfsame Spirit in the burning bush, on the road to Damascus, and on Solomon's porch, respectively, not one wondered if that Spirit was real. Countless believers since then (this author among them) have similarly encountered "the real thing." Changed lives prove it (John 4:23–24; 1 Cor. 15:45; Acts 1:8; 2; 9:3–6; Exod. 3:2,4).

But in the 1830s, one German philosopher, Ludwig Feuerback, surmised that if Hegel were correct in assuming that there is no right or wrong, then it stands to reason that religionists have conceived of a make-believe god. When demoted to mere fabrication, god logically takes on characteristics that suit anyone's fancy.

The church itself has fallen prey to Feuerback's mistaken deduction. Take, for example, Catholic priest Father Thomas Berry. A self-proclaimed geologian and spokesperson for *Gaia*, goddess of Mother Earth, Father Berry draws heavily from the patron saint of the New Age movement, French Jesuit Pierre Teilhard de Chardin. Accordingly, Father Berry blames Christians for earth's attrition. His tainted brand of eco-justice scraps the Cartesian Theory, which correctly distinguishes human life from earth, whose resources are intended by God for human consumption and stewardship (Gen. 2:15–16).

Springing from Feuerback's spiritually-iffy contribution to postmodern thought, these concepts spell *hamartia.*

Charles Darwin (1860s and 1870s)
Hamartia: "Science" Preempts Faith

Contrary to God's Word, naturalism is belief that all of life is explicable solely by means of scientific data; therefore, religious verities of any make-believe god are nothing short of illusionary. In the 1860s and 1870s, Unitarian universalist Charles Darwin posed theories of evolution, survival of the fittest, and historic optimism. In so doing, this English biologist volleyed traditional scientific thinking into the welcoming court of postmodern thought (1 Tim. 6:20).

When interviewed in Seattle on a public affairs presentation of KTBW (6 March 2000), physicist and Boeing systems engineer Mike Sabourin asked the provocative question, "Can a scientist *not* believe in God?" Indeed, the founder of the Scientific Method, Francis Bacon, was a devout believer. The same is true of numbers of eminent scientists responsible for scientific astronomy, Boyle's Law, Newtonian mechanics, calculus, modern taxonomy, galactic astronomy, electromagnetic theory, the Second Law of Thermodynamics, bacteriology, immunology, genetics, Maxwell's Equations in physics, modern computer science principles, and more.

By definition, science is systemized knowledge gained objectively, minus bias and emotions. It comprises an inductive method of searching, examining, measuring, collecting data, forming hypotheses, testing, and verifying.

Ideally, science deals with facts, but, as Mike pointed out, scientists are fallible humans with emotions and egos. Charles Darwin himself admitted that his rationale led him to the astonishing conclusion that the universe is *not* the result of chance. But, he reasoned further, his own mind is not to be trusted. Why not? Because it evolved from a monkey!

Dr. John F. Ashton has compiled decisive statements from fifty highly educated, critically thinking contemporary scientists who have joined the swelling ranks of those who believe in the biblical version of creation. According to *World* magazine (26 February 2000), scientists today are increasingly endorsing design as opposed to random chance.

Mistakenly, many presume that the Bible somehow wars against science. Intimidated and shamed by evolutionists and their noisy, though misguided rhetoric, many well-meaning Christians cower and, then, nod at the presumption of so-called theistic evolution. This they do by using ecclesiastical terms to mask their tacit endorsement of Darwin's godless, flimsy science (1 Tim. 6:20).

The truth is that reality is greater than science. You see, scientists who embrace naturalism give credence only to the physical realm. Their arbitrary assumption is reminiscent of an ambitious fisherman who cast his net repeatedly to collect and subsequently measure all fish caught. That none measured less than two inches led this fisherman to the flawed "scientific" conclusion over time that *all* fish measure at least two inches in length. Never mind that the weave of his fishing net allowed smaller fish to slip through. By ignoring the greater reality, our fisherman erred. The same is true of scientists who fail to recognize life's spiritual dimension.

Springing from Darwin's scientifically-iffy contribution to postmodern thought, Darwinian theory spells *hamartia*.

Karl Marx (late 1800s)
Hamartia: Science Governs Life on Planet Earth

In the late 1800s, German philosopher, economist, and social theorist Karl Marx devised dialectical materialism (or communism) and the *Communist Manifesto.* The Marxist-Leninist maxim of "earning one's keep on Planet Earth" is at the heart of today's love affair with sustainable development.

An United Nations buzzword, sustainable development holds to the underlying belief that humankind is a cancer, all of whose activities like eating meat and using appliances or air conditioning are deemed unsustainable. This central organizing and ruling principle of the global community insists that wealth must be redistributed and populations controlled.

Despite the fact that current population growth is slowing, many Christians buy into the myth of global overpopulation. Some mistake redistribution of the world's wealth for cheerful, voluntary giving orchestrated by God. Others blush without cause at their alleged guilt for marring the face of "Mother Earth." In hopes of establishing themselves as responsible world citizens, these exchange truth for lies.

Springing from Marx's socially-iffy contribution to postmodern thought, such concepts spell *hamartia.*

Sigmond Freud (early 1900s)
Hamartia: Sexual Pleasure is Life's Richest Reward

In likening union of Christ and His church to intimacy between a man and his wife, Paul typifies ultimate bliss—that of spiritual relationship with the altogether lovely one, Jesus Christ (Eph. 5).

In the early 1900s, Austrian physician and prolific writer Sigmond Freud perverted this biblical picture by inspiring worship of the god of sexuality. In formulating the concepts of *id, ego, superego,* and having studied the sub-and un-conscious mind, Freud perceived sexual conflict to be the source of mental and neurotic illness.

Neuroscience does not support Freud's foundational principle, repression of unwanted thought. Furthermore, his so-called science draws from literature and philosophy. Nevertheless, no other single theorist has equaled Freud's profound impact on the world's psychiatrists, psychologists, and social workers.

Although Freud dismissed all religious belief as a form of mental illness, his own psychobabble unveiled more of an ecclesiastical than a rationalistic bent. Given Freud's "war with God," as he termed it, it is ironic that psychoanalysis continues today in some religious circles. Liberal theologians, as Prussian-born Paul Tillich of Union Theological Seminary and Harvard Divinity School, give Freud place. In need of deliverance, many Christians, even ministers, worship at the altar of sexual gratification.

Today, Freud's bias is evident in Planned Parenthood's safer sex campaign, rampant Kinseyan sexuality, and the gay rights movement. Some enlightened postmodernists feel free to abandon their families for self-interest; to terminate an infant's life, if for no more compelling reason than convenience; and even to rape, rob, and rumble at will.

Springing from Freud's medically-iffy contribution to postmodern thought, these concepts spell *hamartia*.

Grave Consequences Following

For a season in Hebrew history, there was no king in Israel. Each one served self by doing what was deemed right in his own eyes. As a result, idolatry and confusion abounded. Things aren't much different today. If it is true that we are products of evolution, with sexual pleasure being our richest reward, it stands to reason that we are accountable to no god other than Self (Judges 17:6).

Preoccupied with self-esteem and self-fulfillment, groupies of the secular talk show circuit purport that nothing takes priority over self-will, wants, and desires. As in days of old, idolatry and confusion attend today's "Me Generation." For example, in the throes of recent presidential scandal, self-serving relativism contributed to feigned confusion as to what the linking verb "is" means! Doing what is right in one's own eyes not only undermines the sanctity of our nation's highest office. It also gives sway to Columbine-magnitude tragedies, not to mention the egregious merchandising of baby parts.

The church has not escaped the enemy's lies. Take the Laodicean Church of Revelation, Chapter 3. Significantly, Laodicea means "rule of the people." God soundly rebukes even this end-time church for missing the mark. Her spiritual indifference, self-sufficiency, and shameless materialism are embodied today in Christian gurus of "name it-claim it" fame.

My prayer is that we, as believers, might equip ourselves "to act as athletes in concert" for the faith of the Gospel. In order to sidestep sin that easily entangles, I invite you to join me in honing biblical focus as we stroll together through the alphabet of deceitful cultural-*isms* (Phil. 1:27; Heb. 12:1).

CHAPTER 2

HAMARTIA
ANTI-SEMITISM

> But now being made free from sin *(hamartia)*, and become servants to [the one true] God, ye have your fruit unto holiness, and the end everlasting life (Rom. 6:22).

Anti-Semitism Defined

Literally speaking, anti-Semitism is prejudice against Semitic people. A Semite is a member of any of the Near-or Middle-East peoples whose languages are related. Semites are descended from Shem (meaning "name" or "fame"), born the second son of Noah some ninety-eight years before the Flood (Gen. 11:10).

In ancient historical times, the world of the Semites was the Fertile Crescent. Principal Semitic peoples of ancient times included Babylonians and Assyrians (Akkadians); the Arameans of Syria; the Canaanites, including Palestinians and Hebrews; the Arabs and Ethiopians.

In practice, anti-Semitism means prejudice resulting in discrimination and/or persecution leveled specifically against the Jews as an ethnic group. A form of racism, anti-Semitism is widely spread, even in contemporary society.

Anti-Semitism at Work: Ancient Blood Feud

Today, extreme right-wing groups foster anti-Semitism throughout the world. Examples include the National Front in the U.K. and France, neo-Nazis in the U.S. and Germany, and the Palestine Liberation Organization (PLO) in Arab nations. The latter operates as a guerrilla army.

Anti-Semitic racism likewise exists in what appears to be less malignant form—namely, as an unconscious attitude based on preconceived notions or negative stereotypes. Though mere typecasting seems benign enough, history proves that impulsive reactions to stereotypes can be tragic. Such was the case in Hitler's Germany, where about six million Jews suffered extermination in the Holocaust of 1933–1945.

As a resident of Kuwait, I personally witnessed residuals of the infamous four-thousand-year-old blood feud between Ishmael (Arab Muslims) and Isaac (Jews)—all of whom vie tirelessly for the position of God's elect and for the land of promise. Muslim Arabs claim descent from Ishmael, whom they erroneously assign first-born status over Isaac as "seed of promise." This being the case, Ishmaelites do not acknowledge national Israel; any reference requires instead the politically preferred term, "Occupied Palestine."

A primary reason for my Bible's not being welcome in that area was its repeated use of the word, "Israel." Moreover, it failed to substantiate the faulty claim that Israel today is on Islamic sacred ground and must be retaken as a Palestinian-Arab state.

According to fundamental Islamic belief, every human is born Muslim and, if necessary, must be forced into submission. In general, Christians and Jews may be permitted to live, but only under Islamic domination. You see, *Dar al Islam* (House of Islam) is a form of cultural imperialism, elevating to the status of divine mandate the spirituality and culture of seventh-century Arabia. Its global charge is "one Arab nation with an eternal mission." Hyper-fundamentalist religious warriors take anti-Semitism one step further. They believe that the war is open until Israel ceases to exist and the last Jew in the world is eliminated. Only then will Islam's eternal mission be realized.

With these tenets in view, I undertook an adventurous journey by VW Bug in the summer of 1973. My AAA-assisted itinerary for this venture paralleled the Fertile Crescent with London its final destination. Upon entering Israel from Kuwait, Iraq, Jordan, Lebanon, and then Syria, I necessarily refused a stamp on my passport, lest I be forbidden reentry to the Arab countries from whence I came. While bold to share my faith in Jesus Christ, I intentionally avoided political discussions that would serve to inflame passions.

Anti-Semitism throughout History

Many may be surprised to learn that, historically, European Christians practiced anti-Semitism for nearly two thousand years. In the fourth century, when Christianity was adopted as the official religion of the Roman Empire, prejudice intensified against Jews who refused to convert. Because of the Crusades (1096–1291) and the Inquisition (the 1200s to the 1500s, and beyond), laws were passed forbidding Jews to own land and, in some instances, to earn their living of choice. From the sixteenth century, many cities forced Jews to live in separate areas, or ghettos.

The Jewish plight improved in the eighteenth and early nineteenth centuries. In time, however, anti-Semitism escalated in Austria, France, and Germany. 1881 pogroms (literally, "riots") in Poland and Russia caused many to flee. In the past century, hundreds of thousands have continued to die in Russian pogroms. Fascism and neo-Nazi racial theories resulted in organized persecution and genocide—specifically, the "final solution" to exterminate all "undesirables" in occupied Europe.

Even twenty-first-century tensions and hatred remain high. With intent to bring lasting peace and religious unity to the Middle East, the Pontiff's historic trip in March 2000 placed Pope John Paul II in an unprecedented position of influence; but his mission was to no avail. As is historically the case, name-calling and discriminatory practices escalated to murderous acts in the autumn of 2000. Violence and bloodshed in the West Bank and the Gaza Strip showed no signs of abating. When then Israeli Prime Minister Ehud Barak called for a "timeout" from peace negotiations, his Palestinian counterpart Yasser Arafat allegedly responded, "Go to h—-."

Plain teaching of the Bible affirms that historical patterns repeat themselves. Raul Hilberg's famous quote encapsulates the Jewish story: "First we are told, 'You're not good enough to live among us as Jews.' Then we are told, 'You're not good enough to live among us.' Finally we are told, 'You're not good enough to live'" (See Eccles. 3:15).

It is naive to presume that Islamic interests can be appeased by yielding territory and by reducing the size of Israel. The kingpin of controversy today is not her size, but rather the very existence of Israel.

Twenty-First Century Anti-Semitism Worldwide

Greece

Already, in the tender bloom of the twenty-first century, anti-Semitism has once again reared its head. While desecrating the largest Jewish cemetery in Greece, vandals scribbled their inspirited *mantra*, "Hitler was right!" A similar message appeared on a Jewish community web page. Apparently, this resulted from a presumed Jewish plot to remove the entry, "religious affiliation," from identity cards. 2,500 Greek Orthodox brethren joined protest leader Panayiotis Lyras in a march targeting Greece's small Jewish community. Their stated goal was to oppose an alleged Jewish "conspiracy" with European Union bureaucrats (*The Philadelphia Inquirer*, 1 June 2000, p. A10).

Russia

Today, Russia is divided into fifteen independent republics, much of whose land is too cold or dry for agriculture. Forty percent of Russia's 146 million live below poverty level. With an unemployment rate of 12.4 percent, virtually thousands are addicted to alcohol, drugs, pornography, and gambling. Since the early nineties, Russia has struggled to build a democratic political system and market economy, but inflation tops 86 percent. Prostitution, homelessness, and murder flood the front-page news. Life expectancy averages age sixty-seven. No wonder cynicism grips unregenerate Russian hearts.

While visiting Russia in the early nineties, my husband and I befriended our tour guide, a student at the university. Though manifestly reserved, and appropriately cautious, this young woman articulated the broadly held pessimism of her fellows. Given skyrocketing prices, long lines to secure daily essentials, rampant drunkenness/crime, and low morale, Russia's state of affairs, in fact, was gloomy. Even more, talk of change was deemed just that: *talk*.

Today's news from Russia is increasingly grim. Spokesperson for the Wings of Eagles ministry, Rabbi Yechiel Eckstein has sounded the alarm, suggesting that, any day now, the most virulent form of anti-Semitism the world has known in more than half a century could erupt. President of Chosen People Ministries, Mitch Glaser shares Rabbi Eckstein's concern.

With the nation's economy in shambles and its people lacking even basic necessities of life, a familiar and potentially deadly pattern is emerging. Once again, Jews are poised as scapegoats—this time, for Russian communists, extreme nationalists, and other anti-Semites.

Ultra-nationalist and anti-Semite, Vladimir Zhirinovsky blames increased numbers of Jews in any country as cause for war. Today Russia has the third-largest Jewish population in the world (following the United States and Israel). Consider, too, that in the whole of Russia, especially in the south, one out of three is Muslim. Muslims hold controlling governmental positions. Not surprisingly, leaflets dispersed in Russia call for pogroms (organized, mass killings) of more than a half-million people—just because they are Jews.

As reported in *Forward*, a well-read Jewish newspaper in the U.S., Russian communist lawmaker Albert Makashov parrots black Muslim Louis Farrakhan in labeling Jews as "bloodsuckers." Name-calling accompanies escalating incidents of discrimination and physical harm. In Moscow, Jews face threats of expulsion. Their homes are set ablaze, a synagogue bombed, and General Albert Makashov purposes to "round up all the Jews and send them to the next world."

America

I am told that in Hebrew, "The United States" is rendered *Artzot Habrit*, which means, literally, "lands of the covenant." Bill Cloud contends that in raising up America, God patterned her after His covenant relationship with Israel. Both, he claims, fulfill divine purpose—but not without attending judgment. Indeed, judgment begins in the house of the Lord (1 Pet. 4:17).

God promises to bless those who bless Israel, and to curse those who curse her. Until recent pro-Palestinian rhetoric of Hillary Clinton and James Carvill, America allied unwaveringly with Israel; but America's tide of blessing may be retreating (Gen. 12:3).

To sustain his reign of terror against the U.S., terrorist-financier Osama Bin Laden has stockpiled weapons. His up to twenty thousand followers have declared *jihad* on thousands more. Recently, the FBI in Colorado raided an Islamic retreat, the weapon store for which could amply carry on a revolution in Guatemala. PBS aired *American Jihad* documenting existence of terrorist camps, whose participants shout, "Death to America!" Already, the likes of Bin Laden are associated with embassy bombings in East Africa (1998) and a series of apartment bombings in Moscow (1999), not to mention the unparalleled attack on America (2001).

The number of black Muslims in America is on the rise. Added to that, Islamic fundamentalism is highly organized and funded. Already in America, Muslims outnumber Episcopalians; and 70 percent of Dearborn, Michigan's population is Muslim. By the year 2020, there will be more than twenty-five million Muslims.

Among assets of Muslims in America are news media outlets (UPI and API), Saks' and Tiffany's. Islamic fundamentalists sponsor a Muslim representative in Hollywood so as not to portray Islam in a bad light.

While in office, President Clinton received millions of dollars in oil money. The Muslim month of fasting, Ramadan was observed in the White House; and a Muslim clergyman opened Congress in prayer. While Judeo-Christian literature was outlawed to maintain a so-called "wall of separation," American public school children were handed copies of the *Koran* in the name of diversity.

With the caldron seething—and numbers, assets, and weaponry in place—Muslims in America are looking to revolt. While President, Bill Clinton admitted to strong likelihood in the next few years that terrorist groups will launch a germ or chemical attack on American soil; moreover, America's current defenses are not up to the challenge. The deadly attack of the *USS Cole* off the coast of Aden, Yemen, inaugurated horrifying possibilities as these. Many authorities pinpoint the most destabilizing conflict in the world as the one between Islamic extremism and the Judeo-Christian West.

Anti-Semitism in the Church

Most assuredly, a new wave of anti-Semitism has swept across America—birthed in America's fast-growing Muslim community, yes, but also (unexpectedly so) in her Christian churches.

Because of positive influence of the dispensational view that national Israel has a future in God's plan, most American evangelical Christians today hold Israel and her Jewish people in high esteem. However, in surveying the history of anti-Semitism, David Rausch documents Christendom's bearing responsibility for much of the world's anti-Semitism for some two thousand years (Rausch 1988).

You see, replacement theology holds that the church has permanently replaced Israel as God's instrument. To replacement theologians, God is entirely done with the Jew. Reconstructionist David Chilton claims that "ethnic Israel was excommunicated for its apostasy and will never again be God's Kingdom." Contrary to Scriptures, he believes further that Israel has no future plan as a special nation (Chilton 1985).

Fellow reconstructionist R.J. Rushdoony goes so far as to identify exaltation of Israel with the heresy of "racism," for "every attempt to bring the Jew back into prophecy as a Jew is to give race and works . . . a priority over grace and Christ's work." This, he adds, is "nothing more or less than paganism" (Rushdoony 1970).

To the contrary, after the Reformation, the Reformed Church of Europe widely believed that God's future plan for Israel includes her national restoration. Many even believed and taught that Israel would one day rebuild her Temple. Israel's spiritual future was "a given" in Reformed circles; however, many Reformed brethren today are returning to the error of replacement theology. According to Thomas Ice, when mixed with the right social and political conditions, replacement theology, as embraced by Chilton and Rushdoony, is responsible for theological anti-Semitism.

God's Plan for Israel

The seventy weeks of Daniel confirm that God has not discarded national Israel, as some claim; in fact, He has a continuing plan for her. These seventy weeks apply to 490 years, seventy weeks of seventy years each, as referred to in Daniel 9:24–27. This reference contains a complete history of Israel from Daniel's time to that of the Messiah; furthermore, it discloses Israel's ultimate restoration as a nation.

Clearly, the Bible teaches that God will return the Jews to Israel. In fact, the generation that sees Israel reestablished as a nation will not pass away until the entire Eschatological (end times) Discourse is fulfilled. In time, Israel will endure even greater trial than that imposed upon her by Hitler's Germany (Isa. 11:11–12:6; Ezek. 20:33–44; 22:17–22; Zeph. 1:14–18; 2:1–3; Matt. 24:32–34; Deut. 4:30; Jer. 30:5–9; Dan. 12:1).

The good news is that the last half of the seventieth week of Daniel will take place during the final three and a half years of Great Tribulation. Despite the outpouring of plagues, the Lord will "confirm the covenant" with 144,000 representatives from each of the twelve tribes of Israel. Through this difficult time, God will preserve a remnant, so that before Christ's Second Coming "all Israel will be saved" (Rev. 7:4; Rom. 10:1).

At the advent of Christ with His Bride, God will rescue Israel from world persecution at the onset of Armageddon. Finally, in the Millennial Reign of Christ, Israel's full appropriation of her rightful territory, extending from the Nile to the Euphrates Rivers, will be realized (Dan. 12:1; Zech. 12–14; Matt. 24:29–31; Rev. 19:11–21; Gen. 15:18; Ezek. 38:12).

Conclusion

In sum, anti-Semitism exists throughout history—around the world and at home; in the Antichrist world system and in the church. All Arabs following Mohammed's tradition claim descent from Ishmael, and Ishmael's descendants are among those who promulgate its error. Indeed, Scripture calls Ishmael "a wild ass of a man," not unlike Osama Bin Laden whose hand is against every man; and every man's hand is against him (Gen. 16:12).

While anti-Semitic Muslim Arabs may lead the pack, they are not sole offenders. The Bible refers to carnality as "the lower, Ishmael nature" which, according to Galatians 5:20–21 (NASB), is characterized by enmities, strife, jealousy, outburst of anger, disputes, dissentions, and factions—all of which are likely to attend spiritual anti-Semitism. To produce works-of-the-flesh fruit, as these, is to manifest anti-Semiticlike sin no matter one's historical era, ethnicity, or home base. In stark contrast, servants of God, themselves freed from sin *(hamartia)*, bear holy fruit of a different nature—that of faith, hope, and charity. The greatest of these is charity, God's self-sacrificial love (1 Cor. 13:13).

CHAPTER 3

HAMARTIA
COMPASSIONLESS CONSERVATISM

Be ye angry, and sin *(hamartanō)* not (Eph. 4:26).

Living at the time of the American Revolution, Edmund Burke founded the modern-day conservative movement. He wrote, "When bad men combine, the good must associate else they will fall one by one, an unpitied sacrifice in a contemptible struggle" (Bartlett, *Familiar Quotations*).

President G.W. Bush shares with Professor of Journalism and author-editor Marvin Olasky his view of compassionate conservatism. Furthermore, he applauds Olasky as "the first to show brilliantly how our nation's history is one of compassion." While the phrase's original national identification with George W. was a CNN broadcast in August of 1997, Vernon Jordan first used the phrase "compassionate conservative" when, in 1981, he attacked the Reagan administration for supposedly lacking it.

Compassionate Conservatism Defined

Far from mushy, contentless "crumbs of compassion," or self-aggrandizing altruism, compassionate conservatism is a carefully considered philosophy with a full-fledged program that embraces efforts by religious groups to address social problems associated with poverty, housing, and prisoners. Uniquely so, its "faith-based initiatives" require recipients somehow to examine the way they live. Because government-sponsored programs make no such demand, increased dependency ensues. In the latter case, the slothful becomes "brother to him that is a great waster" (Prov. 18:9).

To the contrary, compassionate conservatism boasts measurable social outcomes; it is both results-driven and cost-effective. Examples include work of the Salvation Army, Samaritan's Purse, Catholic Charities, and World Vision, all of which, for years, have used federal funding effectively.

The former mayor of Indianapolis, Stephen Goldsmith has set an example of innovative, compassionate government that recognizes the tremendous asset of the Christian church within any given community. Himself Jewish, Goldsmith provides an apt model for the nation. Says George W., his Front Porch Alliance represents "the way things ought to be." Similarly, in providing homes for thousands of people, groups like Habitat for Humanity have helped to turn around whole neighborhoods. Its president Millard Fuller invites Americans to change their whole way of thinking; however, keep in mind that his call is based on a globalist, interfaith perspective.

Throughout Campaign 2000 a startling 76 percent of Americans voiced approval for the role of faith-based initiatives called "subsidiarity" by Catholics and "sphere sovereignty" by Protestants. Many others fittingly oppose any entanglement with federal monies and, hence, regulations.

According to Olasky, however, the phrase "compassionate conservatism" is no sugar word for an administration that seeks not to offend, nor does it represent the status quo. It does not institutionalize bad ideas, and (surprising to some) it includes "getting tough on crime." As a result, at Prison Fellowship's Inner Change program in Texas, recidivism is being reduced drastically.

In essence, compassionate conservatism purposes to move from a failing government monopoly to faith-based diversity. It aspires to create what Pope John Paul II calls "a hospitable society" and "a welcoming culture" not based on liberal progressivism, denominational monopoly, or theocracy. The latter is reserved for such a time as the Millennial rule and reign of Christ (Rev. 20:6).

Intrinsically, compassionate conservatism reveres religion and morality as indispensable supports to local grass-roots solutions. By definition, compassion means "suffering with," indisputably a Bible principle. Proponents claim that shifting power from bureaucracy effectively removes barriers from volunteers whose simple mandate is no less than direct charity work (Rom. 12:15).

Distinguished by Free Choice

While compassionate conservatism is unapologetically faith-based, it is distinguished nonetheless by free choice between and among government, secular society, and religion. Synagogues and mosques assume a level playing field with church or even atheistic groups. Under the broad umbrella of compassionate conservatism, each is valued as a "community asset." Notwithstanding, Christians excel in disproportionately performing acts of kindness and mercy that make a measurable difference.

In his first letter to the church at Corinth, Paul allowed using the *cosmos* (whole world order) for godly purposes so long as Christians not overly use it, or rely on it "to the full." While *in* this world, believers are not *of* it. This being the case, they are to maintain focus on the Lord, not this world destined to pass away. Toward this end, Christians rightly use, but do not abuse, the world system. Because theirs is a higher authority, a divine one, believers are wise to avoid as much as possible governmental strangleholds on Spirit-led ministries (1 Cor. 7:31, 35; 1 John 4:5, 17).

Distinguished by Moral Accountability and Personal Responsibility

Say advocates, the idea of compassionate conservatism is more to equip and empower than to redistribute wealth. You see, compassionate conservatism links assistance to moral accountability and personal responsibility—even for Christians who themselves can be as inept as anyone else at charity work. Indeed, "every one of us shall give account . . . to God" (Rom. 14:12).

Participants in the Christian drug treatment program, Teen Challenge, must follow the rule: "If you don't work, you don't eat." In similar fashion, KIPP (Knowledge Is Power Program) is a charter school that receives government funding with some freedom from education bureaucracy. Students commit to excellence, pledging diligence in attendance and homework. Though lacking the all-important spiritual dimension, KIPP shares with its religious counterparts belief in "no short cuts," coupled with personal accountability (2 Thess. 3:10; Job 19:4).

Distinguished by Seven Principles

Olasky pinpoints seven crucial principles. Compassionate conservatism is, first, assertive, then basic, challenging, diverse, effective, faith-based, and gradual.

Assertive

In the 1930s, French historian and politician Alexis de Toqueville studied America's prosperity. What impressed him most was citizen assertiveness rather than waiting for government to act on their behalf. Tocqueville insisted, rightly so, that the American system could not survive without religion to shape and mediate human passions. By way of example, Paul labored day and night to support himself, not waiting upon others, lest he "eat any man's bread for naught" (2 Thess. 3:8).

Basic

Compassionate conservatism taps first the most basic means of assistance—that being family, traditionally the basic unit of every community. Providing for one's own family is a biblical imperative; moreover, the strong are to bear up the weak with "fervent charity" (1 Tim. 5:8; Rom. 15:1; 1 Pet. 4:8).

As the need increases, so do the concentric circles of assistance—from family to neighborhood, from neighborhood to community, from community to government (first, municipal, then county, state, and federal, but only if necessary). Ideally, when government is of the people, by the people, and for the people, and it is righteous, it can serve well its constituency. Even so, good men of God—e.g., Pat Robertson and the Rev. Jerry Falwell—express understandable reticence as details of faith-based programs are ironed out in today's political climate (Rom. 13:1).

CHALLENGING/DIVERSE/EFFECTIVE/FAITH-BASED/GRADUAL

As Olasky puts it, "Compassionate conservatives do not merely give the poor a safety net that may turn into a hammock; they provide instead a trampoline." As such, compassionate conservatism is challenging. As long as individuals have a choice of programs, the Bible must not be excluded by judicial fiat from any antipoverty or other work of charity.

It is documented that well-managed, faith-based programs have a superior track record (even more so than non-religious counterparts). One must start with a limited program boasting gradual, sustainable change, tested at each step along the way. Christians demonstrate faith by a pattern of observable, repeatable, and measurable good works. They remain ever "ready to distribute" and "willing to communicate [share]" (James 2:18; Titus 2:7; 1 Tim. 6:18).

The Conservative Principle of Limited Government

Compassionate conservatism embraces a philosophy of limited government. While it is conservative to cut taxes, it is *compassionately* conservative to help save, give, and build. Rather than simply please oneself, the compassionate gifted are compelled to undergird those not so gifted (Rom. 15:1).

The fight against socialized medicine is conservative, yes, but universal choice in quality health care is *compassionately* conservative. Compassionate Christians do not align with the priest and Levite of Luke 10 (verses 30–37) in "passing by on the other side." Instead, they join the Good Samaritan in showing hospitality, mercy, and liberality. The Lord's compassion fails not, but is new every morning. The same applies to God's faithful within today's Christian community (Luke 10:37; Lam. 3:22–23).

It is conservative to restore parental control of education and, in so doing, to set challenging standards. Even more, it is *compassionately* conservative to "leave no child behind." Welfare reform is conservative; encouraging fervent charity is *compassionately* conservative (Mark 10:14–16; 1 Pet. 4:8).

Sadly, there are many conservatives who lack compassion. In search of limited government, compassionless conservatives look out solely for "me and mine." Without thorough examination, they blanket-judge the less fortunate to be lazy sluggards and do-nothings. In seeking to set their own nest on high, compassionless conservatives cut off many. According to God, fueling covetousness sins against one's own soul (Hab. 2:9–10).

To the Christian, conservatism is most generally deemed good, but compassionate conservatism is even better. In contrast, compassionless conservatism misses the mark completely with grave consequences to society at large. It is *hamartia.*

The Conservative Philosophy of Moral Public Culture

Planned Parenthood

Compassionate conservatives embrace a philosophy of moral public culture. As such, they purpose to eliminate Planned Parenthood, best known for promoting and performing fully-accessible-to-all abortions. The radical social agenda of so-called "safe sex" is its progeny. Though the number of abortions nationally has steadily decreased, Planned Parenthood is performing more, not fewer abortions. Fully one quarter of its funds come from killing unborn (or partially born) children.

Planned Parenthood's founder, Margaret Sanger was an anti-Christian activist involved in the occult (theosophy). Sanger's book, *The Pivot of Civilization,* included eliminating "human weeds" and "sterilizing genetically inferior races." The most merciful thing a large family can do to one of its infant members, said Sanger, is to kill it.

In contrast, *compassionate* conservatism celebrates, facilitates, and protects life. Jesus Himself is "the life," and the way God sets before us is life, not death. To the contrary, compassionless conservatives provide no more redeeming answer to the plight of unwanted pregnancy than casting the first stone. Abortion clinic bombings and threats to attendees demonstrate compassionless conservatism to the extreme. In contrast, Jesus offers a more excellent way (John 11:25; 14:6; Jer. 21:8; John 8:7).

National Endowment for the Arts (NEA)

Decency in the arts provides a second noteworthy example of moral public culture. For good reason, conservatives oppose funding to the National Endowment for the Arts, a kind of federal arbiter signed into existence by former President Johnson (1965). The NEA's $170 million budget funds homo-eroticism, sado-masochism, and blasphemy. For example, the NEA gave Karen Finley a grant to smear chocolate all over her body. Likewise, American tax dollars endorsed *Corpus Christi*, a play in which Jesus is depicted as "queer." Additional grants aired sex lives of homosexual black men, not to mention lesbian peep shows of girls age twelve and under.

In essence, the NEA is an attack on people of faith—some compassionate; some not. While compassionate conservatives admire and voluntarily support arts that are true, honest, just, pure, lovely, and of good report, compassionless conservatives condemn all the arts as vanity. Judgment and censorship are based on personal taste alone, which at best is arbitrary (Phil. 4:8).

The Conservative Philosophy of Fiscal Common Sense

North American Free Trade Agreement (NAFTA)

Its goal ostensibly being equity and social justice achieved by transferring wealth to underdeveloped nations, the North American Free Trade Agreement signed by Bush, Sr. (1992) propels the trend toward global economics. Globalization distributes and then concentrates wealth—therefore, power—into the hands of few wishing to manage masses by means of international law. Among the most prominent insiders, German-born Henry Kissinger describes NAFTA as the first step toward the New World Order.

In fact, and as promised, the agreement has increased trade by some 65 percent, and more trade means more jobs—but, added to that, more agreements and more red tape. Some NAFTA provisions have yet to be fully implemented. NAFTA corridors, for example, are groups of highways from Mexico and Canada to the U.S. They introduce slave labor products and divide our country in half—neither of which is compassionate.

Unholy Trinity: World Trade Organization, International Monetary Fund, World Bank

Hidden in a 22,000-page General Agreement on Tariffs and Trade, the World Trade Organization was rammed without debate through a lame duck Congress, yet it serves as major player in the drive for global governance. Says author Ted Flynn, GATT/WTO causes the world's independent and sovereign governments to be nothing but servants to the money cartel. This represents a very big transfer of power. The Bible warns us that "he that makes haste to be rich shall not be innocent" (Prov. 28:20).

The World Trade Organization acts as a giant international economic Supreme Court in its non-democratic dispute resolution function. Indeed, it locks nations into rules and regulations that exceed authority of their own constitutions. Truthfully, the WTO is not about free trade. Instead, it advances an agenda for central control of world markets. Through the WTO, Americans yield significant control over the domestic economy to an international body that has ruled four times against America.

Senator Jesse Helms (R-North Carolina) complains that the International Monetary Fund (IMF) and World Bank lack sufficient accountability, squander U.S. funds, and impose lending programs resulting in long term bust for poor nations. Nevertheless, the United Nations calls for converting the IMF to a world central bank, providing preferential credit to developing nations. The unholy trinity of WTO, IMF, and World Bank are joined at the hip to enslave us to the state. The simple strategy is this: "no compliance; no loans." Cheerful giving as orchestrated by God altogether evades this compassionless equation (2 Cor. 9:7).

Free Trade; Global Welfare

Free trade and global welfare are not what many presume them to be. Some may be surprised to learn that classic Marxism favors the Robin Hood philosophy of redistributing wealth. Moreover, Karl Marx was fully in favor of free trade because it "breaks up old nationalities" and, thus, "hastens the social revolution."

True, the Golden Age of Immigration (1920-1960) contributed to a successful American melting pot, but the runaway welfare of the last three decades spoiled the broth. Now, many become welfare dependent. They refuse outright to speak English, to contribute to our economy and society, or ever to take the pledge to become U.S. citizens.

The Federation for American Immigration (FAIR) was instrumental in passing the historic 1996 Welfare Reform Act that then-President Clinton signed into law. Nevertheless, the Clinton-Gore administration and Congress worked hand-in-hand to restore millions of dollars in benefits to non-citizens. Those who receive riches wrongly are as the partridge that hatches stolen eggs it has not laid. The benefit is but temporary (Jer. 17:11).

While developing nations and struggling immigrants deserve consideration, it is compassionately conservative, first, to tend to the needs of one's own household, personally and even nationally, then to reach out. But only as an intact family or sovereign nation, respectively—no strings attached (1 Tim. 5:8; Titus 3:1).

The Conservative Philosophy of Strong National Defense

Consider Simon Peter, who smote off Malchus' ear. Careful reading of the biblical account reveals that Jesus never rebuked Peter for having a sword, nor did He insist on licensing, registration, or confiscation of it. Rather, Jesus instructed Peter to put his sword back into its sheath where it rightly belonged. Bearing a sword in readiness was (and is) appropriate; indiscriminate use of it was (and is) not (John 18:10–11).

Compassionate conservatives parrot George Washington, who once said, "If we desire to secure peace, it must be known that we are at all times ready for war." With this in view, conservatives oppose continued dismantling of the armed forces. They further insist on U.S. military presence in Panama. After all, the Panama Canal is vital to strategic passage of naval vessels.

In contrast, compassionless conservatives uplift the morally bankrupt policy of Mutual Assured Destruction, an outdated Cold War posture based not on saving, but rather avenging lives.

Red China considers the U.S. her primary enemy with whom war is inevitable. Moreover, in June of 1999, the CIA fingered China as the single most important supplier of equipment and technology for weapons of mass destruction. With Red China as the new gatekeeper of the Panama Canal, thirteen of her multiple-warhead nuclear missiles are already pointed at U.S. cities. For these reasons, and more, conservatives dispute most favored nation status for Red China.

Compassionate conservatives recognize victims of China's repressive and brutal policies. For example, Chinese women are forced to undergo abortions and sterilization. Furthermore, China traffics in human organs, maintains slave labor camps, and tortures prisoners, including people of faith. Rather than stand firm for human rights, making full proof of their ministry, compassionless conservatives disregard altogether the cry of Chinese people. "Whoso stops his ears at the cry of the poor, he also shall cry himself, but shall not be heard" (Prov. 21:13).

Conclusion

In *Zorach v. Clauson* (1952), the Supreme Court ruled "We are a religious people whose institutions presuppose a Supreme Being. . . . We cannot read into the *Bill of Rights* . . . philosophy of hostility to religion." Research demonstrates that church attendance parallels lower drop out rates, diminished drug abuse, and overall falling crime rates. It stands to reason that church ministry has a rightful place in society.

Be assured that faith-based, grassroots efforts are credited with eliminating neighborhood prostitution and drug houses, not to mention adding street lights and viable, successful youth programs. Even more than non-religious counterparts, well managed, faith-based programs are proven to be effective.

Texas was first to establish the option of employing private and religious charities to deliver welfare services. Take, for example, an unpaid Texas couple, Calvin and Johnnie Mae Carter, who run a community center in Sunny Acres. With "God in charge," their welfare program works just fine.

Those who disallow "intrusion" of the church in matters of state on the basis of the Establishment Clause of the First Amendment should reflect on these words of Chief Justice William Rehnquist: "[Separation between church and state] is a metaphor based on bad history." The original idea was to bar the state from establishing or favoring one religious view over another. To the extent the state intervened, it used its authority to further aims of the church.

In God's eyes, it is sin knowing to do good, but failing to act on that knowledge. As Edmund Burke once said, "All that is necessary for the triumph of evil is for good men to do nothing." Christians justifiably incensed at social ills as poverty, prostitution, substance abuse, and violent crime must not fail to act. Nor should they use their anger as an occasion to sin. Instead, they should act upon Bible truth that God is well pleased with compassionate sacrifice of those who "do good" in His Name (Heb. 13:16; James 4:17; Eph. 4:26–32).

CHAPTER 4

Hamartia Cultism

If Christ has not been raised, your faith is worthless; you are still in your sins *[hamartia]* (1 Cor. 15:17, NASB).

"To Be or not To Be?"—That is the Question

When threatened by Israel, King Balak of Moab sent messengers to a renowned diviner, Balaam, that he might curse Israel. After the Lord opened the mouth of Balaam's ass, He opened Balaam's eyes to see before him the angel of the Lord with sword in hand. Subsequently, God communicated to Balaam extraordinarily pointed prophecies foretelling Israel's happiness (Adam Clarke).

In religious circles, Balaam has been called everything from a genuine, true prophet of God, who fell through covetousness and ambition (Tertullian, Jerome, Adam Clarke) to a "numb-skulled, money-grubbing, heathen seer" (Wenham). The question is still posed: Was Balaam a saint, an irreligious charlatan, or a novice in faith, lacking power over passion, as suggested by Jamieson, Fausset, and Brown?

According to Scripture, cults, as tares, grow alongside wheat, the true church (Matt. 13:38). This being the case, a similar question is posed today about suspect churches and cults that have visibly proliferated, especially since the mid-1800s. Are they groups of saints, charlatans, or novices?

Although liberal Protestant churches may deny the virgin birth of Christ, His Deity, and bodily resurrection, that does not make them cults—only unbelievers. Research shows that 71–80 percent of all cult members previously graced the pews of traditional mainline churches (Martin, Williams, Chambers, Langone, Dole, and Grice). Take, for example, Mary Baker Eddy, founder of Christian Science. Though she eventually claimed to supersede Christ, Eddy nonetheless was reared as a strict Congregationalist in Bow, New Hampshire. U.S. founder of the Mormon religious sect, Joseph Smith is yet another notable example. In the early 1800s, when Joseph was a pre-teen, his family associated with the Presbyterian Church not far from Rochester, New York. In 1828, Smith joined the Methodist Church.

Most Christians agree that Eddy and Smith eventually became cultists; but what about others who, like Balaam, cause us wonder? Around the turn of the century, for instance, William Booth's evangelistic ministry among outcasts of London rejected traditional theology with regard to baptism and communion. If doctrinal deviation is proof of cultism, then the Salvation Army and Quakers, too, are cults. But most agree that is not the case. So, just what *is* a cult?

Cultism Defined

A cult is organized heresy with sub-Christian views, extra-biblical revelation, and no rightful claim to salvation. Though some pose as Christians, cultists deny the born again experience. Isolationism, exclusivity, and psychological conditioning earmark cults. Surprisingly so, many cults hold to some degree of orthodoxy in doctrine; however, they magnify an order, a principle, or a leader over and above Jesus Christ (John 3:3).

By definition, cults are recently founded systems with entangling organizational structure. They require compulsive, unreasonable preoccupation with, and obsessive devotion to, their human leader who, in turn, claims special revelation and authority to interpret the Word of God to his own liking. Contrary to Psalm 119:89, cult leaders often reject all or part of the Bible and substitute or add their own books of teachings. These false teachers make merchandise of followers by exploiting them financially. Members often turn over all rights, individual opinions, and/or property to leaders, whom they obey without question (2 Pet. 2:3).

While followers release personal wealth to the cult, cult leaders stockpile it. At one time, Oregon cult leader Bhagwan Shree Rajneesh was believed to be the world's largest collector of luxury Rolls Royces. When U.S. founder of the Christian Science movement Mary Baker Eddy died, her fortune exceeded three million dollars, not a penny of which was left to charity.

A Korean born, self-proclaimed messiah, the Rev. Sun Myung Moon of the Unification Church boasts hundreds of millions of dollars in investments. Among them include a shipyard, meat packing plant, printing company, and hotel. For a quarter of a century, Moon has spread his business empire alongside his apostate gospel. In 1982 Moon was convicted of tax fraud in the U.S.; nonetheless, former President Bush and former Canadian Prime Minister Brian Mulroney accepted large honorariums to speak at Moon's black-tie dinner to launch his Buenos Aires-based daily newspaper.

Having "itching ears," many among us satisfy our own lusts by seeking out false teachers, as these, who "will not endure sound doctrine" (e.g., the resurrection and blood atonement for sin). Needy folks from traditional churches crave the love, care, and acceptance initially promised by cults out to ensnare them. By failing to exercise due caution, even sincere, but sentimental Christians fall prey (2 Tim. 4:3; Gal. 1:6–7).

In His Eschatological Discourse, Jesus predicted proliferation of cults in these end times. A cult-exit program, Wellspring Retreat and Resource Center, claims that some 185,000 Americans join cults each year; and more than three thousand destructive cults currently exist in the United States alone (Matt. 24; Mark 13; Luke 21).

While the Lord puts primary blame on cult leaders (shepherds), not on members of the group (sheep), the victim's pain is no less felt. In time, victims may reject not only the group in question, but also anything and everything having to do with Christianity. The way of truth becomes maligned—all because of well-molded words and teachings designed to manipulate, exploit, and take unfair advantage (Ezek. 34:1–4; 2 Pet. 2:1–3).

Cult Tragedies

The destructive element of cults must not be underestimated. Northwest of Georgetown, Guyana, Jonestown was a commune of the People's Temple Sect founded in 1974 by American Jim Jones, who incited murder and mass suicide. Tragically, cyanide drinks took the lives of 914 followers with 240 children among them.

Marshall Applewhite's Heaven's Gate Cult was a flying-saucer cult comprised of computer experts who, in search of the next level in human evolution, also committed eerily ritualistic mass suicide in Rancho Santa Fe, California (1997). The Doomsday Ugandan Suicide Cult likewise anticipated a happy journey to heaven when its victims remained nailed inside a church set ablaze. This tragic "homecoming" of ex-Catholics followed an alleged vision of the Virgin Mary experienced by the cult's sixty-eight-year-old leader. While that leader was believed to have fled the deadly conflagration, some five hundred monks, nuns, and children died in it.

The Charles Manson family slaughtered strangers at cult leader Charlie's bidding. In 1969, Manson's young followers perpetrated the grisly and apparently motiveless murders of actress Sharon Tate and California businessman Leno La Bianca, among others. In March 1995, Aum Shinri Kyo cult members were accused of killing twelve people and sickening thousands by releasing sarin nerve gas in the Tokyo subway. Allegedly acting under orders of cult guru Shoko Asahara, Akira Yamagata was convicted of dropping a toxic liquid chemical over his victim, whom he killed. Yamagata is a former member of the ground self-defense force in Japan's army.

Confusing Cult Practices

Not all cult practices are limited to cults. Some wrongly equate strong preaching with mind control and cultism. Were this the case, all the great evangelists of the last three centuries, Billy Graham included, would be tagged cultists. Others finger excessive devotion.

If so, every martyr throughout history would qualify as a cultist. Neither the former nor the latter applies.

While cults do have strong leadership, so do good churches. Many mainline churches (e.g., Lutheran, Presbyterian) have stalwart, authoritative leaders—for example, Luther, Calvin, and Knox. The Bible teaches plainly about church government and delegated authority. That Paul was not "a whit behind the very chiefest apostles" in no way brands him as a cult leader. Nevertheless, the apostle Paul was willing to come with a rod if need be; furthermore, in no uncertain terms, he commanded that he be followed (Heb. 13:17; 2 Cor. 11:5; 1 Cor. 4:21; 11:1).

Cults may well exhibit a "we-they" mentality, but so does the true church. In the latter case, the "we" are wheat; and "they" are tares. "Coming out from among them" is Bible truth, not cult-like snobbery. The same applies to "putting away" those who fail to walk in step with Bible truth (2 Cor. 6:17; 1 Cor. 5:13; 2 Thess. 3:6).

Dangers of Crying "Cult"

Rather than combat the real enemy, well meaning, but misguided Christians all too often slander one another. Keeping in mind that God forbids rumors, slander, and gossip, believers are to steer clear of talebearers. Never should a Christian brand brethren as cultists, for it is the Devil's work to accuse believers—if not falsely, certainly presumptuously (Exod. 23:7; Rom. 8:33–34).

Many believers wrongly assume that their safety from cult deception lies in doctrinal orthodoxy, unwavering commitment, and freedom from character flaws. However, anyone can be deceived and manipulated. Ironically, some overly zealous pastors have so recklessly maligned practices of cults that inadvertently they implicate their own churches.

In reaction to the Jonestown massacre of 1978, alarmists cried for government control of religious cults. Thereafter, a legislative push threatened cults and, at the same time, Christian fundamentalists falsely aligned with cultists. Along with cult mania came the unsavory practice of "deprogramming." Not discerning the nature of cults, secularists denounced even sound Christian organizations, as *Maranatha* and Campus Crusade for Christ. Deprogramming "authorities" targeted, among others, converts of Jerry Falwell and Billy Graham.

A study by Professor Irving Hexham and Rudy Dirks of Regent College found that among thirteen religious groups victimized by deprogrammers were Baptists (*Evangelical Newsletter*, 4 September 1981). In the early 1980s, an Alabama court attacked the Friendship Baptist Church in Montgomery for its Christian school ministry. Its students were alleged to be isolated, controlled, degraded, and bored with Bible reading, prayer, and memorizing Scripture. Allegations of "cultism" and "brainwash" formed a substantial part of that legal case. Similar charges were leveled against Faith Baptist Church of Louisville, Nebraska, where Pastor Sileven was jailed after refusing to subject a ministry of the church, his Christian school, to state licensing. Antagonists likened the good pastor to Jim Jones.

One cult expert has made a specialty of what he calls "Bible-based cults." Himself an accused kidnapper and convicted criminal, Rick Allen Ross served as adviser to the BATF and FBI during the Waco siege. He joined other deprogrammers to make sure that stories of Waco survivors conform to the official party line of the Clinton-Gore administration.

Targeting mainstream Christianity, Dr. Cathy Moses of the Dallas Center for Religious Addiction and Abuse directly connected the Waco massacre with Christian fundamentalism. A pamphlet offered by the Dallas Center reads, "There is nothing FUN about FUNdamentalism." Following Waco, former President Clinton warned, "We may have to confront [this sort of fanaticism] again." No doubt "we" will.

The Waco tragedy may well represent a growing federal intolerance toward religious faith in general. Tal Brooke of the Spiritual Counterfeits Project explains that "the government had to search out an anti-hero—someone nobody likes—to set a precedent for taking religious liberty away." Indeed, media coverage has freely associated conservative Christians with David Koresh. Having conducted a computer search of newspaper articles to learn how often the media had linked the name David Koresh with the term "fundamentalist," Dr. Marvin Olasky cited 148 examples.

Cultish Christians

Cult tendencies include preoccupation with leadership, micro-management of lives, pet doctrines, and fear mongering. But beware, these very attributes likewise characterize many good Christians.

Preoccupation with Leadership

Excessive veneration of man is a common cult practice, but one that Christians fall prey to as well. Rather than seek the Lord and His Word for guidance, many Christians seek endorsement, or a "final word," from a single respected Bible teacher, mentor, prayer leader, pastor, or counselor. They ask permission to make adult decisions as to what we believe, how we should vote, or how to keep house and raise children.

When a fellow Christian under another's leadership offers a word of testimony, or biblical truth, these run to their leader, not the Word, to weigh the worth of what has been shared. Yes, there is wisdom in a multitude of counsel, but personal accountability is paramount to a Christian's maturation process. As one grows in Christ, he progresses from infancy to full-stature sonship with ability and mandate to think independently and to live responsibly (Acts 17:11; Eph. 4:13–14).

Micro-management of Lives

While the Bible is specific on a number of issues pertaining to one's personal daily life, it remains silent on others. For example, Scriptures address hair length and clothing choices, but only in general terms. While it does not insist upon how and when to conduct one's "quiet time," there are Christian fellowships that enforce parameters for personal devotions and badger members to participate in activities or ministries that hold no special interest or calling (1 Cor. 11:4, 5, 7, 14, 15; Deut. 22:5; 1 Tim. 2:9).

To them, the "law of group conformity" outweighs the "law of love." Before embracing a brother or sister, some would first judge that one's appearance, body of knowledge, and habit patterns. They censure brethren who may or may not dress within bounds of biblical propriety and whose taste varies from their own. Superficial choices invite stiff-arming—for example, a woman's using (or not using) make up, earrings, or nail polish and a man's having (or not having) a mustache or beard. Christians with cultlike tendencies micro-manage their own lives, not to mention lives of family members and friends.

Pet Doctrines

Years ago, I frequented a lovely Bible study group. Lessons taught were more devotional than analytical in nature, suiting the tastes and needs of participants who, for the most part, were blessed to be stay-at-home wives and moms or retirees. After some time, however, themes and Scripture passages repeated themselves. For years, in fact, we heard the same lessons—nothing new.

Mind you, these Christian women were well connected to higher education. Many had reached professional heights in their chosen careers; nonetheless, any mention of deeper life theology was brushed aside, even discouraged. Some labeled current events as being "worldly" even when issues affected the cause of Christ. Dark subjects, though scriptural, were shunned. Apparently only pet doctrines passed muster.

Not given to the group view, nonconformists tended to peel off and gravitate elsewhere. This served only to reinforce established collaborative consciousness. In no way was this edifying gathering of godly women a cult, but its preoccupation with pet doctrines might be considered cultlike. You see, God's Word is explored precept upon precept, line upon line, here a little, there a little (Isa. 28:10). This passage in Isaiah speaks to systematic correlation and comparison of Scripture, not limited to any favored passage or doctrine. It behooves Christians to avoid the cultlike tendency of limiting one's theological grid to hand picked doctrines, precious as they might be.

Fear Mongering

Our home is located in an earthquake-prone area. With this in view, many responsible citizens—ourselves included—plan and prepare for needs of family, friends, and neighbors should an emergency ensue.

As Y2K fast approached, many reliable sources warned that the much-publicized Millennium Bug threatened a worldwide economic depression of such monumental proportion that opportunistic, manipulative measures would be warranted. In anticipation of a possible crisis, the Fed increased currency in banks by up to $50 billion, and many citizens undertook exhaustive preparations with regard to finances, food, drink, first aid, and waste management.

As a result, in the event of a short-lived winter storm, a good number of families could live comfortably even without electricity. When February and March 2000 spelled relief, few regretted sensible preparations they had made.

Many proactive Christians approached their preparatory tasks with unruffled trust. Others who heralded gloom and doom attracted and drew together the fearful. Although a sky-is-falling mentality has no place among secure believers, many overly anxious Christians practiced the cult motivation of fear mongering when the dreaded Y2K bug loomed on the horizon.

In conclusion, believers are wise to steer clear of the wayward ways of cults lest they, too, miss the mark of sound Bible truth. To remain free from deception and its grave consequences, faithful followers of Christ never fail to examine themselves in light of God's Holy Word and to live their lives according to Spirit-anointed principles contained therein.

CHAPTER 5

Hamartia
Darwinism

For whatever is not of faith [in the one true God] is sin *[hamartia]* (Rom. 14:23).

In the twentieth century, Unitarianism became closely linked with liberal politics and the cause of world peace. A sort of mystical, religious humanism, Unitarianism denies the deity of Christ all the while it upholds reason as one's guide to right action. English biologist Charles Robert Darwin was an Unitarian universalist. For good reason, Darwin is one said to rule from the grave, for his theories of scientific, social, and mystical evolution effectively mold postmodern thought and spirituality.

"Scientific" Darwinism

In 1925, Dayton, Tennessee's William Jennings Bryan prosecuted a secondary-level science teacher for violating state law in his classes. According to author-speaker Chuck Missler, this "monkey trial" was never about John Scopes' guilt or innocence in teaching that humans descended from lower life forms. Its purpose rather was to disseminate Darwinism, and that it did quite effectively.

In a nutshell, the liberal, faith-driven system of Darwinism rejects God Himself. For this reason, the battle between evolution and creation is no minor one. If in fact humans are mere products of time and chance, it stands to reason that life is devoid of elevated meaning. Consequently, arguments against abortion and euthanasia seemingly lose their punch.

Scientific Evolution: Presumptuous

Natural selection is the alleged process whereby gene frequencies in a population gradually change to adapt to the environment. Only the most fit survive and thrive. Indeed, Darwin's disciples believe that the weakest link among us deserves to be expunged.

A transplant from Great Britain, the popular television game show, *The Weakest Link,* demonstrates in a limited time slot how survival of the fittest works. Seemingly self-centered competition coupled with feigned animosity toward competitors take priority over the show's supposed component of team play. Fairness not much counts in eliminating those deemed to be "one French fry short of a 'Happy Meal.'"

Scientific Evolution: Unscientific

Scientific Darwinism maintains that, without master design, a single cell is responsible for all of life—this, through a process of random changes over some 4.5 billion years—and yet, suspiciously, major groups of plants and animals have no transitional forms in the fossil records. Darwin offers no satisfactory answer as to why assemblages of complex animals appear in the geological record without ancestors. Additionally, both simple and complex fossilized organisms coexist in every strata of rock. Were evolution true, neither would be the case.

Said Darwin, evolution from simple to increasingly complex forms is affected by means of mutations and survival of the fittest. But evolutionary transition from simple to complex life forms is unrealizable. You see, even at the cellular level, many structures are "irreducibly complex," meaning that *all* parts of a structure must be present in order for that structure to function at all. This reality negates Darwin's theory of gradual, random change.

Furthermore, the "simple cell" turns out to be a miniaturized city of unparalleled intricacy and adaptive design. The most primitive one-cell life form exceeds in complexity even the most advanced computer. Remarkably, the human body houses fifty-five trillion cooperating cells with countless energy exchanges. Even more astonishing, each feature of every cell is bio-chemically dependent on others.

In no way are we mere accidents of nature. To the contrary, that we are "fearfully and wonderfully made" is self-evident (Ps. 139:14). Even secular scientists, as astronomers, are compelled by their data to recognize existence of a Creator-God. Science historian Frederic B. Burnham further observes that scientists embrace intelligent design as "a more respectable hypothesis today than at any time in the last hundred years."

Written by Yale-and Berkeley-trained developmental biologist, a brilliant new book by Jonathan Wells (*Icons of Evolution: Science or Myth?*) exposes Darwinian fables. Nevertheless, evolutionary theory is considered to be fact among intellectuals, some of whom identify with the faith community. These would do well to heed popular biologist and creationist speaker, Dr. Gary Parker, who correctly identifies one significant shortfall: Darwin's missing link remains just that—*missing*. It seems that despite broad acceptance, Darwinism itself remains "one French fry short of a 'Happy Meal'"!

Scientific Evolution: Dishonest

Dating methods are controlled by factors of temperature, pressure, humidity, and light, none of which are constant; nevertheless, evolutionists wrongly assume a uniform decay rate. Besides that, commonly employed carbon decomposition and radioactive decay dating methods are notoriously inaccurate. The case for Darwinism further weakens given the shameful exposure of fraudulent "Peking" and "Piltdown" men, among others.

Even if all mutations were beneficial, which they are not, statistical odds for life's creating itself through chance mutations (one in ten-to-the-billionth power) prove the theory's folly. Additionally, scientists know of no mutational change that has effectively produced increasingly complex heredity in chromosomes or DNA.

Finally, an idea is in the realm of science if, by but one example, it has potential of being falsified by an experiment. No matter the volume of evidence supporting a theory, it takes only one proof that it is false. Much of what is taught in schools as evolution is not falsifiable and, thus, cannot qualify as science.

Scientific Evolution: Foolish

For fifteen years, my husband decorated prize-winning cakes on local television. It is as inconceivable to imagine that scientific evolution is any more likely to have occurred than it is for flour, sugar, eggs, milk, and food coloring to coalesce gradually into one of my husband's designer cakes apart from his masterful touch.

Such inanity prompts the questions, "If natural law gave rise to life, where did the natural law come from?" or, better yet, "If humankind evolved from monkeys and apes, why do we still have monkeys and apes?"

Without doubt, sound evidence overwhelmingly favors a young earth and Noah's Flood, as recounted in Scripture. Indeed, the earth's constantly decreasing magnetic field points to its being no more than ten thousand years old. Even Einstein and non-Christian biologists, as Britain's Brian Goodwin, agree that Darwinism is inconsistent with evidence.

Astrophysicists view the universe as a vast natural laboratory for studying matter under conditions of temperature, pressure, and density that are unattainable on earth. Astrophysicist Heinz Oberhummer testifies, "I am not a religious person, but I could say this universe is *designed* [emphasis added] very well for the existence of life." Nature's delicate balance unmistakably supports teleology (design) rather than evolution (random chance). To assume otherwise is nonsense.

Scientific Evolution: Faith-Based

Speaking to intelligent design, not random chance, the anthropic principle in science suggests that "the universe is the way it is because, if it were different, we would not be here to observe it." That the DNA molecule exhibits "specified complexity" makes it even harder to believe in naturalistic origins. Nonetheless, Christian theorists are quick to offer as compromise explanation the improbability of "theistic evolution" so as not to appear out of touch with worldly wisdom. They conclude, wrongly so, that science has to be a search for naturalistic explanations. To the contrary, reputable science is best viewed as an honest search for truth.

Given that origins are not observable, repeatable, and measurable, to embrace Darwinism at any level dismisses the scientific method of inquiry. Even more importantly to Christians, doing so trashes authenticity of Scripture while, at the same time, it marginalizes the God of the Bible. If "in the beginning, God . . ." fails to carry full punch, the same applies to any, and perhaps all, of the Bible's thirty thousand promises to believers.

Known as "Darwin's Bulldog" in the late 1800s, Thomas Huxley coined the term, "agnostic," to soften his then socially unacceptable posturing as an atheist. Simply put, Darwinism helped Huxley ignore his Creator; however, as a scientist, Huxley was compelled to admit, rightly so, that evolution is no more than "tentative hypothesis."

Keeping this in view, contemporary Darwinian dogma clearly aligns with "vain babbling" and "oppositions of science falsely so-called" (1 Tim. 6:20). Take, for example, the phrase, "ontogeny recapitulates phylogeny," faulty notion that, throughout its development, the human embryo replays steps of evolution. German biologist Ernst Haeckel coined the phrase; and, astonishingly, his famous fake drawings still appear in biology textbooks.

Since the early stages of the embryo are supposedly not fully human, Haeckel's incredible belief is used to justify abortion. "It-is-written" patriarchal language of Isaiah 49:1, then, gives way to "I-feel" matriarchal language that demotes the human fetus to the nefarious status of non-person. Philosophy professor at the American University, Jeffrey Reiman goes a step further claiming that "infants do not possess in their own right a property that makes it wrong to kill them." God disagrees. In fact, He "hates hands that shed innocent blood" (Prov. 6:16a–19).

Fifty-six men who signed the *Declaration of Independence* believed in the Creator, who alone endows inalienable rights. Notwithstanding, Darwinists apparently prefer to be identified with apes than with fallen humanity in need of a Savior. This assertion is seemingly well reasoned. Embracing the religion of "scientific" Darwinism conveniently invites humans to transfer blame for their failings. After all, human actions result from brain states produced by some combination of chance and physical law. Presumed to be no more than accidents of natural selection, it stands to reason that humans lack power of moral choice to heed Rabbi Daniel Lapin's plea to return to "founding moral imperatives"—i.e., the Ten Commandments.

Social Darwinism

Some may be surprised to learn that Darwin's true claim to fame is not scientific evolution but rather historic optimism. The latter contends that, apart from God, and with the passing of time, human thinking, philosophy, and destiny are improving progressively toward the New World Order, a sort of utopia. The Bible calls it differently. The major prophet, Isaiah, instructs that human effort apart from God produces nothing of significant, lasting value (Isa. 26:18).

Social Darwinism: Rooted in Plato

Some four hundred years before Christ, Plato advocated using needed force to wipe out existing government and social structures to provide a blank slate upon which to develop the portrait of a great new society ruled by philosopher-kings. Plato's ideal society eliminated marriage and family. Children were to be raised by the State. New York Senator Hillary Clinton has embraced Plato's mistaken supposition that "it takes a village."

In *Tragedy and Hope: A History of the World in Our Time,* Harvard-trained Professor Carroll Quigley of Georgetown University identified powerful elitists who wish to control what Americans see, read, and think. Quigley mentored former President Clinton, introducing him to a permanent shadow government whose powerful bankers, businessmen, and government officials (i.e., philosopher-kings) control the agenda of our political life from behind the scenes.

Social Darwinism: Promulgated and Popularized

The apostle Peter made reference to cults, as gnosticism, when warning believers not to be led away with the error of the wicked.

Gnosticism is an esoteric cult of divine enlightenment. It is precursor to other cults (e.g., Mormonism), contemporary mysticism (e.g., New Age movement), and secret societies (e.g., illumined Freemasonry). All of these reflect error of the wicked; all are popular in the burgeoning New World Order; and all are rooted in Plato's *New Republic*. Finally, all reflect social Darwinism, resting on the mistaken assumption that the strong flourish and have claim to rule over the less gifted (2 Pet. 3:17).

Based on the work of Darwin and Herbert Spencer, social Darwinism was popularized by turn-of-the-century entrepreneurs, as Andrew Carnegie, whose brand of socialism disdained truly free enterprise while, at the same time, it created a ruling class. Carnegie offered scientific justification for late nineteenth-century *laissez-faire* capitalism (the principle of unrestricted freedom in commerce). According to historian Dr. Stanley Monteith, however, *laissez-faire* capitalism is non-existent. Most internationalist bankers/financiers ("kings without kingdoms," Rev. 17:12–13) favor monopoly capitalism. These work in concert to get the government to expand its reach of control so as to discourage competition.

Himself a spiritualist, Sir Andrew Carnegie joined his friend, Cecil Rhodes, in hope of realizing objectives to reduce the United States to a colony of the New World Order and to promote transformational Marxism. German philosopher, economist, and social theorist, Karl Marx argued for transformation of human life and nature, tacitly assigning an egalitarian super-status for the mass proletariat, which was to be reflected in the State.

SOCIAL DARWINISM: REALIZED UNDER A RULING ELITE

Social Darwinism is realized under a ruling elite, modeled in secret societies as Skull and Bones. Chartered at Yale University and organized in 1832, Skull and Bones is no mere debating society, as some presume. It is rather a group of moneyed soldiers in a secret war for power. At a 1991 Bilderberg Group meeting, David Rockefeller observed that "the world is now more sophisticated and prepared to march toward a world government. The supernational sovereignty of an intellectual elite and world bankers is surely preferable to the national auto-determination practiced in past centuries." While the vast Rockefeller family influence cannot compare to the centuries-long, pervasive influence of Skull and Bones, their goals nonetheless are similar.

By definition, global governance supposes voluntary submission to a system of supranational world management. Social engineers serve as ideal point men for social change or paradigm shift. Advocating Plato utopianism under a ruling elite, Cecil Rhodes formulated a plan for world dominion, including the foundation of "so great a power as to hereafter render wars impossible." Even today, his group is dominated by financial elitists. Bright, young Rhodes scholars, as William Clinton, are rewarded for like-mindedness.

U.S. politician and diplomat, Colonel Edward Mandell House acted as President Wilson's closest adviser. The Colonel was part of a cabal of one hundred social engineers, known as the Inquiry. The Inquiry contributed to formation of the Council on Foreign Relations, America's preeminent non-governmental foreign affairs organization. In a letter sent to House on 21 November 1933, President Roosevelt wrote of "a financial element in the larger centers" that "has owned the Government ever since the days of Andrew Jackson."

More recently, Phyllis Schlafly wrote of "some of the biggest names in American politics, business, and the press" who were not "heads of state," but those who give orders to them—in other words, the "king-makers." This was partly in reference to the Bilderberg Group, a coterie of about one hundred elite globalists within the stalwart of the Eastern Liberal Establishment of Insiders, euphemism for a deliberately anonymous and prestigious membership whose collective viewpoint is globalism.

Harper's Magazine (1958) spoke of this "government in exile" as a group whose participants are similar in interest and outlook. They form what some would term "the power elite, shaping events from invulnerable positions behind the scenes." Exceptional talents and aptitude guarantee this elitist cabal their alleged right to rule over less gifted counterparts deemed unaware of what is good for them.

Social Darwinism: Realized through a Super-master Race

Based on supremacy of the State over the individual, Nazism obsesses on a racist version of Darwin's survival of the fittest. In the 1930s and 1940s, Nazi Germany erroneously promulgated the notion of Aryans as a white-skinned, blue-eyed, fair-haired super-master race. Even today, humanists look for a superior race, their motto being, "one world; one species."

Secular humanists hope to control evolution by means of genetic engineering—namely, deliberate manipulation of genetic material by biochemical techniques. Often achieved by introducing new DNA, genetic engineering is used to improve hereditary qualities. Accordingly, today's trend in e-commerce is to assist women in their aspiration to give birth to smart or beautiful babies—this, by artificial insemination.

On the other hand, international population reduction plans eliminate undesirables, those not so smart or beautiful, including the comatose, disabled, or terminally ill; those severely depressed or mentally impaired; the elderly, and eventually all independent thinkers. To neo-Darwinists, abortion is no more than lopping off the top of the food chain to enable nature to reconstitute itself.

The goal is not only to eliminate the unworthy, but also to pinpoint, nurture, and place illumined, group conscious, politically correct world citizens in the viable work force of the global community. The desired outcome is global human resource development.

Mystical Darwinism

In brief, mystical Darwinism holds promise of "becoming god." Of some six million Freemasons around the world, many attain to positions of world leadership as presidents, justices, prime ministers, and military men. Unbeknownst to some, esoteric Masonic belief focuses on recovering the "Lost Word" so as to possess the divine self, or christ-state.

It is alleged that signs, key words, tokens, and points of entrance carry the initiate through ninety-seven degrees of illumined Freemasonry. At the thirty-first degree, the Masonic candidate expresses hope for a better incarnation in the next life. His bidding is to advance in the New Age cycle of reincarnation. Freemasonry's ninetieth degree ostensibly takes one "over the abyss," transcending good and evil. At this point, he supposedly becomes a god. An additional six million Mormons worldwide aspire to this very hope.

With offices in New York City, London, and Geneva, Lucis (formerly, Lucifer) Trust promotes belief in an assumed hierarchy of wise men who, over time, have evolved through successive reincarnations to reach this coveted state of christhood, or divinity. Established in 1923, Lucis Trust is recognized as a powerful nongovernmental organization (NGO), acting as key player at recent United Nations summits. Henry Kissinger is among its most prestigious members, and Robert MacNamara serves at director level. Chancellor of the University of Peace, Costa Rica, and self-proclaimed "Father of United Religions," Robert Muller also belongs. It was Muller who spurred the United Religions Initiative (URI), a sort of spiritual UN.

New Age occultists, as Muller, aspire to achieve the higher self through a series of reincarnations. Mystical evolution, as embraced by secret societies, has to do with *karma* (fate). New Age occultists trust that multiple reincarnations with upward mobility provide needed opportunities to progress from embryo-god to ultimate oneness with the universal god-force.

According to Eastern thought, a human's highest destiny is "extinction"—that is, absorption of the finite self into the infinite absolute, called *Nirvana*. Becoming god, they believe, produces balanced communities boasting "group fusion" and "alignment." For the phenomenon to be realized, one must discard individual thinking for group think.

"Group think" is collaborative consciousness sacrificing absolutes (e.g., the Ten Commandments) to ensure social harmony in balanced communities. A Soviet term, meaning "collective opinion," consensus is mandatory. It employs the Marxist decision-making process of dialectics, featuring three stages of fact-based "thesis," feeling-based "antithesis," and compromise "synthesis." Group think finds place in liberal theology, the political correctness movement, social engineering processes employed in today's education reform movement, and in New Age mysticism.

To traditionalists, mystical Darwinism sounds preposterous; nonetheless, its error is broadly embraced in powerful circles around the world. *The Eugenic Manifesto* expresses interest in competing with Jesus Christ and Buddha for the "destiny of man. . . . It is now time for you to meet God," it reads. "Here is God. That God is you" (Hart 1997).

In 1996, researchers at Case Western Reserve University and the University of Virginia found that high self-esteem is characteristic of violent criminals, spouse abusers, rapists, gang members, and the sociopath. Nevertheless, self-esteem increasingly takes front-row seat to academics in today's public education system. One of the students responsible for the Columbine massacre of 1999 wrote in a schoolmate's yearbook "I *am* God [in German]." Curiously, Paul characterizes end-time world citizens as being "lovers of their own selves" (2 Tim. 3:1–2).

Sadly, the life and work of one Charles Darwin has contributed significantly to spread of such *hamartia.*

New Paradigm, Developmental Stages

Old:

God-centered Judeo-Christianity (Col. 1:16–18)

- *Anthropocentricity* (Humans, crown of creation, Heb. 2:6–8)
- *Teleology* (Master design, Gen. 1:1)
- *Accountability to God* (Resulting in the abundant life, John 10:10, 27)
- *Bio-stewardship* (Cartesian Theory, earth's resources for human good, Gen. 1:28; 2:15–16)

Transition:

Me-centered Secular Humanism (Ps. 53:1; 2 Tim. 3:1–2,4)

- *Egocentricity* ("Man is the measure of all things," Obad. 4)
- *Scientific Evolution* (Random chance, 1 Tim. 6:20)
- *Self-will* (Resulting in death culture intended to ensure sustainability, 2 Pet. 2:10; Rev. 9:6)
- *Bio-downplay* (Characterized by *laissez-faire* capitalism, 1 Tim. 6:17, and isolationism, Prov. 28:26)

New:

Earth-centered Mystical Humanism (2 Tim. 3:13; Isa. 42:8)

- *Biocentricity* (Planet above humans, Rom. 1:25)
- *Mystical Evolution* (From embryo god to "christhood," Heb. 9:27)
- *Extinction* (*Nirvana*/cosmic illumination, 1 John 5:19)
- *Bio-socialism* (Product of sustainability, specious UN term for controlling population and redistributing the world's wealth, Isa. 55:8–9)

CHAPTER 6

HAMARTIA DEMOCRATIC TRANSNATIONALISM

And I heard another voice from heaven saying, "Come out of her, my people, that you may not participate in her sins *(hamartia)* and that you may not receive of her plagues, for her sins *(hamartia)* have piled up as high as heaven . . ." (Rev. 18:4–5, NASB).

Prophesied

According to John, the Revelator, an end-time "mother" is forthcoming. This woman is described as a whore sitting upon many waters, representing a transnational mix of peoples, multitudes, nations, and tongues. "Mystery, Babylon the Great" (a title with which this whore is associated) represents the False Prophet and religious system of Revelation 17. Pictured as seated upon a beast bedecked with finery, this whore is inebriated with the blood of true believers. Her adulterated doctrine corrupts the minds of multitudes (Rev. 17:1,5,15).

While at the same time subservient to her, kings and great men of the earth, identified as "merchants," fornicate with her. These political and economic unions [of kings and merchants] with spiritual blasphemy [of the whore] produce "abominations of the earth" (Rev. 17:5; 18:23).

Accordingly, worship of Mother Earth *(Gaia)* is the basis for today's fashionable eco-theology. Many Christians buy into error promulgated by Father Thomas Berry, New Age Catholic priest and spokesperson for *Gaia*. Proponents view *Gaia*-Earth as an interconnected, living ecosystem whose divine nature prompts worship and whose delicate nature requires protection of world government. Berry's beliefs support the very big business of radical environmentalism, as expounded by Al Gore in *Earth in the Balance.*

Disassociation from the whore of Revelation 18 is imperative for safety's sake because "her sins have piled up as high as heaven." In the end, God will see to the destruction of this latter-day global "eco"-menical religion and its system of global governance. Having become rich off "the abundance of her delicacies," merchants of the earth will greatly mourn her ultimate demise. No longer will she promise limitless prosperity while wrongly "swearing by those who are no gods" (Jer. 5:7; Rev. 17:16,17, 18:3,11).

Until that time, she takes form in burgeoning democratic transnationalism, another name for globalism, but with specific attributes pertaining to the present context.

Contemporary Plutocracy

Simply put, a plutocracy is government by a controlling class of wealthy elitists. Curiously, Pluto in Greek mythology was Lord of Hades. Similarly of the underworld, "Mystery, Babylon the Great" melds politics (kings) with economics (merchants) to produce ecological fraud with religious overtures (abominations of the earth).

Many believe a central issue for America's future is emergence of a contemporary plutocracy, wedded to corporate power, which even renowned humanist Paul Kurtz admits to increasingly espousing "a spiritual/religious/supernatural mystique." In excess of twelve thousand environmental groups own huge stock portfolios and real estate holdings. It is they who control the legislative process that regulates developers and competing companies. Therefore, this emerging plutocracy weds spiritual, economic, and political components—all reflective of end-time, one-world government, as delineated in Bible prophecy.

"Collaborative commerce" may sound magnanimous, but cooperative capitalism among the world's leading corporate competitors eventually creates a new hierarchy of concentrated economic power, not necessarily in the best interest of our nation. The Bible calls those who fail to prioritize care of their own household (in this case, a nation) "worse than infidels" (1 Tim. 5:8).

Former Soviet President Mikhail Gorbachev publicly testified that the *cosmos* (world order) is his God. Gorbachev further advances environmental crisis as the international disaster key justifying *perestroika,* or global restructuring. His ideal is a contemporary plutocracy, and he is not alone.

Global Governance and the UN Millennium Summit

In August 2000, world religious leaders met in New York for the Millennium Summit of Religious Leaders. The summit was financed by billionaire Ted Turner—the same media and real estate mogul who calls the Ten Commandments "out of date." Hundreds of Zoroastrians, Shiite Muslims, Buddhists, Christian clerics, and tribal representatives (again, a transnational mix of "peoples, multitudes, nations, and tongues") endorsed specific measures that targeted world peace, easing poverty, and helping the environment—all principles of the *Charter for Global Democracy (Charter 99).*

The *Charter* was presented in September at the United Nations Millennium Assembly and Summit, whose objectives mirrored and expanded upon those of the Millennium Summit of Religious Leaders. According to radio host-historian Dr. Stan Monteith, this summit was "the most important gathering held in North America since our forefathers signed the *Declaration of Independence* 224 years ago."

The fifty-fifth annual meeting of the UN General Assembly, the Millennium Summit was the largest gathering of world leaders ever held. Funded in over 119 countries, spanning five continents, the summit drew generals, prime ministers, presidents, premiers, potentates—yes, kings and merchants—from all over the world.

Global governance is an ancient concept resurrected in 1991 by the International Socialist Party. With a vision to transform the

United Nations from a debating conglomerate to a sovereign entity, a seat of global governance, this New York gathering forged the future of the UN. The goal is to use existing national, state, and local governments as mere conduits to carry out UN policy.

A publication of the Democratic Socialists of America pinpointed now as "the time to press for the subordination of national sovereignty to democratic transnationalism." Given blessing and funding from once UN secretary-general Butrous-Butrous Ghali, Willy Brandt, former Chair of Socialist International, appointed twenty-eight members to his Commission on Global Governance.

After three years, the Commission published its 410-page report, *Our Global Neighborhood* (1995). A network of NGOs (nongovernmental organizations) advanced the report's agenda by simplifying the Commission's recommendations into a *Charter for Global Democracy (or Charter 99)*. Once again, the idea was (and is) to restructure and retool the UN, empowering it to implement global governance on three levels—economic, political, and spiritual.

The Charter for Global Democracy (Charter 99)

The *Charter* reflects official UN *economic* policy to consolidate all global agencies under direct authority of the UN, which in turn will regulate all transnational corporations and financial institutions. It demands an independent source of revenue for the UN (enter, global taxation) and calls for cancellation of all debt owed by the poorest nations (enter, redistribution of wealth). Its economic and environmental government-managed (i.e., sustainable) development falls under jurisdiction of an International Environmental Court.

In like fashion, the *Charter* reflects official UN *political* policy to eliminate America's veto power and permanent member status of the Security Council. Moreover, it authorizes a UN standing army, with reduction of all national armies and required registration of all arms.

Finally, it reflects official UN *ethical-moral* policy to require compliance with UN human rights treaties, some of which limit parental authority, and all of which are to be upheld by the International Court of Justice, compulsory for every nation.

As is the case with "Mystery Babylon, the Great," emerging democratic transnationalism mates merchants of the earth, and kings thereof, with a false religious system. Its *eco*-nomics is an industry involving many billions of dollars per year. At its root is pantheism (Greek: *pan,* "all"; *theos,* "God"), assigning greater intrinsic value to a presumably divine eco-system than to humans, whom God honors as crown of His creation. Some proponents outwardly call for worship of the goddess of Mother Earth, *Gaia,* whom Al Gore reveres as "fount of all life."

While the *Charter 99* agenda will take many years to implement, several very effective tactics propel it. The first is creating a perception of crisis that can be solved only by international cooperation. Hysteria linked to global warming and/or terrorism serves well this purpose. The second is to create perception of overwhelming public support, as has been attempted by proponents of global taxation. The third is use of double speak. Who would readily recognize that "freedom from fear" really addresses global gun control, or that "sustaining America's future" speaks to absolute authority over the global commons (environmental systems that support life)?

When resolution meets with the appearance of consensus, this is interpreted as authorization to move forward. The real impact of the UN's Millennium Summit is that, for the first time, extreme notions channeled through NGOs have been officially transformed into policy that the UN uses as sanction to pursue its ungodly plans.

Beware: Deception

Under Catholic leadership, the *Louvain Declaration* (1974) appeals to the religious community to propagandize planetary citizenship. Father Thomas Berry of the Temple of Understanding envisions a new Ecozoic Age, which he believes will transcend God. Protestant counterparts join Eco-Catholics in foreseeing "one church for one world." Sadly, this religiously pluralistic international community affords no rightful promise of salvation. Along with secular globalists, it calls for international accountability, peace, equality, justice, sustainable development, and democracy—all of which appeal even to born-again Christians who may fail to comprehend the underlying agenda and spiritual implications of each.

International Accountability

International accountability is not, as some wrongly presume, merely monitoring brutes guilty of genocide, war crimes, and aggression. It is instead international control. At his historic address to the UN in January of 2000, Senator Jesse Helms (R, North Carolina) called international law "make believe justification for hindering freedom."

The framework for enforcing world law is the International Criminal Court (ICC). Americans did not create the ICC, nor is it comprised of American judges—*nor* does it guarantee trial by a jury of peers, right to face one's accusers, or even right to know charges leveled. Nonetheless, the court prosecutes purported crimes against UN treaties. Even the Pentagon fears that, given the ICC, our military men and women could be subject to the judicial whim of foreign dictators, as Castro. But these are not the only ones at risk.

Take, for example, the *United Nations Convention on the Rights of the Child* (1989). Under it, American parents could be prosecuted for keeping away from their children violent movies, music, videos, or computer games. The *Convention on Elimination of All Forms of Discrimination against Women* (CEDAW) similarly usurps parental authority. Vague by design, CEDAW supersedes our *U.S. Constitution* in its effort to redefine the family. Indeed, the UN Fourth World Conference on Women (1995) and Beijing +5 in New York City (2000) include homo-, bi-, and trans-sexuals in defining "gender." In contrast, the Bible makes it clear that God acknowledges only two: "male and female" (Gen. 1:27).

Promised Peace

However appealing, promised peace is unattainable when it omits the Prince of Peace Himself. The worldly counterfeit for Christ's theocratic rule of peace is a multilateral global security system authorized to invade even America's borders, if deemed necessary. The Bible warns that the world's brand of pseudo-peace will destroy many (1 Thess. 5:3; Dan. 8:25).

Equality/Justice

In June of 2000, the Human Genome Project unveiled the first near-complete record of human DNA with promise of developing new therapies for genetically based illnesses. Cause for rejoicing was tempered by the threat of multiplied abortion in its wake. Given mapping of the human genome, some fear resultant practices of genetic engineering, determinism, and discrimination. In a genetically engineered world, faceless multinational corporations control virtually every aspect of life.

The United Nations Educational, Scientific, and Cultural Organization (UNESCO) *Declaration of Tolerance* (1995) essentially elevates rejection of moral absolutism to the status of legal requirement. With this in view, the bio-ethics program associated with the project may be dangerously compromised to embody the New Earth Ethic, which blatantly ignores fundamental Judeo-Christian values.

To the globalist, equality holds true exclusively for those to whom it applies. In a word, some are deemed "more equal" than others. In fact, for the sake of population control, many of the "less equal" among us are systematically eliminated by means of abortion on demand, infanticide (partial-birth procedure), and right-to-die advocacy. Industrialized nations provide nearly one and one-half billion dollars annually for UN population control. In time, seekers of death will not be granted this "out"; but for now, death options abound (Rev. 9:6).

Personal usefulness to the global community determines one's value as a citizen of the world. The UN Cairo Conference (1994) identified people as mere human resources whose numbers must be "managed" by international overseers. Clearly, today's eugenics reflects selective breeding practices abused by Nazis in the 1930s.

Foreign Policy Adviser to former President Clinton, Strobe Talbott is quoted as having said this: "Within the next one hundred years, nationhood will be obsolete; and all states will recognize a single, global authority." In the words of Henry Lamb, publisher of *Ēco-Logic,* this interdependent one-world state under global leadership will result in the United States' taking on "the lowest common denominator that forced equity demands."

Bear in mind the UN *Convention on the Elimination of All Forms of Discrimination against Women*. The overly broad language of this international Bill of Rights for women interferes with domestic law of the U.S. regarding adoption, marriage, divorce, child custody, and the like. Under CEDAW, the federal government would appropriate family law under the all-seeing eye of a lowest-common-denominator international bureau that does not embrace the Judeo-Christian model of traditional family.

Sustainable Development

Sustainability is described, not in any of America's founding documents, but rather in the 1997 *USSR Constitution* (Chapter #2; Article 18). It is a Marxist-Leninist principle, ascribing value to producers only. The pre-and new-born, the comatose, disabled, terminally ill, and severely depressed or mentally impaired are among those deemed of lesser value than productive counterparts. Why? Because sustainable communities require producers, not "depleters," as stay-at-home moms and retirees.

Sustainable development is naked socialism in that totalitarianism is necessary to guarantee that humans do not mess with biodiversity. Its impact is felt even in America's Bible belt. Chattanooga, Tennessee, for instance, leads the way as model for neighborhood restructuring toward environmentally friendly urban clusters and community sustainability.

Transferring the world's wealth under the UN principle of sustainable development may sound honorable, but in no way does it parallel voluntary giving urged by Scriptures. Taking away wealth eliminates incentive to create wealth. A better idea is to share the Gospel and freedom technology with a world in need.

To the illumined globalist, abortion is viewed as eco-friendly population control under the UN banner of sustainable development. Sustainable population control translates into sex education campaigns that applaud non-proliferating alternative lifestyles, taxpayer-funded abortions, and UN foreign aid for population control. "Reproductive health" may suggest well being, but in fact, it is an euphemism for legalized abortion on demand, globally.

Global Democracy

Globalists embrace a skewed perception of democracy and representation—in their minds, enjoyed exclusively by global elitists. The democratic component of democratic transnationalism is by no means overlooked in prophetic Scripture.

In a broadly accepted view of Revelation Chapters 2 and 3, the seven churches represent seven stages, or "ages," through which the church goes. Given this interpretation, Revelation 3:14 speaks of the lukewarm Laodicean church on the heels, as it were, of brotherly love and worldwide evangelism—i.e., Philadelphia Church Age.

In the Greek, "democracy" means "sovereign power of the community," not unlike Laodicea, which likewise means "rule of the people." This very church age to which we, as end-time believers, are headed is characterized by being spiritually tepid while fraught with the world's goods. By brazenly defying God's established order, today's cosmic citizens replicate the rebellion of Korah and his band (Rev. 3:14ff; Num. 16).

Democracy as defined by the UN allows citizens to participate in the process of government, true, but that very government is empowered to grant, control, and even withdraw privilege. Sure, people may vote; but rulers control all political parties. Remember that the communist concept of democracy and representation rests both political and economic power in the Communist Party.

Even Karl Marx praised democracy. Classic Marxism holds to the Robin Hood philosophy of distributing wealth. The Marxist/Leninist maxim of earning one's keep on planet earth is at the heart of UN sustainability, and Marx's egalitarian super-status for the mass proletariat is to be reflected in the State.

While many Christians applaud the global spread of democracy, some fail to realize what truly is happening. Today's trend is to transform America's Constitutional Republic into a social democracy headed by un-elected NGOs (non-governmental organizations authorized by the UN) whose decisions override local legislatures.

This social democracy is not to be confused with freedom, which holds that the Creator (not the State) grants unalienable rights of life, liberty, and pursuit of happiness. It is the God-given right to govern oneself, a right that cannot be imposed.

Social Democracy

- *UN Charter*
- NWO Democratic Transnationalism
- Praised by Karl Marx
- Government-granted privilege
- Flexible rule of the people
- Consists of Lukewarm Laodiceans
- Driven by passion of the majority
- Spirit of Korah's band (Numbers 16)
- Total government
- Broad way
- Leads to destruction (1 Thess. 5:3)
- Exemplified in Christ's Crucifixion when Pontius Pilate carried out the majority decree

CONSTITUTIONAL REPUBLIC

- *U. S. Constitution*
- USA Constitutional Republic
- Praised by founding fathers
- God-given right
- Fixed rule of law
- "Made for moral people," John Adams
- Driven by principle
- Spirit of law and order
- Limited government
- Narrow way
- Leads to liberty
- Exemplified in American Republic, providing more freedom to more people than any other government since the days of Samuel

Conclusion

On page 359 of *Our Global Neighborhood*, we read about "the challenge of securing peace, achieving sustainable development, and universalizing democracy." Regarding these lofty aspirations, please allow me to share our family's experience given Seattle's winter blast of 1997.

Living on a bluff, we are blessed with a high-perched view home. In the wake of rain, snow, freezing, and more rain, about one-third of our back yard unexpectedly gave way with incredible force, all in an instant of time. What appeared to be stable was declared "federal disaster area." By all appearances, the loss was sudden, significant, and apparently unrecoverable.

Democratic transnationalism misses the mark with grave consequences following. As Christian patriots, we do well to re-channel its relentless flow lest our national loss be similarly sudden, significant, and unrecoverable. Especially now, when Supreme Court Judges oppose the Ten Commandments and support the murder of viable infants, Christians must obey God's urgent call to "come out" (Rev. 18:4–5).

CHAPTER 7

Hamartia Ecumenicism

> Do not lay hands upon anyone too hastily and thus share responsibility for the sins [*hamartia*] of others; keep yourself free from sin (1 Tim. 5:22, NASB).

Laying on of Hands

Laying on of hands was an Old Covenant custom signifying any one of a number of notable events—for example, the parental bestowal of inheritance rights. In the New Covenant, this act further signifies bestowal of blessings and benediction, the restoration of health, or reception of the Holy Spirit. In both Old and New Covenants, the laying on of hands confers gifts and rights of an office (Matt. 9:18; 19:13, 15; Luke 24:50; Acts 6:6; 8:17, 19; 9:12, 17; 13:3; 19:6; Gen. 48:14–20; Num. 27:18, 23; Deut. 34:9; 1 Tim. 4:14; 2 Tim. 1:6).

Purity, gravity, and sobriety remain prerequisites for Christian service. None is to be ordained into the ministry in haste or unless that one is tested and approved. Continually missing the mark warrants rebuke, not honor. This is to protect followers from repeating the minister's error, doctrinally or morally (1 Tim. 5:20).

When Al Gore selected his vice-presidential running mate, many delighted that a bright, liberal Jew would grace the Democratic ticket. By all accounts, Senator Joseph Lieberman (D-Connecticut) is a man of honor. It was not broadly publicized, however, that a rabbinical court in Brooklyn excommunicated him for unorthodox stands in favor of partial-birth abortion, gay rights, and religious intermarriage of Jews. In an interview with *World* magazine (7 October 2000), cultural warrior William Bennett expressed "big disappointment" in his friend and one-time co-warrior. "There were days I thought I was standing next to Amos and Jeremiah," Bennett mused. "Turns out I was standing next to Seinfeld." Bennett bemoaned the fact that while Lieberman testified of his faith in Tennessee, he laughed about it in Hollywood. It seems that Senator Lieberman did not pass biblical muster for national leadership (Prov. 6:16a–19; Lev. 18:22; Gen. 24:3).

Notwithstanding, today's religious culture remains decidedly syncretistic. In calling upon different religious and cultural traditions to join hands, the World Council of Churches advocates arbitrary "laying on of hands," figuratively, without deference to scriptural protocol.

"One Church for One World" is the slogan of the World Council of Churches. Its standards are outlined in United Nations Education, Science, and Cultural Organization's 1994 *Declaration on the Role of Religion in the Promotion of a Culture of Peace,* signed in Barcelona. UNESCO's "soft" international law calls for respect of "truth and wisdom" found outside Judeo-Christian tradition. Its twenty-first-century ideal wrongly mandates subservience to leadership distinguished by what Paul identifies as "unfruitful works of darkness" (Eph. 5:11).

The Bible View on Ecumenicism

While God celebrates spiritual unity, He opposes pseudo-unity outside of redemption through Jesus Christ. His theocratic plan for peace and harmony will be realized in the forthcoming Millennial rule and reign of Christ, but certainly not by means of a counterfeit New World Order (John 17:21–23).

Although admittedly narrow, in no way is God's plan rooted in human pettiness. It is based instead on God's rightful concern for

His Name above all names, and for the well being of those who bear it. Most assuredly, God excludes no person or group—even sinners—from His boundless love. In Christ, no gender or social class is esteemed above the other; however, Amos 3:3 poses the fitting question, "How can two walk together except they be agreed?" The obvious answer is, "They can't." Today's religious community apparently disagrees (Isa. 55:9; Phil. 2:9–11; Acts 10:34; Rom. 5:8; John 3:16; 1 Cor. 12:13).

The United Religions Initiative (URI)

Founded by Episcopalian Bishop William Swing and permanently based at the Presidio in San Francisco, the United Religions Initiative is a sort of spiritual United Nations, its motto being, "unity in diversity." Fairly new to the interfaith scene, the URI is spurred from ideas of self-proclaimed "Father of United Religions" Dr. Robert Muller and Catholic theologian Hans Küng. The latter authored *Global Responsibility in Search of a New World Ethic*. From 31 December 1999 until 2 January 2000, the URI's "72 Hours" interfaith, bridge-building project drew groups from around the world.

Paving the way for the URI global assembly, bold new religious initiatives were presented in Budapest, Hungary in June 2000. This gathering witnessed the signing of an official URI charter based on principles of universalism (*non-selective* in endorsing varied paths to God) coupled with tolerance (*selective* for its exclusion of fundamental Christianity). Whatever is done in word or deed should be done in the name of the Lord Jesus; significantly, the name of Jesus was never once mentioned at the URI's charter-signing summit (Col. 3:17; Phil. 2:9–11).

The URI works at the grassroots level by means of Cooperation Circles, local church-like interfaith settings bringing together URI members for inter-religious worship and community planning. Eighty founding Cooperation Circles are "locally rooted and globally connected."

The URI is potentially a controlling factor within the global interfaith movement. Through its charter, URI members agree not to proselytize each other. Its Preamble supports religious expression rights only "as set forth in international law." Even proponents admit to the danger of suppressing genuine religious freedom.

Among UNESCO's decrees is identifying as a global threat any form of intolerance, as demonstrated by Bible-toting Christians. For example, to embrace a biblical view of homosexuality and lesbianism is deemed inappropriate intolerance, even hate. The URI's Emergency Response Network prides itself in responding to alleged hate against homosexuals, women, and minority races (Lev. 18:22; Rom. 1:24–27; 1 Cor. 5:9–10).

Jesus spoke of a time when persecutors of committed Christians would think they are serving God's purposes. Many of His followers correctly believe it is immoral to endow different groups with rights based on nothing other than gender or sexual orientation. Nonetheless, liberals in Congress are attempting to pass hate-crime legislation designed to punish *attitude* crimes motivated by "prejudice" more harshly than *behavior* crimes of greed or cruelty (John. 16:2).

True, God holds us accountable for our thought lives. It was Christ's mission not to undo the Law, but rather to bring it "to the full." In God's economy, anger with one's brother and lust of the heart are likened to murder and adultery, respectively. Hate-crimes advocates play God by presuming to know the hearts of others. This is evidenced throughout federally funded hate-crimes prevention curriculum, portraying Bible-honoring Christians as racist; Baptists and Pentecostals as murderous Nazis (Matt. 5:17, 21–24, 28).

UN World Peace Summit of Religious and Spiritual Leaders

In August of 2000, world religious leaders met in New York at the Millennium Summit of Religious Leaders to discuss and celebrate global interfaithism in tenor with Catholicism's Great Jubilee at the turn of the century. Leaders from the ranks of Buddhism, Hinduism, Jainism, Zoroastrianism, and Taoism heavily outnumbered representation from monotheistic faiths (Judaism, Islam, Christianity). Despite its peace and harmony theme, the summit was marred by manifest hostility. Chinese delegates walked out when a message from the uninvited Dalai Lama was read.

Three men made the UN World Peace Summit of Religious and Spiritual Leaders a reality. One was occultist Maurice Strong whose wife is a practicing Wiccan. UN Secretary-General Kofi Annan gave his blessing to the summit, but media mogul Ted Turner was its brainchild. Strongly antagonistic against biblical Christianity, Turner calls the Ten Commandments out of date. "If you're going to have to have ten rules," he adds, "I don't know if [prohibiting] adultery should be one of them" (Ex. 20:14).

World Council of Churches (WCC) and Political Correctness

For needed reforms to be fully implemented worldwide, Ross McCluney recommends a central guiding principle, or a new set of core values, that the entire human species can agree upon (McCluney 1994).

Toward this end, the WCC seeks to reunify various branches of today's diverse religious community into what Christian author Dave Hunt calls a "religiously pluralistic international community," not unlike that achieved under Constantine, ruler of the Roman world (AD 324). Today, however, its common denominator and major test of orthodoxy is the eco-theology of radical environmentalism. Guilt for human abuse of the environment, especially by Christians, provides motivation for the global call to exaggerated stewardship. Eco-justice demands our asking Earth, not necessarily God, for forgiveness.

Today's eco-menical movement has provided cover stories for all major religious publications from the Unitarian universalist magazine, *Word*, to *Christianity Today*. The movement's primary proponent is Upper Manhattan's Cathedral of St. John, the Divine, otherwise known as the Green Cathedral. Parishioners called for global convergence of world religions at the turn of the millennium.

Franklin D. Roosevelt was one of the Cathedral's chief fundraisers, and Al Gore frequently serves there as lay minister. Additional associates include top environmental activist and mystic Maurice Strong, not to mention the New Age movement's shining star, occultist David Spangler, who performs the Eucharist there.

An esoteric order connected to the Knights Templar, the *Gaia* Institute resides within the Cathedral. It applies Earth-worship's concept of interdependence to ecological cleanup for the federal Environmental Protection Agency.

Surrounded by Shinto and Native American shrines, Cathedral "worshippers" demonstrate a trendy pan-religious bent by performing *Tai Chi* rituals and Earth masses. Forces of Nature dancers leap up and down its aisles while the Howl-eluia Chorus of some two hundred politically correct Episcopalians display dubious oneness with Earth by literally howling at the moon.

WCC, Catholicism, and Baha'i Faith

The Greek term for "ecumenical" means "of the whole world." Ecumenicism is global unity of the entire religious community. Known as the first ecumenical council of the church, the Council of Nicaea issued its famous creed, sanctioned by the Emperor Constantine (AD 325). Under Constantine, his aides, and the papacy, a type of ecumenical unity, promising no licit salvation, was successfully achieved at the dear price of religious syncretism, as is the case today.

Formed in Holland (1948), the World Council of Churches continues to push privately for unification with the Church of Rome, whose ecumenical goals are revealed by ongoing dialogue with representatives of four major non-Christian religions. Under Catholic (meaning universal) leadership, the *Louvain Declaration* of 1974 appealed to religious communities of the world to propagandize the decidedly New Age perspective of "planetary citizenship."

Planetary Citizens is a Baha'i movement connected with the United Nations International Children's Emergency Fund (UNICEF). The Baha'i faith wholeheartedly supports UN empowerment and global governance.

During a recent trip to Dubai, my husband and I hired a guide. Formerly a Muslim, but recently converted to the Baha'i faith, Kamir was bright-faced, clear-eyed, and exceptionally fit and handsome. His devotion was reminiscent of a newly saved Christian. Freely, boldly he expounded tenants of his faith inclusive of pantheism, globalism, and harmonization coupled with spiritual unity, growth, and ultimate maturity. A Filipino, Kamir's wife is Catholic but nonetheless is "opening up" to the presumed upward mobility of egoic advancement, as espoused by her husband.

Years earlier, while living and ministering in the Arabian Gulf area, I often gazed into the eyes of Muslims. Time and again, I noted absence of that distinguishing twinkle which invariably accompanies one's having been with Jesus. In Kamir's case, it was different, disturbingly so, for his eyes virtually danced with light. In fact, Kamir sees himself as having become "enlightened."

With Kamir, his wife, and two beautiful children in view, I left Dubai feeling pensive and saddened by the powerful, but false light Kamir exuded with a devotion that puts to shame many a sleeping Christian. While promising peace and harmony among all cosmic citizens, Kamir's new, illumined worldview is destined instead to "sudden destruction" (1 Thess. 5:3).

WCC and Universalism

Perhaps not surprisingly, the World Council of Churches is strongly influenced by the largest secret society in the world, Freemasonry. Masonic authority Carl H. Claudy boasts of the society's tolerance for all religions. Upon the altar of the thirty-third degree initiation ceremony are four "holy books"—namely, the Bible, the *Koran*, the *Book of Law*, and the *Hindu Scriptures*. According to many acknowledged Masonic authors, "any god will do." No matter their personal beliefs, all men in the brotherhood are seen as "spiritual sons of God," who swear to protect the brotherhood, right or wrong. To the contrary, Jesus told Thomas, "I am the way, the truth, and the life; no man cometh unto the Father but by me" (John 14:6).

WCC and Islamic Fundamentalism

Once head of Middle Eastern studies at Cambridge, Dr. Arthur J. Arberry is an outstanding professor of Arabic and Persian studies. In his famous two-volume work, *Religion in the Middle East*, Arberry shows Islamic religion and culture to be fundamentally one. Even the former Foreign Minister of Iran, Dr. Ali Dashi, a Muslim scholar, agrees that Islam must be understood in terms of its seventh-century Arab culture, imposed worldwide without conscience by means of tribal brutality.

Of the world's six billion inhabitants, about 20 percent embrace Islam. Many Muslims hold controlling governmental positions in Russia, for example, where one out of three, especially in the south, professes the faith of Islam.

Given that the dominant religion in Great Britain is fast becoming Islam, the Prince of Wales has called for better understanding of its "important message for the West"—that being, preservation of an integrated, spiritual view of the world. With this in mind, Prince Charles calls for increased recruitment of Muslim teachers in Britain's schools in hopes of bringing Christianity and Islam closer together.

Even in America, throughout the Clinton-Gore administration, a Muslim clergyman opened Congress in prayer; and the Muslim month of *Ramadan* (fasting) was observed in the White House. According to Islam expert Dr. Robert Morey, public schools distribute the *Koran* in a show of diversity; moreover, a Muslim representative in Hollywood ensures that Islam is not portrayed in any bad light. Since the attack on America (11 September 2001), many people in the public arena have made concerted effort to liken good Muslims to good Christians, as if their respective faiths were equal (which they are not).

Says Dr. Morey, Muslims in the U.S. already outnumber Episcopalians. As many as 70 percent of the residents in Dearborn, Michigan are Muslim. By 2020, more than twenty-five million Muslims will join America's faith community, thus elevating Islam to a position second only to Roman Catholicism.

Many applaud such inclusiveness, but consider this. Anywhere in the world that Islam is practiced as the majority religion, human rights and freedom are implicitly impossible. Take, for example, Robert Hussein. Raised a Kuwaiti Muslim, Hussein later converted to Christ. As a result, a Shiite Islamic court judged him guilty of apostasy and, therefore, worthy of divorce from his wife, redistribution of his wealth, and even execution.

According to Michael Horowitz of the Hudson Institute, Islamic regimes are most guilty of persecuting Christians. Donald MacAlvany of *Voice of the Martyrs* fingers Saudi Arabia as the worst persecutor of Christians—with North Korea coming in second.

Furious because Muslims are converting to Christ, militant Muslims in Jakarta, Indonesia declared *jihad* against Christians; furthermore, their anti-Christian pogroms meet with little government interference. Similarly, the "Baghdad Butcher," Saddam Hussein, maintains brutal power for one reason—that being, the Islamic religious establishment backs him.

Iran funds some thirty terrorism schools in Sudan, and its Muslim government is waging a brutal war against Christians. As a result, millions have been killed, displaced, tortured, or sold into slavery. In Nigeria, some two thousand were killed in religious violence spearheaded by Muslims seeking to impose Islamic law on all.

One U.S. official has reported, "It has been a long time since I have seen such strong anti-American feelings in the Middle East." Arab rage over "decadent" U.S. support of Israel insures continued Islamic terrorism against the U.S. and Jewish targets worldwide.

WCC and the New World Order

Nevertheless, the Washington State Interfaith Council purposes to set aside religious differences on behalf of the New World Order. Similar councils are springing up around the world as never before. There are more than seventy in the U.S. alone, and the number is growing. Toward achieving shared one-world goals, the World Council of Churches collaborates with the World Constitution and Parliamentary Association, a forefront association poised to realize the global agenda. Called "Positive Christianity," the push for global unity proclaims a sort of mish-mash "good news" that most can affirm.

The year 2000 ushered in the United Nations' International Year of the Culture of Peace. With it comes new pressure to establish the Third Wave global management system, allowing governments to yield responsibilities, albeit not control, to civil society. Non-governmental organizations (NGOs) are required to implement the vision, conforming churches to demands in UNESCO's *Declaration on Religion in a Culture of Peace.*

An United Methodist leader of the North Illinois Conference, Bishop C. Joseph Sprague founded Communities of Shalom, committed to guard against "the offense of the Cross" (that is, presuming Jesus to be the only way, as Scripture maintains). He further promotes a public program that includes mental health based on politically correct standards. To many, politically correct spirituality and world convergence appear both normal and necessary.

Global solidarity is no new notion to Bible scholars. The book of Revelation warns of Great Apostasy earmarked by nations coming together into "one mind." The apostle Paul describes members of this united global community as demonstrating misplaced love of money, self, and pleasure. Furthermore, this single-minded conglomerate will exercise a form of religion devoid of God's power and marked by drug abuse, profanity, and moral laxity. Orthodox Rabbi Daniel Lapin and his colleague, Michael Medved, tag this phenomenon "America's Real War"—a culture war. More accurately, it is spiritual warfare against *poneros*, or "active evil" (2 Tim. 3:1–5; Eph. 6:12).

Despite a show of global consensus, coupled with premature celebration of universal harmony and peace, the one-world system will be plagued with wars and rumors of war, many of which are ethnic in nature. Already, there are over thirty ethnic wars ongoing in the world (Matt. 24:7).

In a word, ecumenicism is not what it is cracked up to be. Light cannot possibly fellowship with darkness and still remain light. For this reason, the clear command of Scripture is not to link hands, but rather to withdraw from those who walk "out of the ranks." This includes, but is not limited to New Age idolaters and Earth-worshippers (Rom. 1:25; 2 Thess. 3:6; 14).

Christians, be warned. Interfaith ecumenism, as embraced by the World Council of Churches, neutralizes the inspired Word of God and must not be embraced. Tragically, universalists will miss out on the blessing of worldwide unity under rule of the very Prince of Peace Himself. Added to that, they will experience certain wrath of God for participating in blasphemy and for compelling others to do so (Rev. 14:9–11).

CHAPTER 8

Hamartia
Pseudo Egalitarianism

And having come, He will reprove the world concerning sin *(hamartia),* and concerning righteousness, and concerning judgment (John 16:8, Rotherham).

In 1945, English novelist and essayist George Orwell wrote the satire *Animal Farm* in which he declared all animals to be equal, "but some are more equal than others." Guided by the United Nations' ruling principle of sustainable development, today's brand of egalitarianism is similarly lop-sided. You see, some are considered to be "more equal" than others. In contrast, God pairs true equity with righteousness, viewing a just weight as "His delight" and a false balance as "abomination" (Prov. 2:9; 11:1).

Egalitarianism may sound good for its supposed advocacy of political, economic, and legal equality for all. In fact, it is no more than a specious buzzword for nepotism (or favoritism), demonstrated in affirmative action's styling of reverse discrimination and its prevailing culture of entitlement. In 1949, Orwell wrote *1984* to portray dangers of excessive State control over individuals. How true his uncanny predictions proved to be.

Ruling Elite "More Equal" than the Masses Versus James 2:1–9

The Lord's brother, James, exposed the folly of partiality. To honor the rich and powerful over the poor is wrong. Take, for example, those recommended for special training in internationalism by being awarded Rhodes Scholarships. These are persuaded that exceptional talents and aptitude guarantee their right to rule over less gifted masses judged to be unaware of what is good for them. A former special assistant in the U.S. Department of Education's Office of Educational Research and Improvement, Charlotte Thomson Iserbyt wrote *The Deliberate Dumbing Down of America*. In it, she unveiled the global charge to produce compliant, subservient workers for a collectivist society—more specifically an oligarchy, government by a ruling elite (James 2:1–9).

In his masterpiece, *Tragedy and Hope: A History of the World in our Time*, Harvard trained Professor Carol Quigley fingered a power-elite network of Round Table Groups. Quigley referenced the secret society of Cecil John Rhodes, whose prestigious scholastic fund was founded at Oxford University for scholars from the Commonwealth, Germany, and the U.S.

According to Rhodes, America's charge is to join in helping England establish Anglo-Saxon imperialism. To elitists, the "white man's burden" is a sacred trust undertaken by the Anglo-American Establishment to provide for the well being of peoples unfitted for self-government. It is alleged that this Anglophile network controls what Americans see, read, and think—and rightly so if one were to ask Quigley or his protégé, former President William Clinton. Himself a Rhodes scholar, Clinton accepted the principles of Oxford Professor John Ruskin. It was this self-proclaimed "reddest of the red" who mentored Rhodes along these lines.

Rhodes' Society of the Elect is not alone in its elitist vision. Yale's Skull and Bones represents yet another secret society aiming for world dominion by a ruling elite. Says David Icke, the Society is not an "old boys network," but rather "a vicious group of interbreeding bloodlines seeking to impose their agenda on the global population." Its membership of Republicans and Democrats alike include three U.S. Presidents, not to mention members of the CIA, State Department, Supreme Court, and Senate.

This "government in exile" has a mind to create in today's world community a new culture favoring ruling elitists not unlike Babylon's Nimrod, Egypt's Pharaoh, and Rome's Caesar. Keep in mind that apart from Jesus Christ, every historic case of multinational government under a ruling elite has resulted in tyranny.

In contrast, God opposes those who are "partial in themselves," having become self-appointed "judges of evil thoughts." The Lord is high and lifted up, yet He regards the lowly. Although citizens are to obey rulers, and respect dignitaries, they are not required to cower as inferiors (James 2:4; Ps. 138:6; Heb. 13:17; Rom. 13:1).

Global Citizens "More Equal" than Patriots Versus Acts 10:28

Death of rugged American ideals subjugates the individual to the common heritage of mankind. Toward this end, UN Secretary-General Kofi Annan believes in redefinition of state sovereignty by forces of globalization and international cooperation. With this in view, patriotism is frowned upon; and America's natural competitive nature is discouraged.

To popularize belief that Great Britain had a moral mandate to consolidate the world under Anglo-Saxon rule, Alfred L. Tennyson wrote of the "parliament of men" and "federation of the world." In like fashion, German philosopher and social theorist Karl Marx argued for transformation of human life and nature, tacitly claiming an egalitarian super status for the mass proletariat, which was to be reflected in the State. Some may be surprised to learn that Marx favored democracy.

To "democratize" according to Marx means that government allows certain individuals to partake in some discussions relating to a particular policy proposal. Only those who support the policy, however, are allowed to participate. All rights are granted, controlled, and/or withdrawn by the government. The United Nations shares Karl Marx's praise for democracy. Its push for democratic transnationalism allows world citizens to vote, but ruling elitists maintain control of all political parties. In the words of the Trilateral

Commission's founding director, Zbigniew Brzezinski, "Marxism represents a further vital and creative stage in the maturing of man's universal vision."

The setup for this universal vision of global governance is soft law at the international level. "Soft law" consists of unenforceable agreements between two nations that appear to be consensus and, therefore, have a way of slowly evolving into enforceable world law. Eagle Forum's Phyllis Schlafly joins Trinity law professor, James Hirsen, in sounding the alarm. Both believe that United Nations treaties chip away at American sovereignty, liberties, and freedom to self-govern.

Agreements, executive orders, conventions, pacts, declarations, treaties, and summits all serve to construct a new global bureaucracy exercising undue control over families, schools, businesses, and natural resources. Formerly of the House of Representatives, Helen Chenoweth adds to this list the takeover of our military.

Scriptures encourage individual courage on behalf of fellow countrymen and for the "cities of our God"—namely, our homeland. Christian patriots wisely steer clear of consolidated global powers typified by a one-world, end-time rule. In God's economy, global citizens are not "more equal" than patriots (Rev. 17:11–13; 2 Sam. 10:12).

Multinational Corporations "More Equal" than Consumers Versus 1 Timothy 6:10

According to Phyllis Schlafly, powerful multinational corporations want a world without borders, called harmonization, with increasing concessions to Communist China. Why? Because they are more interested in trade than in preserving freedom, national sovereignty, and human rights. Political dissidents, Christians, and women who violate China's one-child policy are coerced in *gulags* to produce chinaware, artificial Christmas trees, and garments. To be "reformed through labor" requires no trial by a jury of one's peers. Americans nonetheless applaud China and bestow upon her "favored nation" or "permanent normal trading" status. This is true even though, by principle, two cannot rightly walk together "except they be agreed" (Amos 3:3).

By definition, consumerism seeks to protect rights of buyers by requiring honest advertising, fair pricing, and improved safety standards. A powerful new drive in society, consumerism is by and large a good thing. Conspicuous consumption, however, is not. Given preeminence of free trade and fierce materialism attendant to it, consumerism is fast becoming the targeted enemy of sustainability. Increasingly, it is perceived as the primary threat to earth's resources.

For the supposed welfare of all, many demand that responsible citizens voluntarily sacrifice God-given personal liberty. But take a look at the virtuous woman of Proverbs 31. She exemplifies consumerism at its best. This extraordinary woman of ability is likened to merchants' ships that transport goods from afar. In addition to seeking out goods and services, she sells—and supplies merchants with—her own product line of fine linen and garments. As a global trader and resourceful consumer, this industrious homemaker draws praise, not scorn (2 Cor. 3:17; Prov. 31:14, 18, and 24).

Despite God's favorable assessment of her, the politically correct no doubt would juxtapose her entrepreneurial nature opposite sustainable development. Many modernists would criticize the virtuous woman despite her balanced use of the *cosmos*, or whole world order, which God allows (1 Cor. 7:31).

Blacks "More Equal" than Whites Versus Galatians 6:27–29

Harold Koh of the State Department reports that global sex trade surpasses even its drug trade. Especially in the Ukraine, Albania, the Philippines, Thailand, Mexico, and Nigeria, some two million women worldwide are forced into sexual slavery. Incredibly, the UN *Convention on the Elimination of Discrimination Against Women* (CEDAW), signed by Jimmy Carter (1980), but yet to be ratified, encourages legalized voluntary prostitution in the name of advancing women's rights. This, of course, mocks biblical wisdom (Prov. 2:15–19).

Some fear that a crackdown on sexual trafficking will inhibit access to prostitution as a viable "career option." Perhaps for this reason, strategists have shifted attention from sexual slavery to the ills of slavery in America. All the while African-Americans cry for reparations, the Sudanese government persists in killing in excess of 1.9 million—with many more displaced, tortured, and sold into slavery. Startlingly, while the global community applauds reparations for bygone ills, it takes no action to condemn ongoing atrocities, as these.

Politically correct black activist Randall Robinson wrote *The Debt: What Americans Owe to Blacks*. In it, he blames white folks for black poverty. To level the score, Robinson calls for taxpayers to underwrite black reparations. The cost could reach trillions of dollars. This is true even though not a single African-American alive today was ever a slave, nor was a single living white American a slave owner.

Spiritually speaking, neither is more equal than the other. In Christ, we learn that distinctions based on gender, race, or social status do not apply. In God's eyes, there is neither male nor female, Jew nor Greek, bond nor free—black nor white. Because it is not right to do wrongly that somehow good may come, reverse discrimination cannot possibly be a godly solution for the offense of bigotry (Gal. 3:28; Ps. 34:14; Acts 10:28).

Gays "More Equal" than Straight Counterparts Versus Romans 1:26–27

In his second epistle to the Thessalonians, Paul encouraged believers to hold fast the godly traditions they had been taught. Moreover, he commanded them to withdraw from others who refused to do so. Contrary to Paul's instruction, the postmodernist puts forth the concept of "transcending differences" by rising above godly traditionalism (e.g., *U.S. Constitution*, traditional family, and Judeo-Christian ethic). This insurgent view was celebrated on 20 March 2000 at World Citizenship Day in gay-friendly San Francisco (2 Thess. 2:15; 3:6).

UNESCO's *Declaration of Tolerance* decrees the perceived intolerance of Bible believing traditionalists to be "a global threat."

Instead, the UN mandates its own brand of tolerance, even to the point of cheerfully accepting immorality. Accordingly, "the wicked freely strut about when what is vile is honored among [*tolerant*] men," Psalm 12:8 (NIV).

When her television show roused scathing criticism, talk show hostess Dr. Laura Schlessinger learned well the lesson that political correctness effectively excludes the possibility of good-faith dissent. This applies particularly when that dissent is based on traditional Judeo-Christian values. Dr. Laura's moral criticism of homosexual parenting and special rights prompted gay activists to demand that Paramount drop her show.

So-called tolerance was taken a step further when Las Vegas narcotics detective Vinten Hartung sexually molested a boy he had met on the Internet. Rather than face charges, this practicing homosexual was put on administrative leave. According to Deputy District Attorney Doug Herndon, to prosecute would, in effect, "single out homosexuals"; and that would not be "tolerant." It seems that, in this case, gays were considered to be more equal than straight counterparts whose own illicit behaviors pretty much guarantee conviction and incarceration.

To reach out to gays with hope for their deliverance, the national *Truth in Love Campaign* was launched. In response, gay activists falsely accused the religious right of inciting hatred and promoting intolerance. Dozens of United Ways cut off funding to over 6.2 million "morally straight," presumably hate-filled Boy Scouts when, in the summer of 2000, the Supreme Court allowed exclusion of homosexuals from among their ranks. The court ruled correctly that a private organization has every right to set its own standards for leadership.

Incredibly, a federally funded, hate-crimes prevention curriculum that the Justice Department distributes to fifth-through eighth-graders portrays Christians as racists. It specifically equates Baptists and Pentecostals with Nazis and murderers. Ironically, *Healing the Hate: A National Hate Crimes Prevention Curriculum* for middle schools does more to magnify hate than to prevent it. In the realm of political correctness, perceived intolerance simply won't be tolerated! Professing to be wise, some show themselves instead to be foolish (Rom. 1:22).

Fit "More Equal" than the Unfit Versus Proverbs 6:17

Co-founder and first director-general of the United Nations Educational, Scientific, and Cultural Organization, Sir Julian Huxley hoped to improve the human race by denying certain people the ability to reproduce. Planned Parenthood's founder, Margaret Sanger believed similarly. In 1939, she went so far as to identify the unfit as "inferior" blacks and "expendable" fundamentalists and Catholics.

Eliminating the unfit is big business. Industrialized nations provide $1.4 billion annually for UN population control measures. In Holland, there is legal precedence established for mercy killing, even in the case of a depressed teen's suicide. In fact, doctors kill approximately 3,500 per year; furthermore, the Dutch government has documented over one thousand cases a year in which physicians caused or hastened death without patient consent.

America, too, has joined the bandwagon. In 1994, voters in Oregon legalized doctor-prescribed death; and in 1998, Janet Reno declared that, in states permitting assisted suicide, doctors could use federally regulated lethal substances to kill their patients. In God's economy, to the contrary, the very least is counted worthy of comparable human kindness afforded even the fittest among us. Neither is "more equal" than the other (Matt. 25:40).

Women "More Equal" than Men Versus Galatians 3:28

Founded in New York (1966) to promote the women's movement, the National Organization for Women (NOW) boasts up to a half-million members. Its president, Pat Ireland, and other chronically offended feminists advance the haughty notion of female superiority.

Perhaps it is no coincidence that the endtime false, one-world religious system is depicted in Chapter 17 of the book of Revelation as a great whore—not a comely Shulamite bride (Song of

Solomon), nor a virtuous woman (Proverbs 31). From God's perspective, her rebellion is "as the sin of witchcraft" (1 Sam. 15:23).

For women to be among the world's producers, not depleters (as childbearing, dependent housewives), may classify them as pioneer genderists and good global citizens; but they merit no favored distinction in God's Kingdom (Acts 10:34; Gal. 3:28).

Adults "More Equal" than Infants Versus Romans 15:1

Embryonic stemcell research creates tiny humans in petri dishes for the purpose of harvesting their cells for medical treatments. Adults purpose to "create" infants solely for their body parts. Already, collecting, processing, and distributing human tissue (bones, tendons, skin, body parts) is a near billion-dollar national business.

A Melbourne-based company, Stemcell Sciences, for one, allegedly has formed cloned human embryos by implanting human DNA into pigs' eggs. Human clones may well hold out promise for organ/tissue replacement donation, cure of disease, and bringing hope to the childless. But as believers, we are not to please ourselves by sacrificing the weak (Rom. 15:1).

The United Nations twists human rights beyond recognition in defining new rights, such as the "right" to abort. Offering free abortions off the coast of any country that prohibits them, Dr. Rebecca Gompers is raising money to equip a 150-foot ship as a sea-going abortion clinic. Even professing Christians, as the Reverend Deborah McKinley of Old Street Presbyterian Church, escort women to abortion clinics for Planned Parenthood. Keep in mind that one out of four dollars earned by Planned Parenthood comes from killing unborn children.

To justify this chilling trend, philosopher Peter Singer wrote an article entitled, "Killing Babies Isn't Always Wrong." Newborns, he reasoned, are not really persons. They don't acquire a right to live until weeks, even months, after birth. Why? Because they lack "self awareness." MIT evolutionary psychologist Dr. Steven Pinker likewise doubts the full personhood of neonates (infants) for their lack of "morally significant traits." To ensure sustainable development, Pinker proposes infanticide. He wrote in the *New York Times* that an eighteen-year-old who abandoned her newborn in a bathroom was acting on a "genetic imperative." While it is possible for a woman to forget the son of her womb, it is not natural or godly to do so (Isa. 49:15).

Theories put forth by the father of situation ethics, Joseph Fletcher, align with those promulgated by Singer and Pinker. For death lobby advocates, Fletcher has determined fifteen indicators of personhood as qualification for right to life. His list specifically excludes the pre-and new-born, not to mention those seriously developmentally disabled.

In Jeremiah 32:35 and Leviticus 18:21, God expressly forbids volunteering one's child to pass through the fire of death. In no way does He view adults as being "more equal" than their offspring—whether or not they possess "self-awareness," "morally significant traits," or any of Fletcher's phony criteria for "personhood."

Living Ecosystem "More Equal" than Humanity Versus Matthew 6:26, 30

Dr. Reed F. Noss developed the United Nations Wildlands Project, which describes biosphere core-and buffer-zones as places where "collectivist needs of non-human species take precedence over the needs and desires of humans." While God honors mankind over and above His creation, biocentrists do not. Instead, they assign greater intrinsic value to the ecosystem when compared with even a billion human bodies—this, according to Green biologist David Graber (Matt. 6:26, 30; 10:31).

Gorbachev's *Earth Charter* promises to set things straight. A type of *Bill of Rights*, this planetary commandment of sorts binds humans to earth servitude. According to this *Magna Carta* of New World civilization, saving Mother Earth takes preeminence over saving souls for Christ. Matthew 16:26 exposes the falsehood of forfeiting one's soul to gain the world.

To instill ecological consciousness into all spheres of our society, the late David Brower founded the Earth Island Institute (1982). According to this former director and chief executive of the Sierra

Club, mankind no longer qualifies as crown of God's creation. To him, the living ecosystem is "more equal" than humanity. You see, Brower believed that the earth now supports ten times more people than it is able to handle over the long run. With an apparent view to reverse God's mistaken command to be fruitful and multiply, Brower offered his own final solution.

To proponents of eco-justice, as Brower, man is a cancer, all of whose activities are considered unsustainable. Former consultant for our Department of Defense, Barbara Marx Hubbard specifically identifies who among us should be sacrificed to achieve the world's population level for optimum sustainability. In *The Revelation*, Hubbard goes so far as to target Christians as "defective seed." If for this reason alone, it is disturbing to recall that Hubbard ran for the 1984 Democratic vice presidential nomination; and she is linked to the prestigious World Future Society, a kind of clearinghouse for all global conglomerates.

Non-Christians "More Equal" than Christians Versus John 3:36

Embraced by Freemasons, Rosicrucians, theosophists, and universalists, the "any god will do" manner of thinking fails to plumb with God's Word. Nevertheless, today's new tolerance accepts all beliefs as equally valid. Not to offend is its chief virtue—except, of course, when it comes to biblical Christianity. It would appear that the sole form of bigotry considered acceptable in America today is anti-Christian bigotry (Isa. 43:10–12; 44:6, 8).

American secularists sanction free speech for feminists, Marxists, pornographers, and gays, but not for fundamental Christians. Although over seventy million Americans go to church, Christian speech is just about the only expression banned. This applies even though 94 percent of our founding documents are based on the Bible. Of those, 34 percent are direct quotations.

Supreme Court decisions—e.g., *Church of the Holy Trinity v. the U.S.*—prove our nation was founded on Christian principles, one of which is prevailing prayer. Nevertheless, there is a movement underfoot to stop Congress from opening each day with prayer. Added to that, American school children are being suspended for no worse offense than saying grace over lunch (Acts 12:5; 1 Thess. 5:17).

Chester Pierce of Harvard University labels every American child entering school at the age of five as "insane." Why? Because he is presumed to embrace family values as prescribed by traditional Judeo-Christian ethic. Father of Progressive Education, John Dewey likewise perceived each child as a pawn to be trained out of the Bible's allegedly inferior mindset. When in 1952 Dewey died, the overpowering Protestant character of early public schools was extinct.

Though defamed by some, Christians nonetheless are destined to great reward. Truly, eye has not seen, nor ear heard, what God has prepared for the faithful (1 Cor. 4:13; 1 Cor. 2:9).

Global Village "More Equal" than the U.S. of A. Versus 2 Samuel 10:12

In a letter dated 25 December 2000 and published in the *Washington Post,* Mikhail Gorbachev instructed President George W. Bush. As a "citizen of the planet," Gorbachev admonished the President that America's claim to hegemony is not recognized throughout the world. That the twenty-first century can, or even should, be the "American Century," is illusory, "devoid of meaning," and "dangerous." With trendy blame-America-first fervency, Gorbachev further insisted that America's extraordinary privilege is not tenable over the long run.

To build the New Paradigm, and further European unity, U.S. policy must yield to that of an allegedly superior Global Village whose agenda calls for dissolution of national sovereignty. This one-world order promises peace and just redistribution of the world's wealth. In his letter, Gorbachev rebuked the U.S. for her inability to adjust to what he calls this new European reality.

To the undiscerning, the plan sounds good. According to God's Word, however, the New World Order's companion religious system, in time, will require all to worship a coming global despot, called Antichrist. Sadly, proclaimed peace will meet with sudden destruction (1 Thess. 5:3).

Sustainable Development: Environment, Economy, Equity

Sustainable development is the socialist principle of government-managed development. According to Beverly LaHaye of Concerned Women for America, sustainable development is a specious term the UN uses to say that wealth and resources must be redistributed and populations curtailed. Global elitists purpose to ease control of human activities, reproduction, and wealth by "re-mapping modern society's new third-millennium reality." Their expressed plan is to downsize cities and towns into "urban clusters" that blend work places, housing, and nature.

By participating in "collective public visioning," good citizens will be held accountable for achieving rapid transition to community sustainability, green code word for shutting down progress. Tax-exempt foundations, large corporations, the media, and men of wealth who control them back this no-growth, one-world collectivist agenda.

Three E's of the UN concept of sustainable development are *e*nvironment, *e*conomy, and *e*quity.

Environment

Would-be environmentalist Mikhail Gorbachev is a global elitist who looks for a world fascist society. His vision includes "equitable" distribution of the world's resources. An "international disaster key," he believes, is needed to usher in his New Paradigm. Radical environmentalism serves well this purpose. Unknown to many, the movement promotes a radical political agenda that outranks its professed campaign for conservation. The 102-year-old Sierra Club, for example, owns stock in polluting companies. Also, rabid environmentalist Al Gore freely accepted illegal foreign contributions from the world's worst polluter nation, Communist China.

The *Global Biodiversity Assessment* (GBA) is an 1,100-page document put out by Cambridge University to implement policy of a treaty signed at the 1992 Earth Summit. This document ensures global sustainable development by returning to a feudal lifestyle void of amenities, as cars and air conditioners. Executive coordinator for UN reform, Maurice Strong calls for collapse of industrialized civilizations. It was he who laid out the GBA. In his goal to limit consumption, reduce standards, and manipulate crisis, Maurice Strong is not alone.

Founded in 1968, an occult-driven spin-off from the Council on Foreign Relations, the Club of Rome issued the 1972 report, *Limits of Growth*. In *Limits to Growth*, COR elitists admit to creating artificial shortages, as affirmed by the *1992 Rio Report to the Club of Rome*. In retrospect, the 1973 fuel crisis demonstrated ability of our government to manipulate world events and create crisis situations for one major purpose—that being, control.

Economy

Keep in mind that ours is a totally wired civilization, thoroughly dependent on electricity for daily comforts, true, but also for industry and production, transportation and communication. No doubt the very complex and vital issues relating to energy serve well an agenda of elitist control.

For over a century, the Rockefeller family and banks they control have dominated the oil industry in the United States. Aware that nuclear power threatens their holdings, the Rockefeller family manipulate most media outlets to convince the public, wrongly so, of the danger of nuclear reactors. In fact, it is they who propel radical environmentalism to oppose viable nuclear options to supply needed energy. Theirs appear to be motives of deceit, profit, and control by means of collusion and manipulation of the "power pool."

Equity

Curiously, affluent environmental activists rarely, if ever, live in communities they maim by stripping ranchers, loggers, timber mill workers, miners, and farmers of their livelihoods—all in the name of uncompromising ideology. In the Southwest, they reside in artsy Santa Fe or the university town, Tucson. Many live well off of generous grants received from establishment institutions like the Rockefeller and Pew Foundations, not to mention billionaires, as Ted Turner.

Aptly dubbed "Prince Albert" by colleagues, Al Gore considers the automobile a "mortal threat." In fact, over a twenty-five year period, his dream is to eliminate the internal combustion engine. Nonetheless, Gore relishes the luxury of being transported by chauffeur-driven (even air-conditioned) limousine. In Carthage, Tennessee, his tenant Tracy Mayberry calls Mr. Gore a "slum lord," not a friend to the little guy, as he would portray himself. Radical egalitarianism, it seems, applies to the masses only, not to the elite few, who consider themselves to be "more equal" than others.

The Broader Picture

Historian Arnold Toynbee (of the Rhodes' Group) spoke at the Institute for the Study of International Affairs (1931), admitting "we" are "working discreetly with all our might" to extract sovereignty out of the clutches of local nation-states. More recently (Summer 1991, *Eco-Socialist Review*), Democratic Socialists of America designated now as the time to press for subordination of national sovereignty.

The reason for this is elaborated in the *UN Report on Human Development* (1994, page 88), which disparages ability of national governments to solve mankind's problems—e.g., the California energy crisis, global warming hysteria, threat of terrorism, and the like.

Second in command at the UN, Maurice Strong agrees that what is needed instead of nationalism is world government. Because Strong believes the constitutional sovereignty of the United States to be "unfeasible," global governance is necessary. In his book, *A Reporter's Life*, retired CBS anchor Walter Cronkite likewise puts forth a system of world government as "mandatory," even at the expense of sovereignty.

As the *Humanist Manifesto II* (1973) deplores the division of humankind on nationalistic grounds, so do global elitists deplore division on political, economic, and legal grounds. The reason is clear. In a sovereignty-free world order, global elitists are free to manipulate resources (human resources included) for the purpose of control. Of course, they excuse themselves from impact of practices initiated in the name of utopian sustainability and egalitarianism.

Why? Because they are "more equal" than others and therefore more deserving of privilege.

Conclusion

Under socialism, the government takes from each according to ability, and gives to others according to need. A seemingly sincere and benevolent ideal, today's egalitarianism is naked socialism. It is a transition stage between capitalism (free market; open competition) and communism (common ownership of production means; absence of social classes). Through welfare programs, America is getting socialism on the installment.

The fact remains, socialism does not work without force. Elitists in high places are working feverishly to birth a New World Order. To them, the end justifies means. Their brand of pseudo-egalitarianism positions them on the high end of the totem pole. Concerning righteousness and judgment, this represents *hamartia* to which vigilant Christians must not succumb (John 16:8).

CHAPTER 9

Hamartia Extreme Fundamentalism

> But the tax-gatherer, standing some distance away, was even unwilling to lift up his eyes to heaven, but was beating his breast, saying, "God, be merciful to me, the sinner *[hamartolos]*" I tell you, this man went down to his house justified rather than [the Pharisee] (Luke 18:11, 13, 14, NASB).

In a broad sense, fundamentalism is a movement, or point of view, characterized by rigid adherence to any basic principle. While Protestant fundamentalism can be a good thing, it nonetheless represents *hamartia* when taken to extremes.

Dar al Islam, "House of Islam"

Today, fundamentalism is more often than not paired with *Dar al Islam,* or "House of Islam," which is a form of cultural imperialism, elevating to the status of divine mandate the spirituality and culture of seventh-century Arabia.

For good reason, the world community shudders to think that Pakistan represents the first Muslim nuclear power because in geopolitics the Islamic world is a wild card. Allowing no compromise when it comes to personal dogma, Islamic fundamentalists are feared as potential terrorists. Theirs is a sort of theo-mania, not unlike that of Adolph Hitler.

Hitler's "Science of Murder"

Historically, Hitler typifies far-right fundamentalism. Written in prison, and generating great wealth for Hitler, *Mein Kompt* sold second only to the Bible. In time, seventy million fell for Hitler's lies, and eventually Germany chose him as Chancellor (1932). In 1939, Hitler invaded Poland. In less than one year, he and his adherents had enslaved and dominated most of Europe.

In hopes of purifying the European gene pool, the Holocaust was Hitler's eugenics plan to eliminate Jews and Gypsies. His was a "science of murder," complete with specialized labs, business meetings, illusion, and some authentic Satanic technology. Allied prosecution and judges at Nuremberg consciously ignored Hitler's Satanic involvement, which led to killing six million Jews and an additional twelve million others in death camps (e.g., 3.4 million Gypsies and Christians, too).

It is not broadly known that Hitler was a fan of a Russian-born medium, Madam Helena Petrovna Blavatsky, spiritual godmother of the New Age movement. Hitler incorporated a Blavatsky-inspired Tibetan symbol, the *swastika*, and kept her occult classic, *Secret Doctrine,* at his bedside.

Hitler's dogma was a racist version of Social Darwinism in its emphasis on survival of the fittest. The Nazi Party's brand of fundamentalism mixed extreme nationalism with anti-Semitism. While Hitler's efforts failed to breed a super race, and thereafter establish a thousand-year *Reich*, his vision finds perpetuity in the New Age movement. Through New Age occultists, Hitler's hope remains: By means of Luciferic involvement, a Satanic virus will overwrite brains. In the end, a new, allegedly superior species will emerge.

Protestant Fundamentalism

The position of verbal plenary holds that in its original language (Hebrew and Chaldeac, Old Testament; Greek and Aramaic,

New Testament), all of the Bible, Genesis to Revelation, is fully "God breathed" to the slightest stroke of the smallest alphabet letter. Having myself proclaimed belief in verbal plenary while a guest on a radio program, I was met with the deafening silence of incredulity. Nominal Christians scoff at the notion of divine inspiration. In their view, verbal plenary is renegade religion. Uninitiated into Bible truth, some presumptuously pair the perverted fundamentalism of Hitler's *Third Reich* with Protestant fundamentalism (Matt. 5:18; 2 Tim. 3:16).

RELIGIOUS SPIRIT

The Christian's walk is fraught with danger. Thankfully, unfallen angels protect. On the other hand, fallen angels still buffet. Many stalwart souls refuse to succumb to sensual seductions of demons. In response, the enemy seeks entry through other doors—sometimes that of religious fundamentalism (Luke 4:10; 2 Cor. 12:7).

In his desire to appear godly, the religious Christian becomes inordinately fixed on outward appearances. *Do I look the part? Am I attractive or plain enough? Am I prosperous or poor enough? Am I doing enough?* Before long, he applies this measuring stick to others. As a result, religious spirit takes hold and strangles the very life out of zealous, but miscued victims. In time, dry religious fundamentalism supplants altogether one's rightful relationship with Jesus (1 Sam. 16:7; Matt. 23:27; Eph. 2:8; Matt. 7:5; 2 Tim. 3:5).

LEGALISM

Because safety is found in middle-of-the-road balance, the enemy digs potentially deadly ditches on either side. One is that of legalism. By definition, legalism wields the sword of the Spirit, which is the Word of God, without due deference to the Spirit. The "thou shalts" and "thou shalt nots" of Holy Writ are not to be taken lightly. The legalist, however, dissects them under a magnifying glass. He "majors in minors" and expects the same of others. His idea of unity in Spirit is to agree in matters of law (Phil. 4:5; Eph. 6:17; Matt. 23:24).

To the legalist, the spirit realm is threatening. Although he considers himself Spirit-filled and led, the legalist is uncomfortable at best in the presence of spiritual manifestations. As Michal disdained David's animated response to God's returning presence, the legalist disdains his counterparts who demonstrate New Covenant, Acts-of-the-Apostles liberties (1 Cor. 2:14; 2 Sam. 6:14–16; Acts 2:13).

More often than not, the legalist skips over resurrection life Scriptures and lands solidly on fundamental beliefs of righteous suffering and self-denial. When misfortune attends his soul, he knowingly testifies that God put him down for some mysteriously divine purpose. To the legalist, God causes accident, disease, and ill fortune. Not so. More precisely, what God allows to use for good was not necessarily at His initiation. Literally, God works for good in all things (James 1:13; 2 Cor. 12:7; Rom. 8:28).

True, believers daily take up their crosses and share in Christ's sufferings. Nevertheless, liberty, power, deliverance, and provision attend them. The legalist is not much at home in this arena. His way is the cross; at its foot is where he plants himself (1 Pet. 4:13; Rom. 8:21; John 1:12; 8:36; Phil. 4:19).

Fanaticism

This is not the case with fanatics. To them, suffering signals sin. To get on with the glory, fanatics bypass the cross. They expect height without depth, resurrection without crucifixion. Sadly, their path to ecstasy is strewn with trampled brethren, who they surmise must have sinned to remain in suffering (Matt. 16:24; Rom. 8:17; John 9:2–3; Rom. 12:15).

Whereas legalists downplay the Spirit, fanatics deny God's Word its rightful place. This is so because the fanatic alleges to hear directly from God although he frequently doubts similar claims by others. If the Lord's purported leading does not pan out, the fanatic attributes God's apparent indecisiveness to His mysterious ways.

In like manner, the fanatic reads God's direct intervention into mundane matters of no particular consequence. Surely God does not overlook mundane needs. Neither does he violate His own laws of nature, physics, and probability with the frequency fanatics suppose. For example, God may at times provide a convenient parking space; and the Christian is always in order to thank Him for benefits, big or small. But he should not overlook the fact that non-believers receive the best spots with comparable regularity (Col. 3:15b)!

Perhaps in stressing supernatural intervention, the fanatic fails to credit God's gifts of intellect, common sense, free will, and "more sure Word of prophecy." The fanatic, you see, looks for a special word at every turn, a special miracle for every need, and a special leading for every activity. The truth is that all Scripture is profitable—not "my special word" exclusively (2 Pet. 1:19; 2 Tim. 3:16).

Miracles do happen, and with frequency. They may even appear to address concerns lacking apparent spiritual significance; nonetheless, Christians are called to walk by faith, not sight. Honored fleeces are exceptions, not the rule. Believers overcome by the blood of the Lamb, not at the indiscriminate whim of faith-flinging fanatics (2 Cor. 5:7; Matt. 4:7; Rev. 12:11).

Phariseeic Leaven

Jesus admonishes His followers to be "wise as serpents." This is because the dust of man's flesh (specifically, carnality) is the serpent's perpetual meat. Though utterly defeated at Calvary, this enemy virtually feeds on man's sin nature. If the serpent cannot seduce believers into the error of legalism (Word lacking Spirit), he then tries for fanaticism (Spirit lacking Word, Matt. 10:16; Gen. 3:19; Isa. 65:25; Col. 2:15; l Pet. 5:8; Matt. 16:12; 1 Cor. 5:6).

Among others, these two features characterize the Christian life: spiritual fruit and victory. Fruit of the spirit is singular, encompassing love, joy, peace, longsuffering, gentleness, goodness, faith, meekness, and temperance. Victory sparks unspeakable joy; supernatural peace that transcends human grasp; and divinely foreign, outstretched love (1 Cor. 15:57; Gal. 5:1, 22–23; 1 Pet. 1:8; Phil. 4:7; l Pet. 1:22; l John 3:1).

A committed Christian's sincere passion is to represent Christ to a sin-sick world. Falling short is a hard pill to swallow. All too often, the Christian's fruit is found to be bitter, his joy easily speakable, his peace fleeting, and his love flickering. Regretfully, some are tempted into a state of denial. Rather than confess pesky faults, or acknowledge need or weakness, they present themselves as being spiritually together. Expectations of peers mold their image; religious behaviors underscore it. The end result is a cleverly crafted religious icon that sidesteps altogether God's workmanship (Rom. 3:4; Matt. 23:26; James 5:16; Rom. 15:1).

Such Christians are not unlike a notable group of zealots who, at the time of liberation from Babylonian Captivity, most likely started out similarly committed. Having come from bondage, they wanted to make certain, this time, that they would do it right. In this seemingly noble purpose, they embellished God's law with what the Bible calls "doctrine of men." Although their start was admirable, the outcome was Phariseeism.

For their pretense of superior piety, Pharisees missed the mark. Their sin correlated with enforced observances that ignored matters that are highly esteemed by God. Uncharacteristically, Scripture labels them "a brood of vipers," "whited sepulchers," and "blind guides." Plainly, the *hamartia* of Pharisees exceeded that of the Publican who stood afar off in the parable of Luke 18 (Matt. 3:7; 12:34; 23:23, 27).

To the earnest Christian, any association with Phariseeism is unthinkable. He feels no affinity for the legalistic, even venomous ways of the Pharisee, nor does he feel implicated in the least by Phariseeic error. After all, the father of the Pharisee is a liar and murderer from the beginning. This fact alone distances any Christian from familial identity. But does it (John 8:44)?

According to Scripture, the enemy's sin is "active evil." Be assured the Devil and his ranks are not content to suffer alone for their evildoings. To the contrary, their intent is to involve anyone they can, even the elect when possible, in their misdeeds and, ultimately, separation from God. This enemy is as a roaring lion, seeking whom he may devour. Accusation is the Devil's game, for *diabolos* means "to riddle through [with accusation]." The Devil stands before God day and night to accuse those who love the Lord (1 Pet. 5:8; Eph. 6:12; Matt. 24:24; Rev. 12:10).

When Jesus said, "Get thee behind me, Satan," he was not berating His beloved Peter, but rather the Devil whose very words passed Peter's lips. Given these understandings, it becomes evident that error, particularly religious error, is not beyond the reach of genuinely committed believers, Protestant fundamentalists included (Matt. 16:23).

In every respect, the enemy is a great counterfeiter. Whereas God imparts the higher stimulus of Holy Spirit baptism, the enemy offers lower, fleshly stimuli of illicit drugs and alcohol. Whereas God's music edifies and prompts praise, the Devil's music, in contrast, seduces, agitates, and denigrates. Posing as an angel of light, this deft deceiver cleverly uses what is seemingly benign to counterfeit warm, vibrant relationship with cold, dry religion (Acts 2:15–18; Gal. 5:21; Ps. 98:1; 1 John 4:1; 2 Cor. 11:14; Gen. 3:1b).

A counterfeit seems real when, in fact, it is not. Therefore, every Christian must be vigilant lest he, too, be hoodwinked. Religious spirit is the enemy's willing emissary whose mission is to derail even the most resolute of God's people. It furls the brow and elevates the chin while provoking misplaced judgment. It stands to reason that non-Christians are put off by misrepresentation of the glorious testimony God intends (Gal. 1:6; 3:1; Eph. 6:11, 12; John 10:10).

In review, if the Devil cannot trip up the believer in blatant sensuality, he will go for something less obvious, perhaps even excessive and obsessive religious fundamentalism. Religion, you see, is typified by man's efforts; the movement is upward in an attempt somehow to reach and please God. In this sense, Christianity is not religion. Rather, it is relationship, the movement's being downward. God first loved us. Our response back is to love Him in turn and in like fashion (1 John 4:19).

Religious Phariseeism demonstrates the former, but is not always readily discernible. No wonder the Lord admonishes us to beware of the leaven of Pharisees. This leaven typifies false doctrine and sin, which, when present, "leavens the whole lump." That is to say, sin and false doctrine are contagious to those exposed. The insidious leaven of "religious spirit" is generally quite at home among serious Christians. As a result, it represents one of the most prevalent obstructions to victorious Christian living (Matt. 16:6, 12; 1 Cor. 5:6).

OUTWARD FIXATION

It is clear from Scripture that, unlike man, God looks inwardly to one's intent. Nevertheless, He notices outward things, as hairstyles and dress. Just because the Word of God sets a reasonable standard, believers are not free to become overmuch preoccupied with the length of someone's skirt or hair, the value of one's ring, or the make of one's car. Fleeting outward beauty is no spiritual badge, but neither is it a death sentence (1 Sam. 16:7; Matt. 23:27; 1 Cor. 11:4–5, 7,14–16; 1 Tim. 2:9; Isa. 3:16–17; 28:1; Phil. 4:5).

In like manner, excessive love of money may be root to all kinds of evil; but money itself is not evil. We know this because

God uses it for His work. There is no inherent virtue in beauty or plainness, poverty or prosperity. Godly believers exemplify all four categories. It is the Lord who gives and takes away (1 Tim. 6:10; Job 1:21).

External qualities of being dapper, dowdy, wealthy, or wanting are incapable of representing with accuracy inner character, this being God's focus. Freedom from outward fixation frees believers to view their fellows as Christ's beloved, not as their competition or idols, spiritual inferiors or failures (Matt. 23:28; 1 Pet. 1:22; 3:3–4; 1 John 3:1; 2 Cor. 5:16).

Preoccupation with Form

Form is not necessarily all bad. It was, after all, the Lord who instituted the Old Covenant priesthood, rights of cleansing/purification, statutes of holiness, festivals, and the like—all pointing to Jesus. But there is a form of religion that denies the power of it. Religious spirit demands this type of religious form, which is not limited to pomp and circumstance (2 Tim. 3:5).

No believer can rightly dispute the value of seeking God early through His Word, prayer, and devotionals. Christ modeled this pattern, and victorious Christians throughout the centuries have followed suit. How could a daily quiet time possibly be judged as error? The answer is simple. When self-imposed specifications are unattainable with condemnation following, the mark has been missed. To insist upon a specified time, place, and/or format—despite being forced, dry, and dead—demonstrates the error of religious spirit (Mark 1:35; Rom. 8:1).

Keep in mind that our greater Solomon, Jesus, stirs love at His discretion. He may choose to meet His Bride in an unexpectedly spontaneous manner. Be sure, His banqueting table may not always be breakfast! Bondage to religious spirit, however, demands dry form, no matter what. Freedom from it constrains the Bride of Christ to respond with spontaneity to her altogether lovely Bridegroom whenever He wills. To His delight (and hers!), she is free even to initiate spiritual lovemaking, for He is ever desirous of her (Song of Sol. 1:4; 2:7; 5:4, 10, 16; Ps. 45:11).

COMPARISON

Remember the parable of the Pharisee in the Temple. He prayed *pros*, or toward, self, feigning thanks to God that he was not like other men. While the mistake of prideful comparison trips many, others follow the flawed example of otherwise truly godly men (Luke 18:11–13).

Take Moses, for instance. Most likely with humility, the "meekest man on earth," Moses, decried his speaking ability and deferred to another judged to be more capable than he. In comparing himself to another, Moses forfeited a key facet of his own ministry to Aaron, who by default became Moses' mouthpiece. In like fashion, some Christians wrongly confess ineptitude. As Moses, they bemoan their oral skills (others no doubt speak better than they). As Jeremiah, they lament their youth (surely others have more experience). Such comparison robs God of due praise for His ability to equip, enable, and anoint (Ex. 4:10; Phil. 4:13; Jer. 1:6–7).

FALSE HUMILITY

False humility may prompt a fundamentalist Christian, wrongly so, to insist that execution of his ministry "wasn't me, but it was all God." This seemingly humble, but audacious claim aligns oneself with God-breathed Holy Writ, which cannot be broken (2 Pet. 1:21; John 10:35).

Yes, the aim is "no longer I, but Christ"; but in the same breath, under the same anointing, Paul affirmed, "nevertheless, I live." Knowing his sufficiency was of God, Paul wisely acknowledged God's gifts of free will, intellect, talents, spiritual gifts, calling, personality, physical prowess, upbringing, culture, and more (Gal. 2:20; 2 Cor. 3:5; Rom. 7:18; 2 Cor. 11:5–6; 1 Cor. 14:2, 18; Rom. 1:1; 2 Cor. 11:21–23; Acts 22:3, 28).

Despite popular teaching, co-workers with God cannot accurately be likened to inanimate, empty pipes through which a sovereign God moves. You see, those used by God exercise personal will to commit all to God's glory and to obey Him. Furthermore, they yield and apply their talents and gifts to the task at hand. If someone were to compliment my singing, for example, I can graciously respond, "thank you," without grasping glory from that gift's Giver. My music ministry is not "all God's doing." By His design, I co-work with God, who in turn commends the "good and faithful servant" for singing heartily unto Him. Refusing an honest compliment, however humbly, not only shames the one who thought to give it, but also releases from personal accountability the one who refuses that compliment. After all, God Himself cannot be disputed (Rom. 12:1–2; Eph. 4:8; Matt. 25:21; James 3:2; Luke 19:13; Col. 3:23).

Continuous Assessment/Unsolicited Counsel

Religious fundamentalism presses many to scrutinize and then judge attitudes, behaviors, appearances, and motives. While continuously measuring these against the letter of law, moral zealots suppose they know the thoughts and motives of others. Misplaced enthusiasm drives them to play Holy Spirit by sharing unsolicited counsel. As Job's comforters, they offer rational reasons for lacks and sufferings (Rom. 14:4; Jer. 17:9–10; 2 Thess. 3:11).

If you have missed a church service or prayer meeting—or if your painful circumstance warrants compassion, not counsel—you heave a sigh of relief when you have managed to escape their attention. If not, you feel like a rag doll in their teeth; and it's you who feels condemned. Religious spirit sees to that (Rom. 8:1).

In conclusion, Christians can learn much from the parable of the Publican and Pharisee. The Christian's charge is to embrace truth and to maintain balance in all aspects of life. Doing so dodges ditches of dead, dry religious spirit on one hand and manic fanaticism on the other. As a result, one's spiritual fruit is sweet, his joy unspeakable, his peace incomprehensible, and his love compelling—all to the glory of God (Eph. 6:14; John 8:32, 36).

CHAPTER 10

HAMARTIA GLOBALISM

Let no one deceive or beguile you in any way, for that day will not come except the apostasy comes . . . and the man of lawlessness *[hamartia]* is revealed (2 Thess. 2: 3, AMP).

Globalism Prophesied

A French physician and astrologer, Nostradamus was acclaimed as a sixteenth-century prophet who allegedly prophesied the assassination of J.F. Kennedy and the rise of Adolph Hitler. However, if a prophecy is given in the name of other gods, it is false (Deut. 18:20–22; 1 Cor. 14:37).

God's way is always best. Some six hundred years before Christ, Daniel took his cues from Him and, in so doing, accurately predicted major world governments to follow Babylon (Medo-Persia, Greece, and Rome). In the second and seventh chapters of Daniel, he foresaw yet another future, end-time world rule (specifically, Antichrist's rule). This one-world government will resemble ancient Rome in its syncretistic religion, vast scope of influence, nature of sway as a self-ruling republic, and destined collapse.

Every historic case of multinational government has resulted in departure from truth, tyranny, and suffering. Each missed the mark with grave consequences following. The end-time revived Roman Empire with Antichrist at its helm will follow suit.

In *The Future of Federalism* (1962), Nelson Rockefeller looked to a powerful "free-world supra-national political being" not unlike the scriptural entity known as the "Lawless One," "Man of Sin," "Son of Perdition," "Beast," "Abomination," and "Antichrist." Representing the sum total of all the loathsome beasts described in Revelation 13 and Daniel 7, this "free-world supra-national political being" is a last-days visionary destined to be the most powerful world dictator ever.

While Antichrist is a literal man, he is present in type, or picture, throughout history (e.g., through the lives of Nebuchadnezzar, Antiochus Epiphanes, Nero, Napoleon Bonaparte, Hitler, Lenin, Stalin, and Hussein). Having existed throughout history, Antichrist spirit is companion to love of the world, denial of the Father and Son, and hindrance to true worship. Both John and Paul indicate in their epistles, respectively, that Antichrist was well known to their contemporaries (1 John 4:3 "ye have heard"; 2 Thess. 2:6 "ye know"; 1 John 2:15–18, 22; 4:3; 2 Thess. 2:4).

Destined to become Satan incarnate, Antichrist will oppose Christ at the same time he pretends to be Christ. While promising the world "a more excellent way," Antichrist and his right-hand man, known as the False Prophet, will desecrate all that is holy. Together, they will summon the red horse of warfare, the black horse of famine, and the pale horse of death (Rev. 6:4,5,8).

Perhaps surprisingly, it is God who puts it into hearts of the unregenerate to unite under Antichrist. Thankfully, He will limit the impact and duration of global governance under Antichrist. Notwithstanding, Jesus warned disciples to take heed, for even God's elect, if not watchful, are vulnerable to the false doctrine and signs promulgated by Antichrist. Before the Second Coming of Christ, Antichrist will deceive many with lying wonders; and great apostasy will result in the falling away of true believers (Rev. 17:10, 17; Matt. 24:4–5, 12, 24; 2 Thess. 2:1–12).

To "fall away" presupposes prior right standing with God. Scripture warns that some believers who have known and loved the Savior will succumb to the lie of Antichrist and, as a result, will fall from grace. Biblical prophecy identifies a portion of the end-time church as being increased with the goods of Antichrist's global economy. As such, Laodicean Christians will consider themselves rich and in need of nothing, but erroneously so. Some will end up as wells without water, or clouds carried with a tempest when they return, as dogs, to their own vomit, or sin. To remain safe from delusion, believers must with passion grasp and sustain the victory that overcomes—"even our faith" (Rev. 3:17; 1 John 5:4; 2 Pet. 2:17; 20–22).

Globalism Acclaimed

It comes as no surprise to students of the Bible that world leaders publicly applaud today's global community. In *The Search for a New Beginning,* Mikhail Gorbachev calls for integrated global policies coupled with a new religious paradigm espousing the blatant paganism of Native American Earth servitude. Though lauded for reverence of Mother Earth, Native Americans in reality were responsible for wholesale topsoil and wanton forest destruction. On occasion, they hunted animals into extinction. Even more, some scalped, raped, and tortured.

In no way can Gorbachev or his New Paradigm be construed as allies of biblical Christianity. Although he testifies that "the *cosmos* is my God," Gorbachev boasts of a close friendship with the Pope John Paul II. Furthermore, one of the world's most visible televangelists, Robert Schuller of the famed Crystal Cathedral, presented his communist "friend" as a brother in Christ.

Secular sources join Catholics and Protestants in endorsing Gorbachev's global vision. A direct quote from the *UN Report on Human Development* (1994) reads, "Mankind's problems can no longer be solved by national governments. What is needed is a world government" (page 88).

In *A Reporter's Life,* mainstream media mogul Walter Cronkite agrees. According to this poster boy for the World Federalist Association, a system of world government is mandatory, even at the expense of sovereignty. Considered "the most trusted man in America," this elderly news anchor received the 1999 World Federalist Association Norman Cousins Global Governance Award.

Globalists honored Cronkite for his steadfast support of mandatory world law based on a global lawmaking body and enforcement structure. Among the 150 attending the award ceremony were Nane Annon and Hillary Clinton (by video greeting), *60 Minutes'* Lesley Stahl and Ed Bradley, actress Catherine Zeta-Jones, and actor Michael Douglas, designated "UN Messenger of Peace" (Teichrib 2000).

Global restructuring *à la* Albert Gore has become society's unrelenting *mantra*. According to former Foreign Policy Adviser and personal friend of Bill Clinton, Strobe Talbott, the next one hundred years will render obsolete any concept of nationhood, for "all states will recognize a single, global authority." Hillary's "Global Village," George Bush, Sr.'s "New World Order," and the United Nations' "Sustainable Society" all envision Gorbachev's would-be global utopia.

Attending to the world's poor, globalists extol earth stewardship and responsible procreation. Enthusiasts boast forthcoming harmony among diverse cultures. They affirm women, children, Afro-Americans, and Native American Indians. What's not to like? Read on.

Globalism Precursors

Historical components of globalism include a sequence of "*-isms*" articulated by Jean-Jacques Rousseau, Johann Heinrich Pestalozzi, Horace Mann, William James, Charles Darwin, John Dewey, Charles Judd, Harold Ruggs, George Counts, Scott Nearing, and Sid Simon.

Jean-Jacques Rousseau was a French social philosopher (1712–1777). In *Émile* (1762), Rousseau outlined a new theory of education based on natural development and the power of example. His civil religion worshipped collective human power. Rousseau's contribution to the ultimate secularization of American public education cannot be minimized.

In like manner, Swiss educator, naturalist, and illuminist Johann Heinrich Pestalozzi (1746–1827) furthered Rousseau's secularization of education. Since Pestalozzi believed that chance and natural law govern everything, and all of life is explicable only by means of scientific data, he reasoned further that God is incapable of doing anything (even if He did exist).

U.S. political leader and father of permissivism, Horace Mann (1789–1859) gained admission to the bar in 1823. From Massachusetts, cradle of the public school movement, Mann defined the Hegelian-Unitarian period in America's education history. He believed in the perfectible nature of man and, in 1850, sold Americans on the misguided idea that in one hundred years secular education would solve crime and poverty.

English biologist Charles Darwin (1809–1882) promulgated the fallacy of historic optimism, which anticipates progressive human improvement without need for God. Political internationalists embrace Darwin's theory of natural selection to justify rule of those with special talents and abilities over the less gifted, who are not clearly aware of what is best for them.

Father of American psychology, William James (1842–1910) was a philosopher whose pragmatism interpreted truth in terms of practicality. A member of the Society for Psychical Research, Harvard instructor William James wrote one of the most important works on psychology of religion. Both Horace Mann and William James held tremendous sway with John Dewey.

Best known as the father of progressivism, John Dewey (1859–1952) was an avowed atheist, author-signer of the *Humanist Manifesto I*, and first president of the American Humanist Society. He believed that the political function of the school is to "construct communist society." When Dewey died in 1952, Protestant fundamentalism no longer defined public schools. Instead, the religion of secular humanism stressed self-determination through reason. Dewey's goals included a "science"-based one-world religion, global economics, an interrelated world community, and a new species for a New Age.

Among the countless disciples of Dewey include Charles Judd, Harold Ruggs, George Counts, and Scott Nearing. Through their influence, "pluralism" and "realism" became public education's trendy buzzwords. Ruggs and Counts put forth the revolutionary notion of using public education to shape a new public mind. Additionally, Professor Counts authored a blueprint for socializing America by supplanting competition with cooperation, private capitalism with socialized economy. In *The New World Order* (1949),

Scott Nearing promoted the science of social engineering to achieve one-world economics and politics.

More recently, an humanist who attempted to interject emotional and spiritual components into behavioral psychology, Sid Simon wrote a definitive hand book teaching values, otherwise known as the affective domain. Based on the Raths-Simon theory of relativism, Simon's clarification of values bolstered support for abortion, euthanasia, and assisted suicide.

Secularism, naturalism, permissivism, pragmatism, Darwinism, secular humanism, pluralism, and moral relativism, each in turn, add vital layers that give form to today's flavor of globalism.

Globalism Defined

In brief, globalism is an interdependent, one-world state that specifically rejects biblical Christianity in its quest for so-called enlightened collaborative consciousness. According to Scripture, "peoples, nations, multitudes, and tongues" will ultimately unite. Sharing in common one esoteric mindset, these will submit to a central global authority at odds with the God of the Bible. The empty hope of achieving harmony among diverse cultures will come at the price of doctrinal mix and compromise (syncretism, Rev. 17:12,15).

Global citizens pledge allegiance—not to the United States of America, nor to their heavenly home—but rather to the world community. This is called "collectivism." To date, the Vatican is the only political entity that has not yet joined the United Nations; however, according to best-selling author, Gary Kah, the road to globalism is paved through Rome. The Bible teaches that, in time, world citizens will submit to a world dictator and his cohorts, inclusive of the False Prophet and "kings without kingdoms." These kings could well be mega-magnet international financiers, whose global interests, influence, and connections wield astonishing power (Rev. 17:12–13).

Globalization speaks to redistribution of the world's wealth not to be confused with voluntary, cheerful giving as directed by God. Concentrating that wealth, and therefore power, into the hands of few, who wish to manage masses by means of international law—

called global governance—is nothing short of naked totalitarianism. Regardless of their claims, despots care about control—not the plight of women, children, Afro-Americans, or Native American Indians—all of whom God dearly loves (2 Cor. 9:7).

Would-be environmentalist and notable globalist Mikhail Gorbachev advocates "necessary" environmental regulations worldwide. According to Gorbachev, environmental crisis is an handy international disaster key justifying need for global restructuring, or *peristroika*. Housing the Gorbachev Foundation, the Presidio actively works for Gorbachev's New Paradigm. The Presidio is a former U.S. military base in San Francisco suitably nicknamed the "White House on the West Coast."

Ostensibly to protect Earth, the agenda of radical environmentalism is unquestionably genocidal. Annually, industrialized nations provide $1.4 billion for United Nations population control. UN policies translate into liberal sex-education campaigns, taxpayer-funded abortions, and UN foreign aid programs. Inconceivably, the UN population fund failed to provide indigent Kosovars with life sustaining food, medicine, or clothing. Instead, it provided life curtailing "reproductive health kits."

Octopus Analogy

Globalism can be likened to an octopus with eight arms representing the perhaps unexpectedly interrelated fields of religion, politics, economics, environment, education, philosophy, culture, and technology.

Its religious arm represents enlightened "group think" to be realized in a New Earth Ethic that ignores fundamental Judeo-Christian values in exchange for cosmic consciousness and eco-socialism. The latter specifically excludes national sovereignty and private property rights while presumably giving overriding priority to the world's poor.

Its political arm represents bio-regionally defined, representative federal government again at odds with private property, privacy, entrepreneurial initiative, and resulting prosperity. In restructuring around natural ecosystems, the new society will eliminate state and national boundaries. While the U.S. models state federalism, Europe is today's model for national regionalism. While paving the way for "world peace," international power elitists purpose to regionalize the entire world after Europe's example. With systematic elimination of national sovereignty, regions can be linked effectively into a world government with one-world laws, courts, schools, military complex, and churches (minus biblical Christianity).

Its economic arm represents a collective system of global economics indicated by birth of multinational corporations, the World Bank, World Trade Organization, the G-8 (partners of eight of the richest Western nations, plus Russia), and the International Monetary Fund (global welfare). The Euro represents monetary unification of Europe, and the Bank for International Settlements (BIS) is the global central bank for about 120 national central banks. The BIS's supporting role is to shape and fuel global economics. The non-elected European Central Bank in Frankfurt already exercises unlimited power. Given time, a central end-time authority will control all its citizens' power to buy and sell (Rev. 13:16–17; 18:13).

Its environmental arm distorts the Bible view of responsible stewardship. Environmental crisis justifies need for a new global order; moreover, a political agenda takes front stage to any reputed campaign to save whales and kangaroo rats.

Its educational arm represents cradle-to-grave control of human resources. Lifelong learning is best seen as a psycho-social process of *re*-learning by calling good, "evil" and evil, "good." Anything traditional is the target—e.g., traditional values, family, work ethic, the *U.S. Constitution*, and Judeo-Christian faith. Change agents purpose to replace conventional beliefs, values, attitudes, and individual thinking with collective group think mirroring the new global ideology. The partnership of Global Education Associates joins ninety countries working together to achieve global goals to be accomplished by systematic indoctrination. Successful postmodern students are best viewed as workers, not thinkers; followers, not leaders; group members, not individuals. Ever learning, they fail to discover truth as set forth in Scripture (Isa. 5:20; 2 Tim. 3:7).

Its philosophical arm blends Eastern and Western thought with ancient mysteries from the bowels of Babylon. A French Jesuit paleontologist and philosopher, Pierre Teilhard de Chardin qualifies as "patron saint of the New Age movement." Author Marilyn Ferguson credits Teilhard for the title of her best-selling New Age classic, *The Aquarian Conspiracy*. When asked whose ideas most influence New Age occultists, Ferguson mentioned Pierre Teilhard de Chardin (Rev. 17:5).

Political correctness (PC) forms the philosophical base of globalism while concurrently serving as umbrella under which many "*-isms*" converge. United causes include civil/gender/sexual orientation rights and radical environmentalism.

Its cultural arm represents celebrated diversity. Multiculturalism is selective tolerance that virtually redefines America out of existence while, at the same time, it elevates the right not to be offended to the status of constitutional amendment. The right kind of tolerance excludes fundamental Christianity from the equation.

Its technical-scientific arm represents the Internet—potential resource for depravity, but also used by God for great good.

Globalism Steered

Powerful movers and shakers steer the burgeoning one-world movement. Its *pastors* are Eastern Liberal Establishment Insiders, with "the invisible government," the Council of Foreign Relations (CFR), its brain. As early as 1953, the congressional Reece Committee investigated the CFR. It found that the council "overly propagandizes the globalist concept" in its avowed aim to abolish national sovereignty for a godless secular New World Order. Pastors as these are brutish, quick to destroy their flocks (Jer. 10:21; 23:1, 2).

Its *evangelists* act as societal "change agents" in America's public schools. Many others report the nightly news. In October of 1993, *Washington Post* ombudsman Richard Harwood did a piece about the role of CFR media members. They do not merely analyze and interpret the news, claims Harwood. They "help make" foreign policy compatible with global goals.

Its *deacons* are internationalist bankers and industrial monopolists who are virtual kings without kingdoms. Its spiritual *elders* are New Age mystics who exchange Bible truth for vain, empty deceit. The ancient Celtic doctrine of the druids is remarkably similar to New Age mysticism in its obsession with celestial bodies and belief in reincarnation. Accordingly, the Bohemian Grove in California's Sonoma County hosts an annual two-week gathering of a highly select, all male club whose members have included every Republican President since Calvin Coolidge. There, the likes of George Bush, Sr., Henry Kissinger, Richard Cheney, and Walter Cronkite conduct official business. At the same time, they participate in mock-druidic rituals (Rev. 17:12; Col. 2:8).

Finally, its Bible is the United Nations *Charter*, boasting objectives of tolerance (albeit selective), united strength and armed forces (under the UN banner), and redistribution of the world's wealth (not voluntarily). The *Charter* redefines America's doctrine of original intent, the *U.S. Constitution*, which has served as the supreme law of the federal government since its adoption in 1789.

Rightly viewed, the Preamble of the *Constitution* speaks to forming a more perfect union (*not* the Global Village); establishing justice (*not* exclusively for the world's downtrodden); and insuring domestic tranquility (*not* by militarizing the police force). It provides for the common defense (*not* under the UN banner); promotes general welfare (*not* excluding the unborn and elderly); and secures blessings of liberty (*not* least of which include private property and religious expression).

Functioning as treaties in disguise, executive agreements lack usual constitutional safeguards. For example, the *General Agreement on Tariffs and Trade* (GATT) and *North American Free Trade Agreement* (NAFTA) ignored the requirement of a two-thirds vote by the Senate before ratification by Congress. The World Trade Organization is a significant part of GATT. Through it, Americans have yielded substantial control over the domestic economy to an international body.

Alarmingly, treaties and international agreements are being used increasingly to control domestic matters. By employing words of an international UN treaty, state law already has been invalidated. According to Law Professor James Hirsen, this judicially renders the UN *Charter* the supreme law of the land.

Globalism Exposed

What Bible prophecy anticipates as typical of the last days reads like today's newspaper. John the Revelator and the prophet Daniel warn of a coming cashless economic system, coupled with regionalized global governance. The apostle Paul describes members of the new secular order as demonstrating misplaced love of money, self, and pleasure. Devoid of God's power, they embrace a form of religion defiled by drug abuse, profanity, and moral laxity.

Despite promise of global consensus, harmony, and peace, the one-world system will face endless wars and rumors of war, many ethnic in nature. In tenor with the Eschatological (end-time) Discourse of Jesus Christ, there are already over thirty ethnic wars ongoing in the world (Matt. 24, Mark 13, Luke 21).

The Bible anticipates a time of escalating natural disasters of horrifying magnitude. Since 1987, over 100,000 have died in earthquakes around the world. In 1999 alone, earthquakes in Taiwan, Columbia, and Greece killed thousands. More famines have taken place in the last two hundred years than in all the previous centuries since Christ's first coming; and, at the turn of the millennium, floods in Mozambique left hundreds of thousands homeless among a population that was already one of the poorest in the world. Thousands of lives were claimed while hundreds of thousands faced death from starvation or deadly diseases as cholera and malaria.

Likewise consistent with the Eschatological Discourse, new diseases are on the rise. Not limited to Sexually Transmitted Diseases (STDs) and AIDS, these include killers as Ebola, Lyme and legionnaire's diseases, toxic shock syndrome, and flesh-eating bacteria.

Finally, as Scriptures foretell, Israel commands extraordinary focus in these last days. In March of 2000, Pope John Paul assumed a position of unprecedented influence within the Middle East peace process. His politically correct message emphasized peace and religious unity.

Globalism: *Hamartia*

God's plan elevates yielded men and women from "glory to glory" toward oneness with Christ and the Father. In contrast, the unregenerate progress from "degradation to degradation" as they foolishly pursue mystical oneness with the universal god-force (2 Cor. 3:18; 2 Tim. 3:13).

Hamartia, mark missed with grave consequences following.

God's Word points to a thousand-year global order similar to the Garden of Eden prior to the fall. It gets even better, for a new heaven and earth will follow. This is not so with the secular world order, doomed instead to perish (Rev. 20:1-7; 21:1; Prov. 10:30; 1 Thess. 5:3).

Hamartia, mark missed with grave consequences following.

While the church anticipates a glorious theocratic reign under the headship of Christ and His Bride, global citizens look to the dictatorial reign of Antichrist and his False Prophet (Rev. 11:15; 13:1, 12).

Hamartia, mark missed with grave consequences following.

God provides purchase of wine (blessings of God) and milk (strength of God) without price to anyone who asks of Him in faith. To the contrary, cosmic citizens pay with their lives under Antichrist's tyranny. What's more, redistribution of wealth in the new cashless society will benefit only a few (Isa. 55:1; Dan. 11:39).

Hamartia, mark missed with grave consequences following.

The plan of God is ushered in by believers, supported by unfallen angels, and in union with the higher stimulus of the Holy Spirit. On the other hand, the enemy's counterfeit is ushered in by sinners, supported by fallen angels, and in union with Satan. Moreover, the latter is paired with the lower stimulus of enchantment with drugs (*pharmakeia*, or "sorceries," in Rev. 9:21 and 18:23; 1 Cor. 6:2; Ps. 91:11; Luke 4:10; Acts 1:8; Jude 15; 1 Cor. 10:20–21; 1 Tim. 4:1; Rev. 9:20; 2 Cor. 4:4).

Hamartia, mark missed with grave consequences following.

Whereas the former produces holiness unto the Lord, glorifying Jesus Christ, the latter produces a worldwide pantheistic mystery cult, glorifying Lucifer (Rev. 21:10–11; 13:1, 11–12).

Hamartia, mark missed with grave consequences following.

CHAPTER 11

Hamartia Jingoism

If you are showing partiality [to certain individuals], you are committing a sin *[hamartia]* . . . (James 2:9, *Wuest Expanded Translation of the New Testament*).

The Amplified version of the Bible reads: "But if you show servile regard (that is, prejudice or favoritism) for people, you commit sin *[hamartia]* and are rebuked and convicted by the Law as violators and offenders," James 2:9. Verse 8 of that same chapter mandates the "Royal Law" to love one's neighbor as self. Keep in mind that a neighbor is not limited to an individual; it can also be a group.

Rightful Patriotism

On 25 September 1789, Congress unanimously approved a resolution beseeching George Washington to institute a National Day of Thanksgiving for "many signal favors of Almighty God." To love one's country so blessed is not to offend. In fact, American identity is appropriate for a number of good reasons elucidated by her founding fathers and documents. Many godly heroes honored throughout halls of the Capitol Building exemplify America's rich spiritual heritage. According to public affairs specialist David Barton, faith in Jesus Christ is the driving force behind our nation's birth.

John Adams affirmed that our *Constitution* was made only for "a moral and religious people." While the First Amendment bans a national religion, the Free Exercise Clause of the *U.S. Constitution* guarantees religious freedom. Nonetheless, history revisionists consistently deconstruct any sense of nationalism all the while they portray Americans as moral and ethical inferiors. Knowledgeable patriots rightfully condemn National History Standards of 1994 and 1996 for their warped assaults on historical fact.

America's Founding Father

Take, for example, the life and faith of the father of our country, George Washington. Revisionists claim Washington was Unitarian; facts prove differently. Unitarianism was founded in 1818, but Washington died in 1799; furthermore, Washington maintained strong ties to the Episcopal Church. Washington's own adopted daughter, Nellie, spoke of his true belief, as did Chief-Justice John Marshall and others, whose eyewitness accounts describe Washington as a devoted Christian—not Unitarian or Deist, as some claim.

Washington surrounded himself with likeminded folks of faith. According to a grandson, his wife Martha read from her Bible and prayed for an hour every morning following breakfast. General Washington himself demanded the appointment of regimental chaplains and required that those under his command "attend carefully upon religious exercises." Patriot hero Jonathon Trumbull, Sr., supplied men and munitions to General Washington. At the age of seventy-three, Trumbull returned to ministerial studies and to the service of his God.

Appropriately, the Congressional Prayer Room in the nation's Capitol portrays Washington as one kneeling in prayer. While Dr. Marvin Olasky acknowledges Washington's human weaknesses, he nonetheless identifies Washington as America's "gold standard" for over a century. Publicly, Washington proclaimed fear of the Lord as the beginning of sound public policy. It was he who first added, "So help me, God," to the presidential oath. Every president since has followed Washington's lead. When it was his time, Washington allegedly died "like a Christian and a hero, calm and collected, without a groan and without a sigh."

SUBSEQUENT PRESIDENTS

Washington was not alone as a man of faith among America's presidents. America's second president, John Adams, encouraged succeeding generations to commemorate the "day of deliverance" from Great Britain "by solemn acts of devotion to God Almighty from one end of the Continent to the other, from this time forward forevermore."

It may be that the third president of the United States was very much a product of eighteenth-century enlightenment. Thomas Jefferson was said by some to be a student of Adam Weishaupt, founder of the secret Order of the Illuminati (1776). In the 1780s, the Bavarian government exposed and banned the Order for its Luciferian involvement.

Some claim that the first secretary of the Treasury, Alexander Hamilton, joined Jefferson in similarly dark pursuits, but others disagree. Author of the *Federalist Papers*, Hamilton allegedly purposed to form the Christian Constitutional Society. Although this endeavor was halted by Hamilton's untimely death, its primary goal was to support the Christian religion. By the same token, many speeches of John Quincy Adams sounded like sermons. He credited Christianity as the reason for national independence.

On 29 May 1845, Andrew Jackson assured visitors: "Upon that sacred volume [the Bible] I rest my hope for eternal salvation, through the merits and blood of our blessed Lord and Savior, Jesus Christ." On the day of his death, Jackson referred again to the Bible—this time as "the Rock upon which our republic rests." Thereafter, President James A. Garfield led dozens to Christ and subsequent water baptism.

AMERICA'S FOUNDING DOCUMENTS AND THEIR SIGNERS

According to Rabbi Daniel Lapin, America's religious roots and spiritual destiny are evident in her founding documents. For example, pious pilgrims invoked the name of God in the 1620 *Mayflower Compact*. The first colony clearly purposed to advance the Christian faith. Thereafter, the *Declaration of Independence* acknowledged endowments by the Creator Himself.

Theologians Roger Sherman and Abraham Baldwin both signed the *Constitution*. In fact, the former signed all four of the founding documents, and he helped form the *Bill of Rights*. Additionally, Secretary of Congress Charles Thompson produced into English the first rendering of the *Septuagint*, Greek translation of the Hebrew Old Testament.

Original justice James Wilson signed both the *Constitution* and the *Declaration of Independence*. He called law and religion "twin sisters," for, he claimed, good civil law flows from God's law. America's leading legal authority, Thomas McKean wrote a definitive commentary on the *U.S. Constitution*. He preached a compelling salvation message to John Roberts, sentenced to death in his court. McKean encouraged Roberts to repent, pray, and rely on the dear Redeemer while seeking counsel from pious men.

By the same token, upon speaking at public graduation exercises, *Constitution* signer and first President of Columbia College William Samuel Johnson pointed graduates to God. Both John Hancock and Samuel Adams called citizens to pray.

Declaration of Independence signer Charles Carroll built and funded a house of worship. On his eighty-ninth birthday, Carroll presented Christian faith as the chief reason for America's having entered the American Revolution. Signer Dr. Benjamin Rush founded America's first Bible Society, not to mention the Sunday School Movement in 1791.

The secretary of state under three U.S. presidents, Daniel Webster memorized Scripture and testified of his faith both privately and publicly. One of the greatest orators in American history, Webster spoke in June of 1843 at the Bunker Hill Monument in Charleston, Massachusetts. There he exclaimed: "Thank God! I—I also—am an American!"

America's Greatness

According to famous nineteenth-century French statesman Alexis de Tocqueville, there is no country in the world "where the Christian religion retains a greater influence over the souls of men than in America." This he identified as key to America's greatness. Because (in Patrick Henry's words) "America was founded, not on religions, but on the Gospel of Jesus Christ," people of other faiths have been afforded "asylum, prosperity, and freedom of worship."

In his *Gettysburg Address*, Abraham Lincoln recognized America as a nation under God. The Civil War battlefield became resting place for patriots who sacrificed their lives so that government "of the people, by the people, and for the people should not perish from the earth." The Bible acknowledges no greater love than to lay down one's life for others (John 15:13).

Radical Patriotism (1 John 5:21)

While loving one's country is not to offend, worshipping it is. Let us examine Jingo, legendary empress of Japan until AD 270. Upon death of her husband, Jingo fitted out an army for the invasion of Korea. After an absence of three years, she returned to Japan completely victorious. Subsequently, her son was canonized as "god of war."

In 1877 or 1878, British Prime Minister Disraeli developed a pro-Turk policy, which nearly involved the United Kingdom in war with Russia. At that time, political use of the word, "Jingoism," with reference to the Japanese empress came to indicate warmongering patriotism smacking of idolatry. A London singer known as "the Great MacDermott" popularized a music hall song with the bellicose refrain, "We don't want to fight; but, by Jingo, if we do," etc.

Included within the concept of Jingoism are the following conservative positions: support of a strong national defense, second to none; protection of individual freedoms and private property rights; and use of no foreign commanders in the military. None of these is correctly construed as "extreme." By its broader definition, however, Jingoism *is* extreme for its excessive nationalism and disdain for non-nationals. This, the Bible calls *hamartia,* for God is no respecter of persons.

Partiality in the Pew

A survivor of Nazism and communism, Dr. Balint Vazonyi came to the U.S. from Hungary following the 1956 uprising. Vazonyi identified four points of the American compass—namely, rule of law, individual rights, guaranteed property, and American identity. Today, however, some prophets of social justice demand that national identity give way to multiculturalism. Being American is simply not politically correct. Notwithstanding, a number of stalwart, flag-waving, America-loving patriots fill our church pews. This is good. Some, unfortunately, take patriotism to extremes by mocking different nation-states for cultural peculiarities as relating to diet, perceived work ethic, dress, or adaptations to geographical features. Contrary to the wisdom from above, they judge sights, sounds, smells, tastes, and textures from afar as inferior (James 3:15,17).

Not once in prophetic Scripture is America given preeminence over other nation-states, yet some contend that, if God demonstrates His power, He will invariably choose the United States for its manifestation. Others believe that only their denomination, or home church, qualifies as conduit for Holy Spirit outpouring. God's sending foreign missionaries to minister to *Americans* is scorned as preposterous. In reality, worldwide knowledge of the glory of God will distinguish Christ's Millennial Reign (Hab. 2:14).

For any American to maintain even a degree of identity with his blood heritage is perceived by some as foolish. Christian elitists hold that everyone should speak American English. To these, learning a second language is useless. Such ultra-patriots would do well to reflect upon a striking biblical example. A Moabitess, Ruth demonstrated kindness; moreover, she safekept moral obligation, demonstrated obedience, worked hard in the fields, and willingly received counsel. These attributes no doubt reflected her upbringing and, to some degree, her cultural heritage. Keep in mind that, even in Moab, *Yahweh* visited His people, giving them bread (Ruth 1:6).

Upon marrying Boaz, Ruth transferred her identity with Moab to Judah. Despite her ceded citizenship, Ruth is known among believers to this day as a Moabitess. The same is true of Americans who have a Scotch-Irish, Norwegian, or German background. While "Norwegian-American" may well be deemed inappropriate nomenclature, remnants of Norwegian culture—e.g., propensity to cleanliness—are not entirely dismissible.

Some arrogantly boast that America stands alone as *the* lighthouse, *the* blessed nation, *the* dispenser of all that is good, *the* model to the world, *the* ultimate trendsetter, *the* best and only place to live, *the* center of God's plan and purpose—indeed, *the* center of the universe. Those not born in America, or not legal citizens, are considered of lesser value in God's economy because, bless God, America *is* after all "chosen."

Hamartia Avoided

That America is chosen and called to be a lighthouse to the world is not disputed. Most agree that America is blessed, uniquely so. For this reason, every American should love her and thank God for freedoms and benefits afforded. While extreme nationalism to the disdain of others spells *hamartia,* patriotic civic duty does not.

The bottom line is simple. Christian Americans are in this world, but not of its carnal system. In using the world system for good, they must not abuse it, or imitate its godless ways, for their true citizenship remains in heaven. Even so, as Queen Esther championed her people before King Ahasureus, American believers must likewise defend righteous judgments in the civic arena (John 17:16; 1 Cor. 7:31; Matt. 23:2–3).

According to the Bible, civic responsibilities include prayer, obedience, and godly action. Rendering to Caesar his due, Christians in right standing with God pray for their leaders; moreover, for the Lord's sake, they obey established laws of the land. These things they do respectfully, as Paul before King Herod Agrippa II and Festus in Acts 25:23 through 26:32 (James 5:16; Matt. 22:21; Prov. 24:21; Eccles. 8:2; 1 Pet. 2:13).

Civil authorities are ordained of God, but they are subject to Him as well. In all matters, one's first and primary allegiance is to the Lord, not established earthly governments. Many zealous Christians do not want to hear this, but God commands His people to honor all men—even politicians. Only the impious slander civic leaders. With this in mind, Christians do well to recall that God identified a heathen as "His shepherd," or leader. Ironically, it was Cyrus the Mede, not a Hebrew, who initiated rebuilding the Temple. Election year or not, brawling never befits the Body of Christ; therefore, Christians must not render railing for railing. While Christians are free to hold, express, and promote political opinions, they must not insist upon their own party or candidate. The Israelites learned this lesson well when, contrary to Samuel, they railroaded need for a king to rule over them (Prov. 29:26; Isa. 44:28; 1 Peter 2:17; Rom. 13:1; Jude 8; Exod. 22:28; Acts. 23:5; Eccles. 10:20; Titus 3:2; 1 Pet. 3:9; 2 Tim. 2:16; 1 Sam. 8:19).

To be effective, Christians first must be informed, but never unduly troubled. As workmen that need not be ashamed, well-grounded Christians contribute significantly to the human community. Their courageous leadership benefits all of God's cities throughout the world. Righteousness exalts a nation, *any* nation—not America exclusively. Take, for example, the republic of Fiji in the southwest Pacific Ocean. There, I found the church of Jesus Christ to be very much alive and well. The momentous call to restrain what the Bible calls the "mystery of iniquity" falls to the universal Body of Christ, including Fijian brethren. It is not accomplished by some standing army under Security Counsel directive, nor by American Christians acting alone (Matt. 6:31–34; Luke 10:41; Titus 3:8–9; 2 Tim. 2:15; Prov. 14:34; 2 Sam. 10:12).

In summary, demonstrating partiality to certain individuals or groups is *hamartia*. The "Royal Law" requires more. Scripture instructs us that "God so loved the world, He gave His only begotten son." Following divine example, American Christians are called to love their global neighbors as fervently as they do their own country and fellows. To insist upon the chief seat in the synagogue, so to speak, is to err grievously (John 3:16; Matt. 23:6).

CHAPTER 12

HAMARTIA LIBERALISM

What then shall we say? Shall we habitually sustain an attitude of *dependence upon*, *yieldedness to*, and *cordiality with* the sinful nature *[hamartia]* in order that grace may abound? May such a thing never occur (Rom. 6:1, *Wuest Expanded Translation of the New Testament*).

Core Values of Liberalism

In the minds of many, liberalism speaks to tolerance and generosity—abounding grace, as it were. A dictionary definition of "liberal" is "favoring civil liberties, democratic reforms, and the use of public resources to promote social programs." Praiseworthy as these appear, core values of liberalism likewise include federal deficit spending and high taxes, anti-biblical judicial activism, and unilateral nuclear freezes, not to mention blame-America-first policies.

In a word, liberalism is false dogma purporting that, given ever-escalating taxes and regulations, tax-and-spend government will solve social and economic problems. As such, it mirrors Darwin's hapless theory of historic optimism contending, wrongly so, that with the passing of time human thinking, philosophy, and destiny progressively improve apart from God's timely intervention. America's godless public education system, radical feminism, abortion on demand, gender and racial affirmative action, mandated quotas, and gay rights activism all spring from liberal core values.

America's Godless Public Education System

In 1921, Norman Thomas warned, "Under the name of liberalism, [the American people] will adopt every fragment of the socialist program until one day America will be a socialist nation without knowing how it happened."

According to Congressman Dick Arney, liberals enjoy a near stranglehold on America's college campuses. It is there that proponents promote failed socialist economic policies; furthermore, they work feverishly to undermine traditional moral values. Arney also reminds us that, in making room for the burgeoning global community, America must not love peace more than freedom, unless she is prepared to forfeit both.

Nonetheless, liberal instructors continue to mask their blame-America-first agenda with politically correct multiculturalism, which (in the bogus name of peace and harmony) effectively eliminates America's heritage including Judeo-Christian ethic. That nonbelievers have something of surpassing value to offer contradicts God's warning to "learn not the ways of the heathen" and to "inquire not after their gods" (Jer. 10:2; Deut. 12:30).

Radical Feminism

A tongue-in-cheek liberal bumper sticker reads, "Feminism is the radical notion that women are people, too." While motorists displaying this maxim probably believe the understood message behind it, feminist activist Ellen Willis tells it straight. In a 1981 article published by *The Nation*, Willis admitted, "The objective of every feminist reform, from legal abortion to child-care programs" is—not to humanize women—but rather "to undermine traditional family values."

ABORTION ON DEMAND

As president of the National Abortion and Reproductive Rights Action League (NARAL), feminist Kate Michelman passionately defends abortion on demand. When her husband abandoned the family in 1970, Michelman was pregnant with her fourth child. In reality, she did not feel free to choose. In her estimation, circumstances mandated abortion. For this reason, hers is not the story of a liberated feminist, taking control of her own reproductive destiny. It is instead the story of a woman caught in a trap. Not surprisingly, Michelman clings to the Roe decision in order to vindicate her actions and morality (Reardon and Sobie 1999).

American Civil Liberties Union (ACLU) activists oppose the death penalty in all cases and also the anti-terrorist precaution of airport searches (ACLU Policies #239 and #270, respectively). At the same time, they applaud elimination of some one in four American babies who never make it alive out of the womb. The modern liberal apparently believes in protecting the guilty and killing the innocent. In contrast, God hates "hands that shed innocent blood." In His economy, they that take the sword perish with it (Prov. 6:16a–19; Matt. 26:52).

GENDER AND RACIAL AFFIRMATIVE ACTION/MANDATED QUOTAS

Modern liberals believe standardized tests are "racist," but racial quotas and set-asides—i.e., reverse discrimination and entitlement—are not. In employment and education, minority ethnic groups and women are favored. Sadly, this liberal mentality hurts everyone, especially qualified minorities. With God, there is no partiality. He is no respecter of persons (James 2:9; Acts 10:34).

GAY RIGHTS ACTIVISM

Modern liberals believe that gender roles are artificial, but being gay is natural. To the contrary, the Bible denounces homosexuality as lack of "natural affection." Plainly, "the wicked freely strut about when what is vile is honored among [liberal] men [and women]" (2 Tim. 3:3; Rom. 1:25–28; Ps. 12:8, NIV).

Liberalism Personified

True, a broad range of seemingly valid opinions pad both sides, liberal and conservative; but for the sake of example, we shall look at one high-profile liberal whose political journey qualifies liberalism. In profiling Mr. Al Gore, Jr., there is no intent to dishonor anyone. The purpose rather is to expose *dependence upon*, *yieldedness to*, and *cordiality with* the sinful nature *(hamartia)*. Truth is the objective, no matter the reader's political leanings (1 Pet. 2:17; Rom. 6:1).

Questionable Associations

Among associates of Al Gore, Jr., was the alleged source of the Gore family fortune, the late Armand Hammer. Arguably the Soviet Union's favorite American businessman, Dr. Hammer served well the business needs of Lenin and Stalin. In addition to Hammer, Gore's associates include Taiwanese nationalist Maria Hsia and her clients, front men for the Red Chinese People's Liberation Army. Hsia assisted Gore in organizing the now-infamous White House coffees and Lincoln bedroom visits. It appears that Al Gore has habitually sustained an attitude of *dependence upon* men and women with questionable allegiances.

Gore's Harvard instructor and creator-editor of *The New Republic*, Martin Peretz led the crusade against God-sanctioned sexual mores and restraints, especially those regulating homosexuality and abortion—causes Gore took on. Until he declared his candidacy for Congress, Gore allegedly smoked marijuana laced with opium and hashish in the company of friend John Warnecke. Despite Gore's stalwart reputation as a family man, it could be said, in certain respects, that he has habitually sustained an attitude of *yieldedness to* what the Bible calls the flesh nature.

Astonishingly, Gore toasted Li Peng, who ordered the massacre in 1989 at student demonstrations thronging Tiananmen Square. Having played a big role in the 1990s scandals of the Clinton/Gore administration, mobster-associated Nathan Landow courted Gore as the "White House Southern Hope." Apparently Gore has habitually sustained an attitude of *cordiality with* what the Bible calls the sinful nature and those who emulate it.

A Biblical Example: Lot. The son of Haran, Lot came from a distinguished family. Both Lot and his Uncle Abraham were wealthy and, therefore, privileged. While Abraham was a "friend of God," Lot befriended the world system. Given a choice, Lot lifted up his eyes and saw the well-watered plain of Jordan. At first Lot dwelt in the plain, separate from the "sin that doth so easily beset," but later he pitched his tent toward Sodom, type of debauchery and sin. Lot chose his habitation according to sight, rather than by faith. In so doing, he sought, as many before and after him, to gain the world and what it had to offer.

Make no mistake. Conservatives—some of whom are Christians—likewise depend upon, yield to, and are cordial with the sinful nature *(hamartia)*. If only to fit in and keep from shaking the boat, many well-meaning Christians hob-knob with liberal attitudes, causes, and proponents. In looking, acting, and speaking like worldly contemporaries, these are prone to leap from well-watered plains of safety to the gate of Sodom. The latter may be a comfortable lingering place, but dangerous nonetheless.

EXAGGERATION

While the U.S. Army was the true founder of the Internet, Al Gore claimed that it was he who created it. In similar fashion, after mastering the vocabulary of nuclear strategy, Gore presented himself as having invented the subject. True, Gore got two Nashville Council members indicted for bribery to change zoning laws, but he bragged about having gotten "a bunch of people indicted and sent to jail." Memos by his own staffers warned Gore to stop exaggerating. Gore is not the first world leader to exaggerate. When King Nebuchadnezzar overstated his own greatness by boasting about having built great Babylon, Wonder of the World, his exaggeration pushed him over the brink of reality into insanity (Dan. 4: 29, 33).

Washington Post staff writer Barton Gellman reported: "Convinced that the global spread of AIDS is reaching catastrophic dimensions, the Clinton/Gore administration has formally designated the disease a threat to national security and is planning to dip into already depleted security/military funding to feed special interest groups." Not AIDS, but relinquishing gatekeeper status at both ends of the Panama Canal represents an authentic threat to national security. As a result, the opportunistic Red Chinese now point thirteen multiple-warhead missiles at U.S. cities.

Among many additional exaggerations foisted on America's school children include the need to eliminate automobiles, pesticides, the lumber industry, private property, and—yes—even people. Ironically, the UN is spreading overpopulation hysteria all the while yet another UN agency clearly demonstrates that the real population problem is too few children.

Flip-flop Convictions

Says Rush H. Limbaugh, III, "Liberals don't believe people are capable of thinking for themselves." They need those in the know to bring focus. As a result, lightly held convictions blow hither and yon like feathers in the wind. Liberals are similarly unstable as water, given to flip-flop convictions, as was the case with Jacob's firstborn Reuben, whose tribe never rose to power, probably as a result of his weakness (Gen. 49:3).

While acting as a liberal in Washington, Gore spoke as a conservative in Tennessee. He flip-flopped from tobacco farmer to tobacco fighter; friend of business to friend of Mother Earth; pro-life congressman to pro-abortion senator. Gore once declared that any government official who steals from or lies to the U.S. Congress should be fired immediately; nevertheless, his convictions waned when President Clinton was gnarled in a web of deceit.

Gore's consistent and principled anti-abortion legislation from 1977–1988 ultimately converted to unrestricted abortion. In his early years, Gore opposed homosexuality, but his Campaign 2000 position was to appoint members of the Joint Chiefs of Staff only those who share his then-absolute views on gay liberation.

According to J. Sidlow Baxter, Lot is a type of the worldly believer. As such, he is excluded from the list of seven great men of Genesis. Lot was swept along by Abraham's religion more than he was guided by his own strong convictions. Plainly, Al Gore is not alone in error. When guided more by the state religion of secular humanism and its proponents than by principled adherence to biblical mandate, people of faith betray sanctity of Judeo-Christian values that are vital for America's survival.

Today's New Tolerance

With no absolute standard of truth when it comes to alternative lifestyles, one is inclined to contemplate the provocative question Satan posed to Eve: "Hath God said?" The implied answer, of course, is "surely not." Modern liberals fancy themselves to be more loving and accepting than God, who exposes the gay lifestyle as being vile (Gen. 3:1; Rom. 1:26).

It is far more comfortable to affirm, not repudiate, beloved family members and good neighbors or friends who "come out of the closet." Once homosexuality sports a familiar face, any disapproval of lifestyle appears divisive, even hateful. Today's tolerance attracts people of faith who evidently worry more about offending man than God. Some twenty-eight gay characters on television acclimatize even traditionalists to accept seemingly benign alternative lifestyles.

Contrary to Bible wisdom, the American Psychological Association (APA) removed homosexuality from its list of disorders in 1973. Thereafter, the APA issued a position statement censuring treatment for practicing homosexuals. So advanced is the gay agenda that, by 1999, the APA released a report that stopped short of endorsing pedophilia.

Liberals in Congress are attempting to pass so-called hate crimes legislation, surmising that attitude crimes motivated by prejudice are somehow more serious than mere behavior crimes of greed or cruelty. Hollywood and the liberal media promote a *Gay Bill of Rights*, affording rights to the homosexual that no other American has. As George Orwell observed, when manipulators of mass opinion proclaim a hate campaign, people (especially people of faith) find it hard to resist.

Vermont's high court tends toward giving homosexuals the right to marry, and several states afford domestic partners comparable health benefits as those received by married couples. Although God's Word openly censures homosexual experience and lifestyle, many churches welcome to their pulpits out-of-the-closet clergy. According to *Time* magazine (9 July 1990), Judaism pioneered adoption of a national policy sanctioning homosexuality; and the General Theological Seminary of the Episcopal Church has revised its housing policy to accommodate committed same-sex couples (Lev. 18:22; Rom. 1:24–29; 1 Cor. 6:9–10).

Hypocrisy

Figures compiled by the Congressional Budget Office dispel the liberal myth that sustained growth of the eighties, minus inflation, enlarged the gap between "haves" and "have-nots." To the contrary, facts prove that the seemingly selfish eighties met with remarkable revival of U.S. industry, unprecedented export boom, and a larger percentage of new jobs in higher skill categories. Throughout the eighties, charitable donations by individuals rose by almost 58 percent, as reported in the *National Review.*

While presenting himself as a Tennessee country boy, Gore aligns with liberal colleagues in maligning this prosperous, selfish decade. Notwithstanding, Gore himself enjoys a privileged life. His father was a U.S. senator and his mother a UN delegate. Having spent three-quarters of his youth in Washington, D.C., Gore attended an elitist private school for the American ruling class. His father admitted to having raised his son for the presidency.

Despite praising his father's work on the interstate highway program, Gore assailed bulldozers and road building. When his Tennessee farm was strip-mined for zinc, Gore received personal benefit from industrial exploitation of the earth's resources, but then he crusaded against strip-mining. His own Carthage farm contributes to water pollution and open dumping. Not only does he accept contributions from corporations that contribute to pollution, but also Gore gives favors to the world's leading polluter country, the Peoples' Republic of China. In claiming to have discovered and publicized the Love Canal scandal, Gore overlooked the fact that his family friend, Armand Hammer, chaired the company that created the toxic waste in question.

Gore works to abolish chlorofluorocarbons and to limit automobile use, yet an air-conditioned vehicle transports him to speaking engagements. A vocal defender of racial quotas, Gore vilifies opponents as racists. In doing so, he fails to mention his having lived for four years in a wealthy, whites-only suburb of Nashville. Fathering four children hardly demonstrates Gore's "deep concern" about overpopulation, supposed threat to sustainability.

Seemingly, the broad-minded, tolerant liberal is quick to switch the actor's mask in his own best interest. The same applies to closed-minded, less than tolerant ultra conservatives—for example, scribes and Pharisees whom Christ labeled "pretenders" and "blind guides." Some conservative Christians follow their example by murmuring, gossiping, meddling, and indulging in a life pattern of gluttony while, at the same time, they belittle brethren who fail to grace the pew next to them. A loving, forgiving God will surely forgive *their* trespasses, they reason; but most assuredly God has no time for the unchurched.

"What then shall we say? Shall we habitually sustain an attitude of *dependence upon, yieldedness to,* and *cordiality with* the sinful nature *(hamartia)* in order that grace may abound?" As attorney-author Chuck Crismier says on his daily radio broadcast, *Viewpoint*, "May such a thing never occur in the White House, in the courthouse, in the church house, or in my own house."

CHAPTER 13

Hamartia Materialism

How shall we who died to sin *[hamartia]* still live in it? (Rom. 6:2, NASB).

The Philosophy of Materialism

A philosophy that presumably arose among the early Greek thinkers, materialism theorizes that nothing exists over and above physical matter and matter in motion. Thought, feeling, mind, will, and deities are explained in terms of physical laws alone.

Stoics and Epicureans joined ancient Buddhists as materialists. Stoicism regarded virtue as the highest good. Unmoved by pleasure or pain, stoics exercised austere ethics. They believed that happiness lay in accepting the law of the universe. On the other hand, Epicureans extolled being happy as life's greatest good. Widely held in Christ's day, Epicurean philosophy found its highest joy in intellectual pursuits. For lesser souls, however, sensual satisfaction predominated. When Paul met Epicurean philosophers at Athens, they rejected his teaching of creation, judgment, and resurrection (Acts 17:16–33).

Characterized by excessive worldly and material concerns, the contemporary world brandishes its own brand of materialism, raising profound ethical questions. According to Senator Bob Smith (R-New Hampshire), abortion clinics and the wholesalers are making a killing—literally—off the sale of human baby parts. Disturbingly, the collection, processing, and distribution of human tissue (bones, tendons, skin, body parts) is a near billion-dollar national business. Representative Joe Pitts (R-Pennsylvania) suggests further that the partial-birth abortion procedure was developed to provide this egregious industry with whole body parts. The Anatomic Gift Foundation is but one company that procures organs from aborted babies to sell to researchers.

Materialism: National/International

Shouldering nearly five trillion dollars in debt, America is the largest debtor nation in the world. ABC news has reported that the average family in America wields ten credit cards and accrues, on average, twenty-six thousand dollars in debt. Experts warn that consumer installment debt is propelling the nation toward disaster.

More often than not, luxuries are considered necessities. Many American consumers stockpile TVs, CDs, VCRs, PCs, and SUVs. Numbers of them tote cell phones. Slick magazine ads put forth the latest and greatest products with which to stock closets, pantries, pockets, and purses. President George W. Bush has noted well that ". . . our country will continue to be prosperous and strong, only if we do the right things. Prosperity alone is simple materialism," he added; "[It] must serve a greater purpose."

"All that glitters" extends beyond America's shores. Contemporary goods and services are seemingly limitless along Singapore's famed Orchard Road. Store after store displays all the finest products the world has to offer. While cruising the Bosphorus in 1997, my husband and I marveled at the influx of splendid mansions overlooking its sparkling waters. The next year, we toured the high-tech, newly constructed Convention Center in Hong Kong. There, ceremonies were conducted to welcome her back to the Motherland. Hoisted high on a pole, the Chinese flag proudly caught the wind, making known an unmistakable Red presence. According to our Taoist guide, however, no significant changes will be felt for some fifty years. Indeed, Hong Kong remains as fiercely materialistic as we had remembered from previous visits.

In the spring of 1999, we returned to the Persian Gulf. In Muscat, Oman, the Al Bustan Palace boasts over a quarter-billion dollar price tag. Its atrium is tall enough to stand a Boeing 747 on its nose, and the hotel grounds consist of over two hundred acres of plush gardens replete with spurting and cascading fountains. Muscat's visiting dignitaries luxuriate in astonishing opulence.

Materialism in the Church

To be spiritually prosperous, God's people must choose leaders committed to justice. In Deuteronomy 16, Moses instructed the Israelites to appoint for each of their tribes those judges and officials who "hate dishonest gain." Scripture warns that if we value prosperity over justice, we end up forfeiting both. Sadly, some ministers today merchandise prayer journals, holy water, chopsticks, and miniature "stained-glass" windows that serve only to cloud the simple Gospel. Tithes and offerings are best viewed as sacrifices, not investments; but ministries all too often offer exorbitant return of financial blessings in exchange for a pre-determined love offering.

Her houses of worship sometimes betray America's love affair with affluence. The Crystal Cathedral, the Dino show in Branson, Missouri, and TBN's holiday extravaganza exemplify all that glitters in Christian ventures. Only God knows the heart behind any of these enterprises. While these may or may not be fitting outreaches, the church must keep in view that prosperity, particularly in Christian circles, must serve a greater purpose than to titillate the senses or pad the pocketbook.

Call to Poverty or Prosperity?

True, Peter was a humble fisherman and Joseph, an unassuming carpenter; but there is no inherent virtue in poverty. According to 2 Corinthians 8:9, the Lord became poor for our sakes. Why? That we, through His poverty, might become rich.

Notwithstanding, there are Christians who assert that Christ was poor, having no place to lay his head; therefore, it behooves those who walk in His footsteps to be poor as well. After all, the servant is not greater than his master. But this is not necessarily so. That there was no beauty in Jesus does not condemn Sarah, Esther, Abishag, or the virtuous woman of Proverbs 31 for their extraordinary God-given physical appeal (Luke 9:58; John 13:16; Isa. 53:2; Gen. 12:11; Esther 2:7; Song of Sol. 6:9–10).

For a man or woman of God to be blessed materially might not signify greed, selfishness, or even worldliness. While the poor are with us always, never does Scripture mandate poverty, nor does it put forth poverty as a noble goal. Rather, Job 36:15 proclaims deliverance from being poor (Matt. 26:11).

God Awards Prosperity, Not Poverty

In terms of substance, Job was greatest of all the men of the East; but God allowed everything to be taken from him. In the end, however, He returned to Job twice his original worth (Job 1:3; 42:10).

Job is not alone. Consider Joseph. Due to perceived paternal partiality, Joseph's brothers hated him and subsequently sold him for less than the price of a slave. Even so, Joseph was found faithful. For good reason, the meaning of the name "Joseph" is "he adds." To his credit, Joseph remained unspoiled by sudden prosperity. In the end, God blessed and exalted him (Gen. 37:3–28; 39:1–6, 20–23; 41:14–46).

And, then, there is Mephibosheth. Crippled by a fall, Mephibosheth belonged to a royal line. It appeared that he cared little for material things. Perhaps for that reason God trusted him with a glorious inheritance. This son of Jonathan received all the land of his grandfather, Saul; and he continually ate at the king's sumptuous table (2 Sam. 4:4; 9:7, 9; 19:30).

Upon heeding the call of her bridegroom, Rebekah took on her father-in-law Abraham's great wealth in cattle, silver, and gold. Even Rebekah's brother and mother were gifted in order to bind the marriage contract between Isaac and her. Under similar circumstances, the widowed Moabitess Ruth left behind everything she had previously known in order to embrace the God of Israel. When her kinsman-redeemer, Boaz, married Ruth, he likewise shared with her his great wealth (Gen. 24:53; Ruth 1:16; 2:1).

In response to the faithfulness of Job, Joseph, Mephibosheth, Rebekah, and Ruth, God awarded prosperity, not poverty.

God Sustains Prosperity, Not Poverty

Numbers of Bible characters spent their lives in wealth and yet pleased God and served Him tirelessly. For one, Moses was taken by Hatshepsut, daughter of Thutmose I. As such, he was raised in royal splendor, yet he chose rather to suffer affliction with the people of God than to enjoy the pleasures of sin for a season (Exod. 2; Heb. 11:25).

A man of regal substance, King David, meaning "beloved," was a man after God's own heart. When he died at a ripe old age, David had both riches and honor, despite his sensual failures. By no means had wealth spoiled him (1 Chron. 29:28).

Typifying the very Prince of Peace, Jesus Christ, King Solomon subsequently surpassed all the kings of the earth in riches and wisdom. The testimony of his life's abundance had profound effect on the visiting Queen of Sheba. Virtually speechless, she could not help but bless God for Solomon's unimaginable bounty that more than exceeded her already inflated expectations (2 Chron. 9:6, 22).

Neither Poverty nor Prosperity Crucial

Despite countless scriptural examples of wealthy servants of God, neither poverty nor prosperity is crucial to salvation, sanctification, effective ministry, pleasing God, discipleship, or eligibility for the Rapture.

SALVATION; SANCTIFICATION; EFFECTIVE MINISTRY

According to the Great Commission, the Gospel is to be preached throughout the world to everyone, wealthy or poor. It may be harder for a rich man to be saved than for a camel to go through the eye of a surgeon's needle, but it happens nonetheless. While this feat is impossible with men, it is fully possible with God. The kingdom of God is not meat and drink (or anything material for that matter); but instead it is righteousness, and peace, and joy in the Holy Spirit. As believers, we do not lift up ourselves, our resources, or lack thereof; but rather we exalt Christ Jesus the Lord (Mark 16:15; Matt. 19:23, 26; Rom. 14:17; 2 Cor. 4:5).

Pleasing God; Discipleship

God commended the good servant of Luke 19:17 for his faithfulness in making something more out of what little he had. Clearly, this is no case for the "virtue" of poverty. To the contrary, those who *have* are given even more that they might increasingly magnify and glorify God in all things (verse 26). To love and follow God is to inherit substance. In fact, God promises to load us daily with benefits and, even more, to "fill our treasures" (Prov. 8:21; Ps. 68:19).

Eligibility for Rapture

To be "caught up" or "snatched away" is what Paul identified as the "high, upward calling"—first of the dead in Christ, followed thereafter by fully prepared last-day believers. Of the two in the field and the two grinding at the mill, only one is taken. To be eligible to go, one must be watchful. No mention of worldly status or worth attends the one taken, or the one left behind (Matt. 24:40–42).

Abounding and Abasing

Being good stewards of the manifold grace of God requires trustworthiness. God expects us to make gain, for "to whom much is given, much is required." Remember, too, that riches are prone to fly away as an eagle toward heaven, and ultimately, at death, man's wealth separates completely from him. Hence the maxim, "You can't take it with you." Good men of God learn this lesson well. For example, the increase of Job's house departed for the season of his testing. In like fashion, Paul learned how to abound and abase—being full and being hungry; having abundant resource and suffering need (1 Pet.

4:10; 1 Cor. 4:2; Luke 19:13, 15; 12:48; Prov. 27:24; 23:5; Ps. 49:10; Eccles. 2:18; 1 Tim. 6:7; Job 20:28; Phil. 4:12).

Pitfalls of Wealth

Admittedly, there are pitfalls to wealth. Among them are setting one's heart on fleeting riches and forgetting God. It is possible for wealth, experiential or coveted, to choke the Word and, thus, subject those enslaved by it to powerful temptations and deception. Some misguided entrepreneurs foolishly forfeit integrity to gain (or keep) earthly treasures (Deut. 8:13–14; Ps. 62:10; Prov. 28:20; Matt. 19:23; Mark 4:19; 1 Tim. 6:9; Matt. 6:19; Haggai 1:6; Luke 12:21; 1 Tim. 6:7; Heb. 11:26; Rev. 3:17).

Others give largely—but nonetheless begrudgingly, or of necessity. In contrast, the widow's *lepton* was well received, even when compared to the surplus gifts of the very rich. The *lepton* was a tiny bronze or copper coin that deteriorated easily. It is better known as the "widow's mite" (Mark 12:41–44; Luke 21:2).

Pitfalls of Poverty

As with wealth, there are pitfalls of poverty. Asaph was one of David's chief musicians, who prophesied on the harp. In Psalm 73, he sang of one such pitfall—that of envying the prosperity of the wicked (verse 3). Envy never befits believers (Gal. 5:21).

To respect the rich above less fortunate fellows is partiality, which James calls evil. On the other hand, some pride themselves for their meager means. Even in the case of poverty, pride goes before a fall (James 2:3–4; Prov. 16:18).

The sluggard disregards the diligent ant's industrious example. For instance, the man who received but one talent from his master hid it in the earth, being tempted to slothfulness. For his failing, he lost even the single talent he had been given. In Proverbs 6:6, the root word for sluggard means "to lean." In contemporary America, those who indulge in welfare fraud qualify as leaners. They likewise warrant the uncomely label *Adam belial,* or "worthless mankind." The root word for "wicked man" in verse 12 is "to pant"—that is, to expend energy without producing and, consequently, to facsimile a brute beast, prone to mischief and discord in verse 14 (Matt. 25:25, 29).

Prosperity Testifies of God's Abundant Provision

There is truth in the witty saying, "I've been rich, and I've been poor; but rich is better!" You see, prosperity testifies of God's abundant provision. It is the Lord, after all, who grants power to accumulate wealth. Riches and honor come from Him alone, for He reigns over all. According to Ecclesiastes 5:19, to profit as a result of gainful employment is "the gift of God" to which the Lord in His mercy adds even more (Deut. 8:18; 1 Chron. 29:12).

In willing "above all things" that we might "prosper *in every way,*" God's Word endorses financial success and even commands us to ask God to give us "the uttermost parts of the earth for our possession." This promise in no way warrants a "name it—claim it" theology. Keep in mind that the Lord not only grants wealth; He also "makes poor." No matter, devout believers never cease to praise God, who faithfully regards their prayers, whether from the destitute, or from those with impressive means (3 John 2; Ps. 2:8; 1 Sam. 2:7; Ps. 102:17, AMP).

Life teaches us that rains of blessings and storms of adversity fall upon those justified as well as the unjust. Regardless of circumstances, good or bad, God is worthy of praise. As the bequest of a king suitably reflects his royal stature and means, King Jesus supplies all our needs according to His riches in glory. There is no requirement to "gab it—grab it," for in Christ Jesus believers suffer no genuine long-term lack. If the Father owns the cattle on a thousand hills, as indeed He does, His children will not be found begging bread or abandoned. While God withholds no good thing from those who walk uprightly before Him, it remains His prerogative when to give and when to take away (Phil. 4:19; Ps. 50:10; 37:25; 84:11b; Job 1:21; Matt. 5:45; Ps. 65:4; James 1:4; Ps. 23:1).

Positive Perks Paired with Prosperity

In Scripture, prosperity accompanies a number of godly attributes. For example, it is paired with *obedience and servitude*. The hand of the diligent produces wealth; and Scripture promises that those who obey and serve God shall "spend their days in prosperity, and their years in pleasure" (Prov. 10:4; Job 36:11).

Prosperity is also paired with *meditation on the Word*. To meditate day and night on God's Word is to meet with good success and resulting prosperity (Josh. 1:8).

Prosperity is paired with *uprightness*. "The righteous," we learn, "flourish like a palm tree." Palm trees in Scripture speak of commanding stature and presence (Ps. 92:12).

Prosperity is paired with *love of Jerusalem* (typifying our fellow Bride-Christians, Rev. 21:2). We are to "pray for the peace of Jerusalem." Then shall we prosper as we so love her (Ps. 122:6).

Prosperity is paired with *reverence and seeking God*. "They that seek the Lord shall not want any good thing." Therefore, as we seek first His Kingdom and righteousness, good things are certain to come our way (Ps. 34:9–10b; Matt. 6:33).

Prosperity is paired with *honor*, as was the case with King David, who lived and died full of riches and honor. David's son, Solomon, surpassed all the kings of the earth in riches and wisdom. Prosperity, therefore, is paired with *wisdom* (1 Chron. 29:28; 2 Chron. 9:22).

Finally, prosperity is paired with *self-denial*. Everyone who, for the Lord's sake, forsakes material blessings, as houses or lands, shall receive back a hundred fold. Even more importantly, he shall inherit everlasting life (Matt. 19:29).

Prosperity Not a Fitting Goal

Despite positive perks paired with prosperity, getting rich is not a godly goal. Far from it! Our more excellent inheritance shared equally with Christ is *God Himself*. In Jesus, we partake of the divine nature, fulfilling Christ's prayer for oneness with one another and with the Father. None of us has fully seen, heard, or even dreamed of what God has prepared for those who love Him. Once these truths penetrate the heart, an earthly mansion, sports car, yacht, or designer garment holds little interest (Rom. 8:17; 2 Pet. 1:4; John 17:21–23; 1 Cor. 2:9).

"This may be true," some argue. "But what about well-coifed ministers who apparently use tithes and offerings to amass costly homes, clothes, watches, cars, and planes?" Bear in mind that because something looks costly does not necessarily mean it was excessively expensive. An astute consumer led of the Holy Spirit wields extraordinary buying power. Furthermore, that someone has an earthly treasure does not mean he purchased it with "my tithe." God is known to put it on the hearts of generous men and women to give liberally.

Moreover, what we have is not our own. We are but stewards of God's beneficence. In releasing our tithes and offerings to the work of God, we use the best judgment we can. The receiver, in turn, answers to God for his stewardship of the yielded resource. Simply put, the Bible forbids us to *anakrino,* or cross-examine others, ourselves included, as if we were prosecuting attorneys (Mal. 3:8–10; 1 Cor. 4:3).

Summary

While countless godly men and women are poor, many others are incredibly rich. We learn from Scripture that there is no inherent virtue in prosperity—or in poverty, for that matter. Neither is crucial to salvation, sanctification, or discipleship; and either can ambush and ensnare.

Most Christians experience, as did Paul, abounding and abasing, being full and being hungry; but God's love and valuation of them never vacillates with life's variable circumstances. No matter the quality of life enjoyed or tolerated, as the case may be, everyone needs money to trade for goods and services required in life. We can trust that God remains our faithful provider no matter the need.

A close look at 1 Timothy 6:10 reveals that "the love of money" (not money itself) is a root (more literal to the Greek than "the root") of all kinds of evil. We who died to sin *(hamartia)* upon accepting Christ as our personal Savior and Lord must not remain in sin by indulging covetousness, on one hand, or by refusing God the pleasure of imparting material blessings, on the other. Both miss the mark with grave consequences following.

CHAPTER 14

Hamartia
New Age Mysticism

> And I heard another voice from heaven, saying, "Come out of her, my people, that you may not participate in her sins [*hamartia*] and that you may not receive of her plagues." (Rev. 18:4, NASB)

An *U.S. News and World Report* article, "Running on Faith" (December 6, 1999), revealed that both front-runners to the U.S. Presidency in 2000 hung their political agendas on religion. This had not happened since fundamentalist William Jennings Bryan ran for President, and lost, in 1896.

George W. Bush, Jr., was said to have acknowledged his sin nature, recognizing he was not right with God. In 1985, while traversing Maine's craggy shores, Bush allegedly expressed to Evangelist Billy Graham his desire to be reconciled with God from whom he felt estranged. In his own words, Bush "opened his heart, God changed it," and his life "turned about." If this account is accurate and heartfelt, George W. Bush is "born from above," according to the biblical model (John 3:3).

Al Gore, Jr., likewise presented himself as a faith-friendly candidate—drawing from a year at Vanderbilt University Divinity

School (1971), and choosing an Orthodox Jew as his running mate. But Gore's religious confession bore little resemblance to that of his opponent. Gore claimed to have felt "a transformational relationship with his own interpretation of God." Furthermore, he wrote of pantheistic awareness of "a constant and holy spiritual presence in all people, life, and things." In his book, *Earth in the Balance,* Gore called *Gaia* worship "a religious heritage." He assumed *Gaia*-Mother Earth to be "the fount of all life," representing the living eco-system—which, incidentally, is worthy of being saved and is needful of global oversight.

In starting the National Religious Partnership for the Environment, Gore endorsed eco-justice, assigning humans blame for the earth's alleged attrition. He acts out this belief as an associate and lay minister of the New Age Cathedral of Saint John, the Divine, in Upper Manhattan. This self-proclaimed Green Cathedral calls for global convergence of world religions.

While Bush presumably embraces the biblical, traditional model of right standing with God, Gore's spirituality smacks of neo-pantheistic syncretism. While claiming to be Baptist, Gore's theology is unmistakably New Age. New Age doctrine courts three principles of paganism–namely, pantheism, animism, and polytheism. Pantheism is belief that all life is god, or part of god (e.g., "a constant and holy spiritual presence in all people, life, and things"). Animists contend that stones and trees harbor spirits, thus inspiring many misguided environmentalists to follow Gore's lead in hugging trees. Rooted in pantheism, animism is linked to ancestor and nature (or *Gaia*) worship (i.e., "a religious heritage"). In a word, polytheism honors many gods, vouchsafing Gore's "own interpretation of god."

In Greek mythology, Pan is depicted as a man with horns and hoofed legs of a goat. While the goat is a type of rebellion, and therefore of Lucifer, Pan plays a shepherd's panpipe, counterfeiting the Good Shepherd, Jesus Christ. New Age occultist Marilyn Ferguson and José Arguelles preach a Pan philosophy. Arguelles further identifies Pan as the first son of Mother Earth *(Gaia)* come to save and lead Earth's inhabitants into a New Age of presumed enlightenment.

Gore is not alone in embracing para-biblical beliefs. Over half of all Americans err in presuming a scientific basis for astrology ("star-speak" in Greek). A smaller, but nonetheless substantial number are deluded by obsession with alien abductions and the lost continent of Atlantis. Others wear bracelets promising vain hope for protection, healing, or affluence.

New Age "Enlightenment"

By definition, the New Age movement is a worldwide coalition. Propelled by an esoteric belief system, it is united by global economic and political agendas. Proponents condemn private property as being impossible, free enterprise as exploitation, technology as an abomination against Nature (capital "N" intended), and Judeo-Christian Western culture as the root of all evil.

The movement's English founder is Alice Bailey, co-Masonic hierarch and notable leader of theosophy. Its spiritual godmother is the Russian-born mystic best known for her occult classic, *Secret Doctrine*—namely, Madam Helena Petrovna Blavatsky. French Jesuit paleontologist and philosopher Pierre Teilhard de Chardin qualifies as its patron saint while the founder of analytical psychology, Carl Gustav Jung, stands out among its most avid proponents.

New Age theology is found in the White House, Hollywood, the United Nations, and the public school system, compliments of Al Gore, Jr., actress Shirley McLaine, Maurice Strong, and Robert Muller, respectively.

The number-two man at the United Nations, Canadian socialist and oil/steamship billionaire Maurice Strong dubs his Colorado ranch "the Vatican of the New World Order." A prominent New Age occultist, Strong serves as indomitable director of the World Future Society, the Temple of Understanding, and the International Union for the Conservation of Nature (IUCN), a powerful NGO created in 1948 by Sir Julian Huxley.

Chancellor of the University of Peace, Costa Rica, Dr. Robert Muller was formerly assistant secretary-general at the United Nations. Incredibly, he credited the Tibetan, Alice Bailey's spirit guide, for creation of his prize-winning World Core Curriculum, which forms the base of today's education restructuring movement. Calling for "cosmic education and spirituality," Muller believes in cosmic laws common to all faiths.

New Age Error in the Church

The practitioner of New Age theology is sometimes described as enlightened, illumined, or having "fire in the eyes," a throwback to Sun worship. It seems preposterous that any Christian, or church, would align with such falsity, but sadly many do.

Ecumenicism/Interfaithism

As the term "catholic" means "universal," "ecumenical" means "of the whole world." Today's ecumenical movement seeks global unity of the entire religious community, but always at the price of doctrinal mix, called syncretism. The motto of the World Council of Churches, "One Church for One World," points to a religiously pluralistic international community with no rightful promise of salvation.

True, a recent Gallup survey shows a surge in spirituality among Americans; however, Kevin Manoia, president of the National Association of Evangelicals, warns that many who profess Christ are Bible illiterates. Theirs is a "smorgasbord kind of religion made to suit the individual." Not to offend, many good-hearted Christians fear to draw the line when it comes to clearly divisive words spoken by Christ. Rather than underscore the narrow way, they are quick to welcome broader religious viewpoints, as those held by respectable, but theologically misguided role models.

Mother Teresa's Flawed Theology

Consider the life of Mother Teresa. Who would dare to criticize her? The 1997 death of this notable twentieth-century Nobel Prize-winning humanitarian kindled grief around the world. To her credit, Mother Teresa's work has inspired many to renewed heights of commitment and depths of self-sacrifice. In June of 1985, President Reagan presented Mother Teresa with the Medal of Freedom award, highest civilian honor conferred by the United States. In October of the same year, she elicited the warmest ovation of the United Nation's fortieth anniversary celebration.

In view of her exemplary life, many Christians lightly brush aside Mother Teresa's flawed theology. Attending to human need no doubt honors Jesus; however, Mother Teresa perceived the "dying, the crippled, the mentally ill, the unwanted, and the unloved" as "Jesus in disguise," rather than fallen humanity in need of a Savior-Healer. While Mother Teresa held that all religions hold elements of truth, and no religion or religious teacher is right or wrong, Jesus called Himself "*the* Truth"—never one of many. Access to the Father is through Him alone. No other path or religious leader will do (Matt. 25:40; Rom. 3:10, 23; John 14:6).

UNIVERSALISM

Since the 1962 Second Vatican Council, the Catholic Church has dedicated itself to advancing global inter-religious cooperation. In 1984, at the Pashupati Temple, Mother Teresa sanctioned belief in Hindu gods, Shiva and Ram, the likes of whom Paul called "no gods" (Acts 4:12; 19:26). Clearly, she was an universalist after the example of Pope John Paul II, who vigorously pursues interfaithism. To Mother Teresa, Buddhists, Hindus, and Christians share equal access to the same God, but this is not so (*Time*, 4 December 1989).

At the 1985 Spirit of Peace Conference sponsored by the United Nations University of Peace, Mother Teresa stood shoulder-to-shoulder with the Dalai Lama (self-proclaimed deity), Marilyn Ferguson (New Age author), Prince Bernhard (Bilderberg Group founder), and Robert Muller (New Age "Father of United Religions"). The featured agenda called for a New World Order—not to be mistaken for the Millennial rule and reign of Christ (*Christian Inquirer* April 1985).

PROMISE OF PSEUDO-PEACE

While addressing the United Nations (October 1985), Mother Teresa thanked God for the organization's forty years of what she praised as "beautiful work." Because, she proclaimed, we are all children of God (atheistic communists apparently included), "no color, no religion, no nationality" should divide the human community. To this end, she participated in the Summit for Peace in Assisi, Italy (November 1996). Arranged by the Pope, this meeting was attended by leaders of a hodge-podge of religions, united in prayers for world peace (*Christian News* 11 November 1985; *Time* 10 November 1986).

The conciliatory gospel according to Mother Teresa refutes words of Jesus to the contrary: "I came not to send peace, but a sword. For I am come to set a man at variance against his father and the daughter against her mother, and the daughter-in-law against her mother-in-law." Them's fightin' words, as the saying goes, but *Jesus'* words nonetheless, certainly not enlightened by Mother Teresa's New Age-friendly standards (Matt. 10:34–35).

Mother Teresa further affirmed Vatican II, intimating that adherents to all religions are somehow saved through the Roman Catholic Church. For this reason, Mother Teresa and those who worked with her never attempted to convert the lost to Christ. Her message was rather to become a better Hindu, a better Muslim, a better Catholic, a better whatever we are.

The Bible teaches that peace with God comes solely through Jesus (Rom. 5:1), but Mother Teresa taught, "What god is in your mind you must accept." Tragically, she instructed dying Hindus to pray, not to the one true God, but rather to their own Hindu gods (Doig; Hunt).

Ecumenism, interfaithism, and universalism represent New Age error, not to be embraced by Christ's remnant church. Titus 1:9 reads, ". . . holding firm to the trustworthy message as it has been taught, so that [you] can encourage others by sound doctrine, and refute *[not affirm]* those who oppose it."

Biocentric Thought

The Cartesian Theory properly distinguishes human life from earth, whose resources God intended for human use and consumption. Rather than ascribe humankind its rightful position as crown of God's creation and good stewards of it, biocentricity subjugates humans to the planet. The former reflects biblical, Judeo-Christian thought while the latter defines a New Earth [Global Civic] Ethic (Gen. 2:15–16).

Father Barry's Eco-theology

The principle of good ecological stewardship resonates with biblical Christianity. If we are found wanting in earthly matters, "who will commit to our trust the *true* riches?" God has commanded

His people to tend, keep, and subdue earth for life's necessities, and that we must do (Luke 16:11).

Sadly, today's biocentric thought has infiltrated the church. Father Thomas Barry's eco-theology starts with the erroneous premise that the universe is divine. Eco-justice demands that humans mobilize planetary resources to save Mother Earth and, thereafter, to maintain Nature's fragile balance of energy flow.

French microbiologist René Dubos coined the phrase "think globally; act locally." "Our salvation," he claims, "depends on our ability to create a religion of Nature." When paired with a political agenda that takes front stage to any presumed campaign for clean air or water, eco-theological distortion of stewardship misses the mark spiritually. You see, biocentrism wrongly elevates worth of the eco-system over humans for whom Christ died.

Earth Day

More than 300 million people in 150 nations participated in Earth Day 2000, marking its thirtieth anniversary. This April 22 event represented the largest global environmental celebration in history. Its theme was "New Energy for a New Era." Thousands of local and regional events honored Earth and hoped to ensure sustainable development, which by principle affirms that bears may fish, and wolves may eat meat, but—contrary to scriptural mandate to take dominion—humans may not. Some Earth Day enthusiasts hold to the skewed belief that cutting trees constitutes genocide. Their bumper stickers read, "Meat is murder."

Friends of the Earth, the Audubon Society, and the Sierra Club helped to transform Earth Day into an annual national holiday. Founded by John McConnell, Earth Day is said to belong to the public. Be assured, however, the Sierra Club, for one, is not mainstream. It lobbies to discourage public use of scented products, as deodorant. It also embraces the Wildlands Project, which purposes to return at least half of the land area in America to core wilderness, barring human activity. UN-designated NGOs, as the Audubon Society, represent management behind the United Nations concept of sustainability with intent to re-map modern society's new third-millennium reality.

All year long, politically correct educators across the nation address environmental issues in classrooms by integrating them into science, math, language arts, and social studies. All the while, young eco-warriors are being groomed to parrot politicized messages told them. To honor Earth's indigenous people and to empower youngsters to make a difference, students don Mexican spirit beads and grotesque tribal masks. Their songs encourage Earth worship and tree hugging as if all life were somehow mystically interrelated. Games played are designed more to change attitudes than to model real science.

Parents, too, are cajoled into participation. In the spring of 2000, a character played by Dixie Carter in CBS's "Family Law" received a "D" grade in ecological awareness and, thus, was shamed into renewing her earlier commitment to Earth Day basics. Once having taken extreme measures to comply with eco-correctness, this law associate once again was restored to the status of "cool mom."

A spin-off of the Council on Foreign Relations (CFR), the occult-driven Club of Rome (COR) calls for "a new enemy" to unite humanity. Threats of pollution, global warming, water shortages, species extinction, overpopulation, and famine serve this purpose handily. In reality, the recently formed Interfaith Council on Environmental Stewardship (ICES) released the *Cornwall Declaration on Environmental Stewardship*. Endorsed by scientists and economists, as well as by Jewish, Catholic, and Protestant religious leaders, this declaration asserts that many environmental threats, as those listed above, are greatly exaggerated. A major piece of research from the *U.S. National Assessment of the Potential Consequences of Climate Variability and Change*, for example, found no conclusive evidence of health hazards due to global warming. Ironically, researchers pinpointed some positive outcomes, notably reduced cold-weather mortality.

Despite radical environmentalism's misleading theology, pseudo-science, and leftist political agenda, Christian churches, schools, and parents alike join young Leonardo DiCaprios in what is deemed fashionable support of Earth Day. Even Christian students proudly "pledge allegiance to the Earth, and all its sacred parts—its water, land, and living things and all its human hearts" (Earth Pledge, Global Education Associates).

Religious Experience Preempting the Word

Daughter of a Presbyterian missionary to China, and wife of an Episcopalian rector, Agnes Sanford is a popular Christian author. Some christen her "grandmother of the healing movement in the church." Since its original publication in 1947, *The Healing Light* has sold over half-a-million copies. Even quasi-celebrities as Ruth Carter Stapleton have drawn from Sanford's expertise. On a more personal level, our family friend, a devoted evangelical Christian and victim of unspeakable personal loss, testifies that *The Healing Light* "has given focus" to her belief in God's healing power.

Agnes Sanford: *The Healing Light*

The Healing Light is dedicated to helping people of faith tap the creative energy that God offers. True, Sanford offers a number of illustrations of those whose lives were changed by their willingness to accept God's love, forgiveness, and power. Yet she peppers her work with extra-biblical and decidedly New Age concepts and buzz words—for example, "cosmic healing forces of the body," "higher spiritual energy," "creative life-(and love-) forces."

In so doing, she unreservedly applauds the "new age" and "new order" that earmark an anticipated mystical Omega Point. Accordingly, New Age theology teaches that every 2,160 years of cyclic time, a new age with some new revelation emerges. To the mystic, human planetary light bearers are thrusting the *cosmos* into a so-called age of Aquarius, distinguished by group consciousness, universal brotherhood, and full flowering of human potential. Sanford addresses these from a para-biblical perspective.

Universalism; Pantheism

Contrary to Scripture, Sanford's notion of oneness in Christ wrongly embodies every person in the world, further downgraded to the status of animals. Even more alarmingly, she demotes to mere "primal energy" the unmoved, unchanged, undefeated, and never undone Creator-of-all.

In one illustration, Sanford renounces human dread of snakes as folly. In her theology, the snake is one with humans, and all are one with the divine. Logically, then, the snake is not to be feared.

Pantheists believe similarly that all life is part of God. Given that God is presumed to be the sum total of everything that exists, neo-pantheists likewise humanize animals. To do so is called anthropomorphism.

The Bible teaches differently. God is not some impersonal force, but rather the divine entity to whom humans are accountable and with whom they fellowship. The one true God shares His glory with none—be it animal, vegetable, or even humanity, the veritable crown of creation (Ps. 145:8; Gen. 1:26; James 3:7; Isa. 48:11).

On the other hand, created life forms have origin, limitation, and a certain end. They are not God, or any equal part of God, nor are they to be honored and served as if they were. That our inner being is said to be "part of God," as Sanford claims, is more neo-pantheistic delusion than it is Bible truth (Rom. 1:25).

Superstition/ Religious Syncretism

When Sanford congratulates pain for being one of God's healing agencies, she hints at Shamballa forces. According to New Age mystics, lords of destiny [actually demons] are said to use pain, even death, as instruments to purify and regenerate humanity. Alternatively, the Bible way is to call for elders that they might anoint with oil and pray in the name of Jesus (James 5:14–16).

Sanford's suggested response to a burglar is—by faith—to project into that burglar's psyche the love of God. That alone, she claims, will cause the intruder's mind to change. Added to her mind control tactics, Sanford joins occultist Edgar Cayce in promoting self-hypnosis. While New Age practitioners commonly employ paranormal mind control and hypnotherapy, Bible-honoring believers do not. Such practices are disallowed in Deuteronomy 18:9–12. Among those to suffer the second death of Revelation 21:7–8 are hypnotists (charmers) and idolaters.

Illadvisedly, Sanford presents pioneering scientist Thomas Edison as an example of faith. This is true despite the fact that Edison was known to engage in occult meditation; moreover, he was a disciple of Madam Blavatsky. This Russian-born mystic is known as "spiritual godmother of the New Age movement." Although the London Society for Psychical Research declared Blavatsky to be fraudulent in 1885, she nonetheless convinced a large following of her intuitive insight into the nature of the divine.

"By the Holy Spirit being borne along" (literal Greek), the Bible's forty penmen "spoke from God," not as men (or Episcopalian women) with "cunningly devised fables." While her desire may well be to help, Agnes Sanford is but one of countless Christian ministers who fail to apply the plumb line of God's Word to tenets of faith. In relying heavily on experience, Sanford embraces New Age error, perhaps unwittingly. In so doing, she points other well-meaning folks in the wrong direction (2 Pet. 1:16, 20–21).

Jesus warned believers to take heed lest *anyone* deceive them—including the daughter of a missionary, wife of a minister, and celebrated Christian author. Authenticity applies to the more sure word, not iffy religious experiences or supposedly mainstream belief systems that smack of New Age mysticism (Matt. 24:4).

CHAPTER 15

Hamartia
Occultism

For the Devil sinneth [*hamartanō*] from the beginning (1 John 3:8).

In Latin, occult means "to cover or conceal" from profane public scrutiny. Secrecy, self-god, ritual, degrees of initiation, and a global plan characterize ancient mysteries and modern counterparts of the burgeoning New Age movement, Wicca (witchcraft), and secret societies.

Stated concisely, occultism speaks to surreptitious supernatural influences, phenomena, or knowledge. It presupposes involvement with fortune telling, magic, spiritualism, or false religious teachings. From earliest times, God condemned occultism as spiritually defiling. Scripture forbids all forms of it. Even so, in the last fifteen years, an explosion of interest has resulted in most universities adding parapsychology departments. To explore metaphysical mysteries, many contemporary college students sign up for courses on occult history (Lev. 19:31; Deut. 18:11–12; Lev. 20:6; Gal. 5:19–21; Rev. 21:8).

Secret Societies and Politics

Despite its being banned in the 1780s, the occult Order of the Illuminati lives on today through the Council on Foreign Relations (the invisible government) and its counterparts throughout the world—for example, the British Institute of International Affairs. Founded in 1968 by Italian industrialist Aurelio Peccei, the Club of Rome is an occult-driven spin-off group from the Council on Foreign Relations. Its 1972 report, *Limits of Growth*, served as blueprint for today's bold new economic, military, and political union in Europe.

Recognized as a powerful non-governmental organization (NGO), Lucis Trust is a key player at recent United Nations summits. Established in 1922, Lucis (formerly, Lucifer) Trust is parent organization to the Theosophical Society, which promotes a form of ancient gnosticism, esoteric cult of divine knowledge.

"Doctrines of Demons" and the Church

Paul suggests that even Christians fall prey to "seducing spirits" and "doctrines of devils." Every Labor Day weekend thousands gather in the Nevada desert to celebrate their entrance, one day, into hell. Some are disillusioned Christians who have turned their backs on God. Many associate with the finest universities and corporations around the world. Participants shed their clothes, trance-dance, and exchange idols while celebrating around the burning man, a forty-foot timber giant wrapped in wax-soaked burlap and studded with Roman candles (1 Tim. 4:1).

Inadvertently, some Christians embrace *light* occultism. Supposing they are aligning with philanthropic and humanitarian ideals, good Christian men, women, and youngsters join Orders of Freemasonry, Eastern Star, DeMolay, Job's Daughters, and Rainbow Girls. They are unaware that the author of the *Satanic Bible* and High Priest of the Church of Satan, Anton LaVey, exposed Masonic roots of essentially every occult order.

Former occultist Bill Schnoebelen of With One Accord Ministries claims further that, unbeknownst to most, Freemasonry actually has ninety-seven degrees of initiation. The ninetieth degree takes one "over the abyss," transcending good and evil. At this point, he allegedly becomes god. Signs, key words, and points of entrance grant access to the order's deep secrets.

Having attained to the craft's thirty-third degree, former Mason Jim Shaw never understood the darker side of the craft nor its Luciferic underpinnings. Today a Christian, he works to expose the "fraternity within the fraternity" of the craft.

Occultism Forbidden

According to Deuteronomy 18:9–12, fortunetellers, soothsayers, magicians, witches, hypnotists, psychics, clairvoyants, and those who consult with spirits and contact the dead are all "abominations to God."

Fortunetellers (Diviners)

Repeated use of the phrase "divining the intent" of the voter by means of dimpled or pregnant chads characterized the Presidential "Decision 2000." While this phrase in no way denotes supernatural intervention, its broad use mainstreamed and perhaps even trivialized occult divination. Simply put, divination employs supernatural means to gain information about people or events. An example, laughable to some, is use of a forked stick to divine for oil, minerals, or underground sewer and water lines. This practice is known as "water witching" or "dowsing."

Basic to the Hassid sect of Judaism, Kabbalism presents a decidedly mystical interpretation of the Bible with use of numerical associations. According to the world's leading authority Gershom Scholem, the Kabbalah is related to today's practice of Satanism, white magic, and divination by palm reading. Eliphas Levi was an early nineteenth-century occultist who was among the first to combine fortune telling, tarot, and the Kabbalah into one system.

In 1999, my husband and I enjoyed a Crystal cruise from Mumbai, India, on to the Persian Gulf, Red and Mediterranean Seas. With warm reception, a celebrity guest speaker on board sang the praises of Kabbalism. It seems that in recent years, Kabbalism and "ancient wisdom" have sparked renewed interest, especially among American Jews. Between 1976 and 1997 alone, the number of

Americans who put stock in fortune telling reportedly increased from 4 to 14 percent.

Soothsayers (Observer of Times)

Nostradamus was a sixteenth-century prophet, French physician, and astrologer, claimed by some to have been inspired by God. He reportedly foresaw notable personalities and events, as the rise of Hitler and the assassination of Kennedy, respectively. Even today, his prophecies garnish the tabloids and psychic talk shows on television.

The very foundation of occultism, and a popular practice since the time of ancient Babylon, astrology means "star-speak" in the Greek. It studies the relative position of planets and stars, believing that they influence events on earth. Alerted by an astrologer not to sail the *Titanic*, U.S. financier and investment banker J.P. Morgan allegedly heeded the warning, and his life was spared. Despite the good outcome, Isaiah 47:12–14 warns that astrologers, stargazers, and monthly prognosticators shall be "as stubble." This being the case, seeking their advice is ill advised. Nevertheless, many Christians bypass the Bible in their rush to the horoscope page of daily newspapers and tabloid magazines.

Rumor has it that a "Christian" version of the zodiac has been proposed. The zodiac represents Western astrology based on twelve signs of the zodiac (band of the celestial sphere divided into twelve equal parts, called signs). Pisces and Aquarius are two such signs. New Age occultists believe that humankind is passing from the age of the individual (Pisces) into a New Age (Aquarius)—that of group consciousness.

Druidism is ancient Celtic doctrine remarkably similar to that of New Age mysticism in its fixation on celestial bodies. Appearing in legend as sorcerers and prophets, druids are members of an order of priests in ancient Gaul and Britain. Freemasonry is said to have evolved from druidism, and Halloween is its contemporary expression. Considered to be the day of the year most conducive to demon activity, the Vigil of Samhain, or Halloween, is one of eight major festivals celebrated by witches.

In the original festival of Halloween, it was believed that on the eve of the druidic new year, the Lord of Death permitted wicked souls under his dominion to return to their earthly homes. The living offered sacrifices to appease these wicked dead and, thus, avert any pranks they were inclined to play. A Christian's celebrating Halloween has been likened to a Holocaust survivor's celebrating Hitler's birthday. Yet it happens. Giggly children bedecked as vampires and witches most likely are not involved in the occult; nevertheless, they violate biblical principle to abstain for self-interest from all outward appearance of evil (1 Thess. 5:22).

Magicians (Enchanters, Ones who Interpret Omens)

Magic is the technique of harnessing secret powers to influence events for private purposes. Take, for example, Pharaoh's magicians who duplicated, in succession, each of the miracles God performed through Moses. 2 Thessalonians 2:9–10a warns that Antichrist will engage in similarly deceptive magic to the destruction of many; however, "Christian" writers, as Madeleine L'Engle, cavalierly introduce magical elements into books that parents and teachers alike snatch up for use even in Christian homes and classrooms.

L'Engle's *A Wrinkle in Time* holds not a candle to the fourth installment of seven planned novels about the world's most beloved wizard, Harry Potter. The root of the Hebrew word for "wizard" is "to know." But that knowledge is not of God.

Harry Potter Mania. On Saturday morning, 8 July 2000, the front-page cover story of *The Seattle Times* featured a 734-page children's novel, *Harry Potter and the Goblet of Fire*—largest U.S. first print ever, boasting the highest price paid for release of any children's book to date. With the unprecedented discharge of 3.8 million copies, thousands of parents across the country suspended bedtimes to whisk their children to local bookstores that opened at 12:01 A.M. Dressed as witches and wizards, many adults outnumbered children. Smash sales sent the publisher back to press for an additional two million copies.

While Focus on the Family's critic, Lindy Beam, thinks it best to leave Harry Potter on the shelf, other church leaders "high-five" the beloved Potter novels. Wheaton College professor Alan Jacobs is but one enthusiast. *Christianity Today* apparently bases its approval on popular consensus among Christian leaders, as Chuck Colson, who interprets the Potter craze as longing for "the otherworldly," and hence for God. To many, truth prevails in Harry Potter's presumed-to-be morally ethical universe. However, in Potter's world, it is not at all clear why loyalty is good; and murder is bad.

The British author, a single mom, scribbled Harry's escapades while seated for hours in a public coffee shop. An overnight sensation, J.K. Rowling now boasts a net worth of over two hundred million dollars. She is a literary legend with landmark status globally. For this, she is to be congratulated; her Potter series nonetheless is replete with lessons in practical witchcraft. You see, *Harry Potter and the Goblet of Fire* deals with Harry's escape to Hogwarts School of Witchcraft and Wizardry and his participation in the Triwizard Tournament "to further and promote magical understanding" among "muggles" (non-magical folks). The Dark Lord's evil intent is to self-resurrect and, thus, increase his power over the magic world.

Occult settings, ghoulish characters, and ominous atmosphere fail to reflect divine order—as do use of magic powder, death-defying games, and an enchanted urn. Interpreting omens, calling up dead folks, and casting spells are clearly occult practices unbefitting Christians. In a word, Harry Potter's domain commemorates year-round Halloween. Many charge, rightly so, that the Potter fad flings open the door to occult reality. On the heels of Potter mania, Great Britain's Pagan Federation routinely addresses about one hundred inquiries per month from youngsters who wish to become witches.

Despite the fact that biblical Christianity is in no way compatible with the neo-pagan Potter revival, those who refuse to endorse Potter's brand of occultism are all too often demeaned as unenlightened spoilsports.

Witches (Sorcerers)

While appealing to the forces of nature, modern witches practice occult arts. Some are politically correct, spiritually defunct radical feminists. Former head of Planned Parenthood Faye Wattleton encourages women to feel "the energy" of their womanhood. At Gorbachev's World Forum, where Wattleton spoke in November of 1997, each participant received a pendant showing a circle of female witches dancing naked in the moonlight.

Wiccans frequently work as political activists on Earth's behalf. Incredibly, the United Nations endorses these efforts by sponsoring Environmental Sabbaths for the Earth Goddess, *Gaia*.

While evil intent signals "black magic," benign intent signals "white magic." Shaman practices include white magic powers purportedly to cure illnesses and to control good and evil spirits. In contrast, Tantric Yoga is a sexual form of black magic used for attaining the nefarious, climactic Omega Point. To God, neither "white" nor "black" magic makes a whit of difference. Either way, witchcraft is "a work of the flesh"; and those who engage in it shall not inherit the kingdom of God. Instead, sorcerers shall have their part in the Lake of Fire (Gal. 5:19–21; Rev. 21:8).

Pharmakeia is the Greek word for sorcery, or "enchantments by drugs," for which wrongdoers will not repent in the end times. Overall, domestic consumption of illicit drugs is rising. The markets for heroin, cocaine, and pot are either stable or increasing. Those in a drug-altered state of mind are prone to behave criminally, often with deadly social impact, as felt by about two million known survivors of generational Satanic ritual abuse (Rev. 9:21).

Wiccans and the Church. In July of 1995, retired electronics engineer Pete Davis was elected head of the Interfaith Council of Washington. Founded in 1988, this nonprofit organization represents twelve faith traditions. Davis is the first Wiccan chosen to head such a broadly based religious organization. Purposing to counter religious bias, Davis espouses an earth-centered spirituality. In recognition of his efforts to mainstream Wicca, a colleague ascribed to Davis the nickname, "Pathfinder."

Human Rights Commissioner Michael Chamberlain affirms that neo-pagan witchcraft is a "spiritual movement" in its attempt to revive the ancient religions of Europe and the Middle East. With this in view, he ruled in May of 1995 that trustees of the nonprofit, non-denominational Cathedral of the Pines were remiss in denying access to witches.

In like fashion, a prison Chaplain at Belmont Correctional Institution in St. Clairsville, Ohio, was required by the warden to write a letter of apology to Wiccan inmates. In a Protestant worship service, the chaplain presumably offended them with his biblical teaching correctly establishing the incompatibility of Christianity with Wicca (*Burger v. Belmont Correctional Institution*).

By the year 2000, the famed Episcopal Cathedral of St. John, the Divine, in Upper Manhattan had called for global convergence of world religions, Wiccans included. Leading star of New Age occultism, David Spangler ministers there. Spangler claims himself to be the Great Invocation, calling forth the one-world "savior," whom the Bible identifies as Antichrist. This so-called Green Cathedral houses the *Gaia* Institute, esoteric order connected to Knights Templar (prototype of today's illumined Freemasonry). The Cathedral also houses the Temple of Understanding, whose director is occultist Maurice Strong, second in command at the United Nations. Strong's wife is a practicing witch. Frequented by the likes of Henry Kissinger and Robert McNamera, their Colorado ranch *Baca Grande* is a hotbed for pagan religious activity.

Wiccans and the Military. Today's kinder, gentler military affords Wicca equality as a faith protected under the First Amendment. The largest military base in the U.S., Fort Hood has given official recognition to Wiccans, who now conduct worship services with the sanction of the U.S. Armed Forces. When off duty, Wiccan soldiers wear pentagram pendants, practice candle magic, and attend on-base circle rituals.

Wiccans and Pop Culture. The good news is that a recent Gallup survey showed a surge in U.S. spirituality. The bad news is that pop-culture paganism is the latest fad among young people. Given that 88 percent of America's teens are unchurched, they are all the more susceptible to spiritual error. Many are enticed into the occult by playing demonic games, as *Dungeons and Dragons,* or by means of seductive occult messages in today's popular music, as documented by Al Menconi Ministries.

David Benoit kicked off the 1997 Let's Talk Prophecy Atlanta Conference by exposing witchcraft on children's television and in movies. Take, for example, the Disney film, *Pocahontas.* A prominent Wiccan dubbed it "the most pagan-positive film in history." Poised, well-dressed witches of hit television series *Charmed* and *Sabrina, the Teenage Witch* likewise present witchcraft in favorable light.

Children are not alone in being targeted with pagan-friendly literature by Pocket Books, Citadel Press, and Llewellyn Publications. Brazilian novelist Paulo Coelho is the second best-selling writer in the world, surpassed only by John Grisham. The *Alchemist* established Coelho's global reputation. Among his more famous fans are Bill Clinton, Madonna, and Julia Roberts. Coelho's works have been published in 117 countries and are best sellers in eighteen of them. Significantly, Coelho explores different religions, including Wicca. *The New York Times* reports that Coelho dabbled with satanic teachings of Aleister Crowley, who shaped Wicca. A thirty-third degree Mason, Crowley headed a sex-magic cult claiming illumination to all Masonic secrets.

HYPNOTISTS (CHARMERS)

A charmer in the literal Hebrew is "one who ties knots"—that is, one who casts spells to alter the consciousness of others. Any substance that depresses brain function, inducing sleep, is tagged "hypnotic." Smudge is a well-known, non-regulated drug that produces hallucinations and altered consciousness. Hard-core occultists consider consumption of mind-altering drugs, as LSD and heroin, to be the lazy man's way to this favored state.

More commonly, centering techniques are employed to attain what New Age occultists believe to be a higher state of consciousness. Indeed, Transcendental Meditation (TM) is commonly taught in public schools across America. TM is also offered through churches, Christian retirement communities, and the local YMCA or YWCA.

Hypnosis, autosuggestion, or enchantment is an artificially induced state of relaxation in which suggestibility is heightened. In the act of occult meditation, the term, *mantra*, applies to a special word or phrase repeated over and over again in hopes of inducing the coveted trance. This trend reflects nothing new, for witch doctors, spirit mediums, shamans, Hindus, Buddhists, and yogis have used hypnosis for thousands of years. Again, the idea is to achieve an altered state of consciousness that hypnotism researcher Ernest Higard describes as "demonic possession."

Occultist Edgar Cayce used self-hypnosis to diagnose disease and prescribe treatment. Mind you, neither past-nor future-life hypnotic therapy is a science. Yet, increasingly, even nominal Christian medical doctors, dentists, psychiatrists, and psychologists endorse and/or use hypnosis to battle smoking and eating disorders, manage phobias and pain, and improve one's grades in school or one's sex life.

Consulters with Spirits (Mediums Possessed with a Spirit Guide)

The Bible warns that God will cut off the soul defiled by mediums and spiritualists. In fact, Old Testament law enforced the death penalty on those who consulted with mediums. This verdict was fulfilled literally in the case of King Saul whose great failure was disobedience to God's Word for having summoned the witch of Endor (Lev. 19:31; 20:6; 1 Sam. 28:7–25).

Such practices are not limited to Bible times. Astonishingly, former UN Assistant Secretary-General Robert Muller credits his UNESCO prize-winning World Core Curriculum to the Tibetan, spirit guide to occultist Alice Bailey. Pioneering scientist and inventor Thomas Edison is known to have experimented with spirit communication, and Jungian psychologist Dr. Hal Zina Bennett claimed he never met a person who, within thirty minutes of coaching, could not contact an inner guide.

Superstar John Edward is America's most famous medium. Hundreds of thousands of households tune into his nightly television show. Syndicated nationwide the summer of 2001, *Crossing Over* features ministry to loved ones left behind. Remarkably, half of all Americans believe in the possibility of communicating with the dead. Fully one-third claim to have done so.

Psychics/Clairvoyants (Wizards)

Believers must not seek after wizards, nor be defiled by them. Nevertheless, from experiments in clairvoyance at Duke University, to the *ouiji* board craze of the 1960s, modern man never ceases to demonstrate fascination with psychic powers (Lev. 19:31).

Upon death of his brother Henry, novelist and satirist Mark Twain embraced the paranormal. Deemed psychic, Twain predicted his own death. The late Princess Diana likewise dabbled in physic phenomenon. By the same token, First Lady Nancy Reagan consulted for seven years with psychic Jan Quigley. Even physicist Dr. Albert Einstein believed that psychic abilities deserve sincere consideration. During World War II, he worked for the U.S. Navy Ordnance Bureau. In recent years, psychic espionage and investigation have been broadly implemented globally. In fact, the psychic industry easily draws two billion dollars a year.

So old guard is its use that, in some circles, the term, "psychic," has come to mean no more than keen perception. The more mystically minded seek to emit energy for psychic healing by donning crystals. Trendy stores worldwide market these so-called life beings. Enthusiasts engage dubious psychic services extended to primetime television viewers. Still others endeavor to balance energy forces in the universe by employing the psychic healing practice of aroma therapy. Employed as a sort of cerebral biofeedback application, therapeutic touch originated with New Age mystic, Delores Krieger. Bad forces are presumably eliminated by the flick of the wrist, once again to balance energy forces.

Medium who Contacts the Dead (Necromancer)

Necromancy, or channeling, is a form of witchcraft and part of the black or diabolical arts practiced today by New Age occultists. Etymologically, the term signifies conversing with the dead for purposes of consultation or divination. Mosaic Law sternly forbids its practice (Deut. 18:10–11).

Translation of the Hebrew word for the witch of Endor is a woman that has a familiar spirit—that is, a necromancer. When Saul sought out this medium to determine the outcome of a battle with Philistines, he bit off more than he could chew. The same applies today (1 Sam. 28:7–8).

Spiritualism is worshipping or communicating with supposed spirits of the dead (actually demons posing as their spirits). It became an organized religion in 1848 and, in fact, is practiced by scores of millions worldwide—royalty included. It is reported that Mary Todd Lincoln held séances in the White House, as did the fourteenth President of the U.S., Franklin Pierce. Pierce engaged in private séances with spiritualists out of Rochester, New York—namely, the Fox sisters, who sparked widespread public interest in spiritualism as a modern religious movement.

Following the death of his mother, escapologist and conjurer Harry Houdini took interest in the paranormal. Although he campaigned against fraudulent mind readers and mediums, he, too, conducted séances.

Not long ago, *The Sixth Sense* starring Bruce Willis was a box office success. Its adorable and incredibly talented young star kept a closely held secret. That is, he saw and engaged "dead people." While the plot's discovery process was chilling, its outcome proved heart warming when the boy's mom received precious assurances following alleged visits from the grave of her own deceased mother. Broad validation for necromancy accompanied this riveting film.

Conclusion

Whether by means of secret societies, relaxation practices, entertainment, or literature, the occult has inundated contemporary society. Not uncommonly, corporate executives procure decorators who implement principles of *feng shui*, Mandarin Chinese for "wind" and "water." The idea is that buildings and landscapes are conduits of energy, which can be channeled by the shape and arrangements of a building and its rooms. To wink at what God calls abomination is not to "come out" and "be separate," as Scripture commands. Instead, believers are to avoid touching "the unclean thing." Only then will the Body of Christ be fully armed and empowered for effective spiritual warfare against clever tactics of the enemy. Without exception, camaraderie with the enemy is spiritual *hamartia*. Signaling strong delusion, it induces apostasy. Better to disassociate from, and furthermore reprove, "unfruitful works of darkness" (2 Cor. 6:17; Eph. 5:11; 6:12; 1 John 3:8; 2 Thess. 2:11).

CHAPTER 16

HAMARTIA

POSTMODERNISM

All unrighteousness is sin *[hamartia]* . . . but he that is begotten of God keepeth himself, and that wicked one toucheth him not. . . . The whole world lieth in wickedness (1 John 5:17–19).

A reaction against modernism, postmodernism originated with the Enlightenment, when many intellectuals announced autonomy from God. This clean break demanded that "truth" be found in human reason alone. To make sense of reality, postmodernists believe in no "grand metanarrative"—that is, no big story. For this reason, truth is perceived as nothing more than a social or personal construction. It is more often than not self-serving. Without God and His Plan, reality dissolves into paltry bits and pieces (Isa. 14:12–20; Ezek. 28:11–19).

Postmodern Deconstructionism (Poststructuralism)

According to orthodox Rabbi Daniel Lapin, America no longer represents "one nation under God." Instead, she houses two distinct and incompatible moral visions. The first, America's founding vision, is decidedly Christian. Trinity law professor James Hirsen speaks of "the grand experiment we call America," based upon "a divinely inspired and uniquely political perspective"—that being, individual rights are endowed, not by government, but by the Creator Himself. Today's contrasting moral imperative embraces a new politically correct ethic divorced entirely from the God of the Bible.

Revisionist history aligns with today's alternate ethic. Failing to address the Reformation, revisionists completely ignore Western culture. Developed by the National Center for History in the Schools (1994), the Goals 2000 history standards, once announced, were condemned by the U.S. Senate. To neutralize opposition, the Council for Basic Education reviewed and subsequently tinkered with the standards. As a result of Gary Nash's efforts, more than thirty states adopted them, effectively robbing students of their national heritage.

Now, the Civil War is presented as simply addressing black oppression, and World War II shames America as the unseemly aggressor postmodernists perceive her to be. While George Washington is dismissed as more of a symbol than a hero, former Soviet dictator Gorbachev is credited for single-handedly ending the Cold War. In contrast, Ronald Reagan is scolded as a "cheerleader for selfishness."

Called anti-logic by Plato, deconstructionism is the argument-counter argument ploy of fifth-century sophists who applied spurious reasoning solely to win arguments, never to establish truth. Postmodernism, or high theory, is modern relativism applied to language. In a word, it is cerebral political correctness. In opposing traditional values, postmodernism breaks ground for humanism, diversity, genderism, Afrocentrism, and radical environmentalism.

The new Global Civic Ethic originated in Chicago with Hans Küng and his *Global Responsibility in Search of a New World Ethic*, as brought forth in the 1993 Parliament of the World's Religions. Küng's new ethic promotes illumined, group conscious eco-socialism. It specifically excludes national sovereignty and private property rights while, at the same time, seeming to give overriding priority to the world's poor.

This new ethic encompasses a worldview that ignores fundamental Judeo-Christian values upon which America is founded.

Instead, it endorses biocentrism as opposed to the Cartesian Theory. According to the latter, God allocates earth's resources to be used and consumed by responsible earth stewards. In postmodern thought, to the contrary, consumerism is perceived as the primary threat to earth's resources. As such, it is the targeted enemy of sustainability and, therefore, must be reduced, even at the price of individual liberty.

Postmodern Humanism

Not to be confused with humanitarianism, humanism is a doctrine, attitude, or way of life centered on relativistic human values that exalt human worth based on self-determination through reason. In brief, it is "an exalted view of the solitary, knowing self" (Bruce L. Edwards, Associate Dean of Arts and Science at Bowling Green State University). Furthermore, humanism is a non-theistic religion, as determined by two U.S. Supreme Court cases—one being *Abington v. Schempp*. This 1963 ruling ended a practice that had been in place since the earliest days of the nation—that is, reading the Bible before the start of public school classes.

Humanism's primary documents include two manifestos, written in 1933 and 1973, respectively. Father of progressive education John Dewey signed the earlier manifesto; father of operant conditioning B.F. Skinner signed the latter. Some 7.3 million secular humanists in America find their niche in one of several brands—scientific/rationalistic, mystical/religious (Unitarianism), secular/enlightened, democratic/Marxist. Attracting leading officials of the Trilateral Commission, Rockefeller Foundation, and the White House, the Aspen Institute for Humanistic Studies is a private, non-profit organization in Colorado. Attendees frequent advanced seminars in global ideology. Most materials developed at the institute find their way into public school textbooks. As a result, over forty million children use textbooks whose multi-billion-dollar industry openly promulgates the global agenda, inclusive of humanism.

Humanist goals combine a science-based, one-world religion; global economics featuring redistribution of the world's wealth; a declaration of global interdependence; and a new species. Toward these ends, secular humanists advocate abortion, alternative lifestyles, prisoners' rights, socialism, and world government.

Humanism's Science-based Religion

Christian apologist C.S. Lewis called postmodern hyper-realism "scientism." Scientism is a breed of naturalism, holding that chance and natural law govern everything. According to the naturalist, all of life is explicable only by means of scientific data; therefore, religious verities are illusionary. Even if God really does exist, He is powerless to do anything. In his works, Lewis foretold the Enlightenment's subsequent dissolution into sundry relativisms and constructionisms that defraud humanity out of its humanness, specifically to reflect the image of God. Scientism exchanges sanctification for what Lewis calls "egoistic castle-building" and "incessant autobiography." Indeed, in these last days, postmodern "men shall be lovers of their own selves" (Gen. 1:1–2:25; 2 Tim. 3:1–2).

Riding with the flow, many misled Christians choose encouragement over discipleship, commendation over reproof. Guilt-free pseudo-Christianity is all grace—no duty; all love—no justice; all heaven—no hell. This brand of defunct Christianity may feel good, but it is bereft of the cross, sole gauge for true discipleship (Luke 14:26–27).

The science-based religion of postmodernists invalidates what are deemed outdated notions of right or wrong. One's feelings take priority over morality, certainly as to its traditional meaning. So clarified have postmodern values become that a new global network, *alibi.com*, is gaining popularity. The site's Scottish originator designed it when he needed an excuse for watching a soccer game at the local pub instead of celebrating his mother-in-law's birthday. In hopes of bypassing personal accountability, site visitors obtain useful alibis.

Plainly, the Devil's plan for the world is moral relativism leading to ungodliness, demonstrated as follows (Judges 17:6 with 2 Tim. 3:1–5):

- Misplaced love of self, money, and pleasures—unloving and lacking natural affection.

- Misplaced self-image—being irreconcilable, boastful, arrogant, conceited, lacking in gratitude.
- Misplaced loyalties—being disobedient to parents, treacherous, malicious in gossip, and apt to revile.
- Misplaced godliness—having a form of godliness, but denying its power, and thereby lacking self-control.

Two hundred years of Darwinism, materialistic naturalism, and reductionist psychology have led to the faulty conclusion that humans are no more or less than animals. In fact, animal law has become the next legal frontier. Says Gene Edward Veith, "With the support of some of our most prestigious law schools, the Great Ape Legal Project is laying legal groundwork to classify apes as a type of 'person,' rather than as a type of property" (*World* Magazine, 27 May 2000). As such, the law now safeguards the life and liberty of apes at the same time it legitimizes dismembering and killing unborn human children, wrongly tagged "non-persons."

HUMANISM'S GLOBAL ECONOMICS

In 1995, Congress issued a *Declaration of Interdependence* permitting the U.S. economy to be regulated by international authorization. In today's corporate dictatorship-in-the-making, government allows tremendous concentration of money and power. In time, as the Bible predicts, an ultimate central end-time authority will control its citizens' ability to buy and sell.

The "mark of the Beast" is Antichrist's stamp or brand indicating ownership or subservience. To acquire this mark signifies volitional pledge of allegiance to the New World Order, coupled with willful worship of Antichrist. Serving as a de facto national identification card, or smart card, the mark in time will authorize its bearer to buy or sell (Rev. 6:11; 7:14; 13:16–17; 18:13).

On the *Today Show* in May of 2002, Dr. Wilkin implanted silicon identification chips in upper right shoulders of each member of a family in Boca Raton, Florida. The so-called verichip from Applied Digital Solutions is an advanced verification system that, when scanned, displays the bearer's FDA-compliant database. Although we have yet to experience the "mark of the Beast," this implanted chip is undoubtedly a precursor.

Humanism's goal of global economics featuring redistribution of wealth bears little resemblance to the cheerful (literally, "hilarious") giving put forth in Scripture. Bible prophecy identifies a portion of the end-time church as being increased with the goods of this global economy. Contemporary Laodiceans consider themselves to be rich and in need of nothing, but erroneously so (2 Cor. 9:7; Rev. 3:17).

Humanism's *Homonoeticus*

A decade ago, the *Williamsburg Charter Survey on Religion and Public Life* found that one-third of surveyed academics finger evangelicals as "threats to democracy." Indeed, America's Education and Justice Departments argue that Christianity is a major source of bigotry and hate crime. Many liberal Protestant churches are the most "Christophobic" of all.

What is needed, humanists believe, is a modern and superior species fitted for higher level of existence on planet earth. When humanity takes a "quantum leap" to its higher destiny, it presumably will receive mystical powers; and the New World Order will fully emerge. A significant segment of humanity will, in fact, take this leap, thereby creating a new species, called *homonoeticus*. However, a great number [probably referring to Christians] will not yet be ready to participate. Mystical humanists believe that, suddenly, these will be removed to a nonphysical dimension, where their *karma* can catch up before they are allowed back to the physical plane. This scenario no doubt will be offered to explain the Rapture (Phil. 3:11, 14; Rev. 20:5–6; Titus 2:13; 1 Thess. 4:15; Rev. 3:10; Song of Sol. 2:8–14; Matt. 24:39).

Postmodern Diversity

Diversity Celebrated

Alluding to Antichrist's kingdom in the end times, Daniel described the fourth beast of his well-known vision as "diverse" (Dan. 7:7, KJV, Rotherham). Its nature is distinguished by the pride, syncretism, and godless unity expressed well in 1995 by a lesbian minister from the United Church of Christ.

When she addressed the meeting for the first Gay/Straight Youth Alliance Pride Rally and March in Boston, Nancy Stillman announced:

> I am so proud . . . of all of us for being out . . . [and] for standing together to say "Yes" to love and "No" to hate. "Yes" to the glory of diversity of creation and "No" to stereotypes, labels, and narrow mindedness. . . . We gather in the name of many divinities and philosophies. . . . In whatever way that you believe in this moment, I invite you to join your hearts and your minds as we pray together.

With these words, Stillman illustrated multiculturalism (or diversity). Multiculturalism is a postmodern notion with an explicitly liberal political agenda. It elevates to the status of constitutional amendment the right for a select few not to be offended while they themselves are free to berate others as "hate-mongers," "breeders," and "homophobes." To make room for the burgeoning global community, multiculturalism virtually redefines America and biblical Christianity out of existence "in the name of many divinities and philosophies" (See 2 Tim. 3:1–7).

Although today's diversity is touted as tolerance, its tolerance at best is selective, for it blatantly excludes fundamental Christians. Stillman's call was to join hearts and minds of believers of any faith—except, of course, the faith that heeds "the straight gate" and "narrow way" of Matthew 7:14. When it comes to Bible belief, *tolerant* postmodernists furl their brows, point their fingers, and shake their heads in disgust.

The recent Supreme Court verdict banning prayer before high school football games intimates that the motto, "In God We Trust," lacks relevance in today's pluralistic society. Indeed, a federal court recently ruled that the state of Ohio must remove from all license plates the phrase, "With God, all things are possible." Controversy in Colorado promised to turn this motto into church-state fodder. Dissenter Gully Stanford uplifted diversity as reason enough to question its proclamation.

Given today's legal climate, it becomes increasingly clear that biblical Christianity is excluded from the world's celebrated diversity. Daily, public school educators deny American youth auditory access to student-led voluntary prayer and visual access to the Ten Commandments. Nevertheless, under misguided belief that even minors have a constitutional right to view obscene material, library boards across America refuse to block Internet pornography. Throughout the entire Clinton-Gore administration, not a single Internet-based obscenity case was brought.

Diversity, Global Goal

There is a worldwide system of checks and balances based on nation-states. However, from Arnold Toynbee (1931), to H.G. Wells (1939), to Assistant Secretary of State William Benton (1945–1947) to the Democratic Socialists of America (1991), the cry goes forth to relinquish America's rugged independence in exchange for multicultural interdependence.

One of the world's largest bureaucracies, the United Nations is an association of nation-states joining more than 126 diverse organizations and agencies worldwide. Serving as a giant international economic Supreme Court in its non-democratic dispute resolution function, the World Trade Organization (WTO) is but one of many UN attempts at undermining American sovereignty. A major player in the drive for global governance, the WTO is not about free trade, but rather an agenda for central control of world markets. Says Director of the Polaris Institute Tony Clarke, the WTO is the closest thing we have to world government on this planet. In the name of diversity, Americans have yielded significant control over the domestic economy to this international body.

Postmodern Genderism

Many hostile feminists unfairly attack traditional Christianity for its supposed put down of women. To the contrary, the virtuous woman of Proverbs 31 is literally "a woman of ability." Verse 10 identifies her as "a force" or "a power." Even so, the feminist movement campaigns for social, political, and economic equality for such oppressed women. Afoot for decades, genderism is one of many politically correct "*-isms*" that champions population control (e.g., managed death options as abortion, childless lesbianism, eugenics).

In 1981, *The Nation* published an article by feminist activist Ellen Willis, who pinpointed the objective of every feminist reform from legal abortion on demand to child-care programs—that objective being "to undermine traditional family values." Another prominent feminist and supposed intellectual depicts all heterosexual sex as "rape." The truth is that the godly marriage bed is "undefiled" (Heb. 13:4).

Author of *Psychology as Religion: The Cult of Self-Worship,* Dr. Paul Vitz illustrates today's "selfism," the only ethical tenet for which is self-gratification. To selfists, personal autonomy becomes life's greatest good—surpassing even love of God, spouse, and children. Unfortunately, the radical feminist movement and selfism have not escaped the church. On 11 September 1995, Oxford University Press published *The New Testament and Psalms: An Inclusive Version.* In it, the Lord's prayer commences with "Our Father-Mother in heaven . . ." No reference is made to "God, the Father," and the "Son of Man" is now "the human one." Contrary to biblical text, this revised New Testament has children "heeding" (not obeying) parents and wives committed (not submitted) to husbands. Incredibly, references to Christ's being at the right hand of God have been omitted. Why? So as not to offend left-handed people!

Postmodern Afrocentrism

Afrocentrism is the politically correct theme that applauds indiscriminately all that comes out of Africa, while at the same time condemning Euro-American culture. The idea is to supplant Judeo-Christian thought by establishing instead an all-embracing Global Civic Ethic at odds with Bible truth.

Because it is not right to do evil that somehow good may come, reverse discrimination cannot possibly be a godly solution for the offense of bigotry. Nevertheless, many inadvertently buy into the falsehood that it is the flesh color and not its nature that yields bondage. Color lines are being drawn all the more today, but this time by some blacks (Ps. 34:14; Acts 10:28; Gal. 5: 19–21).

Postmodern Radical Environmentalism

Not to be confused with good stewardship of the earth, radical environmentalism is foremost among united causes under the banner of political correctness. Its political agenda surpasses any professed campaign to safeguard our grandchildren. Radical environmentalists put forward sustainable urban clusters in an ordered agrarian society with intent to ease totalitarian control of human activities, reproduction, and wealth. In so doing, the movement provides the primary argument for world government. Toward this end, radical environmentalism demands action, even in the face of scientific uncertainty. For example, the scientific community has reached no consensus to warrant need for nearly three hundred environmental treaties already administered by the United Nations.

Because of the *Endangered Species Act*, the *UN Biodiversity Treaty*, and the *President's Commission on Sustainable Development*, public officials are hindered from taking action without first considering the well-being of spotted owls, kangaroo rats, or the Delhi Sands flower-loving fly. A multi-billion dollar per year industry, radical environmentalism is driven by great foundations whose money buys unfair and unlawful access to bureaucrats who make rules everybody should have a voice in, but only a few have influence over.

Abolition of Private Property

Postmodern thought insists that Western culture is the root of all evil; moreover, private property is impossible. Notwithstanding, America's greatness has come from the idea that individuals have the right to own and control their own property. Depicting the radical environmentalist's position, Point One of the *Communist Manifesto* altogether abolishes private property. Helen Chenoweth-Hage (R-Idaho) warns of escalating takeover of America's land base. Already, the federal government owns forty percent of the entire landmass of the nation; states likewise own a sizable chunk. Furthermore, simply by changing legal definitions, millions of acres in the Western United States have been taken from multiple use and public access.

In the biblical account of Lucifer's fall from grace, the outcome of his error includes the godless enterprise of weakening nations by destroying the cities thereof and by making the world "as a wilderness." Along these lines, the *UN Biodiversity Treaty* supports the Wildlands Project, calling for half of U.S. land to become wilderness, disallowing human activity (Isa. 14:16–18).

UN treaties have placed some 68 percent of America's national parks, preserves, and monuments under UN regulation. When it comes to land use under UN control, there is no distinction between federal and privately owned land. Contained in *Agenda 21*, the *Desertification Treaty* claims jurisdiction over fully 70 percent of the earth's land area. Although no enforcement mechanism is in place, the UN works to prevent any land use that lends to desertification—e.g., converting forests to pasture, or pasture to row crops, or crop lands to sub-divisions. A convention adopted in Paris (1994), the *Desertification Treaty* is an integral part of the global environmental agenda. In the last days of the 106th Congress, the treaty slipped through without adequate review. Its ill-advised ratification mocks the advice and consent responsibility that the *Constitution* places squarely upon the Senate.

OVERRIDING PRIORITY FOR THE WORLD'S POOR

In a 1974 report entitled, the *New International Economic Order*, the UN General Assembly outlined a plan to redistribute the world's wealth. The global commons, including outer space, the atmosphere, non-territorial seas, and environmental systems that support life—all under United Nations trusteeship—are considered the common property of the world community. This is true, too, of raw materials (including people).

Globalization is transferring the world's wealth under the UN principle of sustainable development (Green code word for shutting down progress). While this ecological ideal sounds honorable, it actually expands poverty by taking away wealth and the incentive to produce it. A better idea is to share with the world the Gospel ("good news") of Jesus Christ coupled with America's unsurpassed freedom technology (2 Cor. 9:7).

Conclusion

In the 1820s, gifted orator Daniel Webster warned, "If the power of the Gospel is not felt throughout the length and breadth of the land, anarchy and misrule, degradation and misery, corruption and darkness will reign without mitigation or end." Bible wisdom warns that the whole world lies in a bed of wickedness. In lamenting loss of America's founding values, Jewish medical educator David C. Stolinsky rightly reasons that hesitancy to go out after dark is not for fear of evangelicals forcing us to read the Bible. Rather, it is in fear of gangs taught that nothing is superior to their own needs, wants, or feelings (1 John 5:17–19).

Embracing no big story and no God of Creation, postmodernists clarify values based on the imperial Self. The worldview, at best, offers relativism and situation ethics. In so doing, it undermines the biblical principle that "*all* unrighteousness is sin *(hamartia)*," as in Judges 17:6 and 1 John 5:17. Simply put, postmodern thought may sit well with the world community, but it still misses the mark. For this reason, consecrated Christians should steer clear of its multi-faceted seduction (Jer. 10:2).

CHAPTER 17

Hamartia
Progressivism

Some men's sins *[hamartia]* are openly evident, leading on into judgment; with some, however, they even follow after (1 Tim. 5:24, Rotherham).

Progressivism is best known as a turn-of-the-century trend in education, fathered by socialist revolutionary John Dewey, who called for carefully structured attitude adjustment and behavioral modification—all in the interest of collectivism.

Historically, however, progressivism is distinguished by three time periods, the first of which is its biblical-Calvinist period, dating from colonial times to the 1840s. The next Unitarian/Hegelian period started in the 1840s and lasted until World War I. Dating from World War I, the final period continues even today. Contemporary educational trends include anti-authoritarianism; early-, open-, and bilingual-models; full educational services in the least restrictive environment; and Robin Hood plans to shift money from property-rich districts to poor ones.

Progressive Education

An avowed atheist, John Dewey was author-signer of the *Humanist Manifesto I* and served as first president of the American Humanist Society. A Marxist-Fabian socialist, he was professor of philosophy at the distinguished Teachers' College at Columbia University in New York. To Dewey, the political function of schools is "to construct communist society" (1928). Toward this end, his experimental schools—e.g., the Organic School in Fairhope, Alabama—did away with tests, grades, rewards, punishments, and promotions.

Produced by Columbia University's Teachers College, the first issue of *The Social Frontier* urged restructuring of American society and heralded the burgeoning age of collectivism. "Educational workers" (no longer "teachers") were commissioned to join into "a mighty instrument of group consensus, harmonious expression, and collective action."

Organized in 1919, the Progressive Education Association denounced rote learning, recitation, and conventional textbooks while promoting affective and holistic curricula, cultural relativism, and cooperative consciousness. "Pluralism" and "realism" surfaced as public education's latest buzzwords.

Dewey's network continues to exercise incredible power throughout the education establishment. Best known as father of progressive education, Dewey maintained that the only reality is experience. He made inquiry the essence of logic. Through the influence of Dewey and his disciples (Charles Judd, Harold Ruggs, George Counts, and Scott Nearing), traditional education with its God-fearing, Bible-based instruction toppled. When Dewey died in 1952, the Protestant character of the early public schools withered.

Dewey's brand of Hegelianism elevated the State as supreme. The child became no more than a pawn to be trained. A German philosopher, Hegel believed that "man is best when serving the State." Hegelian dialectics is a behavior modification technique of group consensus under peer pressure. It undermines the notion of fixed rights or wrongs. In the dialectic process, the end justifies means.

Outcome-Based Education (OBE)

Consensus, or conflict resolution, is a Soviet term for "collective opinion." First developed in the late 1950s, the Delphi technique represents a psychological process in which a predetermined outcome is decided. All discussions and decisions are made to lead the group to that consensus. This brand of group accord under peer pressure is promoted through today's Outcome-Based Education model. OBE is a component of former President Bush's America 2000 and Clinton's Goals 2000. In brief, OBE changes the way children are trained, evaluated, and graduated. It minimizes academics while maximizing labor skills to facilitate human resource development for the universal good of the global community.

Enacted by Congress in 1994, the *Goals 2000: Educate America Act* claims to have set "high standards," but used heavy-handed phrases some forty-five times as to what the "states will do." Federal control of local schools makes OBE a national curriculum. For some three decades, the Department of Education has supported OBE although its own research suggests that most well known OBE/Mastery Learning schools do not warrant emulation. Sadly, American students have fallen behind—placing nineteenth out of twenty-one in math, sixteenth in science, and dead last in physics. Perhaps not surprisingly, 20 percent of all public school educators send their own children to private schools.

For well over a decade, the *National Assessment of Educational Progress* has been administered, usually in March, to selected students in public education. Called the "Nation's Report Card," the *National Assessment of Educational Progress* (NAEP) surveys knowledge and skills, yes—but also attitudes. Targeted students fill out "background questions" that have nothing whatsoever to do with the three R's, but everything to do with family affluence, activities, and attitudes. Even in testing, the certain shift from academics to the affective domain is evident.

Human Resources Development and Management are accomplished by means of lifelong learning, interdisciplinary approaches, systems thinking, partnerships, multicultural perspectives, and empowerment principles.

Lifelong Learning

At most, an American child spends less than 10 percent of his time in school. To accomplish today's educational goals, lifelong learning is decreed necessary. Created in 1946 by its first secretary-general, Sir Julian Huxley, the United Nations Educational, Scientific, and Cultural Organization (UNESCO) is tantamount to a global version of our National Education Association (NEA). In the 1970s, UNESCO outlined cradle-to-grave lifelong learning, best described as a psychosocial process of re-learning. Its intent is to supplant traditional beliefs, values, attitudes, and individual thinking with new global ideology and collective thinking, called "group think." All the while little Johnny cannot read, schools focus on self-esteem, ethnic pride, alternative lifestyles, global citizenship, visualizing death, diversity, drugs, sexually transmitted diseases, and safe sex.

Through efforts of the Heritage Foundation, the Reagan administration withdrew membership; however, UNESCO's impact is no less felt today. Indeed, UNESCO has innovated biosphere reserves, the right kind of tolerance, cosmic education for global citizenship, not to mention lifelong learning. Through Goals 2000, OBE, one-stop social clinics, school-to-work, and lifelong learning programs, educrats mold America's children, called "human resources," to their liking.

Interdisciplinary Approaches

Integration of the disciplines is best suited to thematic teaching resulting in fewer courses presented. While de-emphasizing facts and knowledge—that is, content—interdisciplinary approaches feature process instead. They emphasize higher-order thinking accomplished through cooperative learning. No longer are Carnegie Units needed to graduate; demonstrated outcomes do the trick. Futurist-educator Benjamin Bloom is applauded for his *Taxonomy of Educational Objectives* (1956), forming the basis for OBE. Also used in communist China, Bloom's taxonomy presents moral relativism as the ultimate cognitive goal.

SYSTEMS THINKING

Forbes magazine recognizes the National Education Association (NEA) as America's "largest and richest brass-knuckled labor union." The NEA saturates most of the nation with its fifty-two state-level and thirteen thousand local-level affiliates—all of which champion systems thinking, coupled with political activism. New-fashioned, revolutionary, and politically correct systems thinking defines the burgeoning New Earth Ethic. This global civic endorses biocentrism (planet before people)—excluding national sovereignty and private property rights, all the while appearing to give overwhelming priority to the world's poor. Former U.S. Education Secretary William Bennett identifies the nation's chief education lobby as "the absolute heart and center of the Democratic Party." He warns further that OBE eliminates standardized tests, does away with traditional subject-based curriculum, and advances a social agenda that is both radical and indulgent.

GLOBAL PARTNERSHIPS: "IT TAKES A VILLAGE"

Vague by design, the *Elimination of All Forms of Discrimination against Women* treaty supersedes our *Constitution* in its effort to redefine the family and usurp parental authority. The UN Fourth World Conference on Women (1995) and Beijing +5 worked to extend reproductive health to adolescents (ten to nineteen years of age) and to youth (nineteen to twenty-five). "Reproductive health" is a deceptive euphemism for legalized abortion on demand.

In accordance with the 1990 *Convention on the Rights of the Child*, "competent authorities" may interfere in families when a child desires to exercise his rights. This yet-to-be-ratified convention endorses a national system of day care and sets children's rights in opposition to those of their parents. If ratified, it will grant children the "right" to read, listen to, see, or write about content of their own choosing. Furthermore, the convention takes away a parent's option to use corporal punishment in biblically appropriate ways. Without parental intrusion, children may choose their own religious bent and engage in sexual activities of choice. They may attend their preferred school and, as needed, sue parents in a court of law.

Partnerships are put forth in Goals 2000 and UN global plans for action. The idea is to create alliances between the United Nations and local communities without knowledge or approval of state or federal legislatures. The brainchild of Prevent Child Abuse America, Healthy Families America allows government monitors to enter homes of first-time parents. It promotes up to fifty in-home visits annually per family until a child reaches the age of five.

Multicultural Perspectives: Gay Rights/Revisionist History

Simply put, the word "diversity" means having a certain number of ethnic minorities, women, handicapped, and homosexuals represented in the workplace, school, or any group for that matter. In contrast, God is no respecter of persons. Multiculturalism actually emphasizes differences based on ethnicity, race, gender, disability, and sexual orientation. In the OBE model, individual liberty and limited government take back seat to tenets of multiculturalism (Acts 10:34).

While only 2.8 percent of men and 1.4 percent of women practice homosexuality, pro-gay Project 10-type counseling programs are offered junior and senior high school students. "Ten" stands for falsification that fully 10 percent of teens are gay. Astonishingly, the *Gay Manifesto* insists on adult sex with children (Demand #55, 1993, March on Washington).

After the 1994 National History Standards were released by UCLA's National Center for History in the Schools, Lynne V. Cheney branded them a revisionist assault on historical fact. You see, revisionist history deconstructs any sense of nationalism or patriotism. Being American is not part of the agenda, for multiculturalism virtually defines America out of existence. Even more alarmingly, progressives denigrate Western culture, distinguished by Judeo-Christian morality and market capitalism.

By dividing American society and culture against itself, diversity contributes to dissolution of national definition and sovereignty. Those who oppose diversity are berated as racist, sexist, homophobic, and oppressive in their lame attempt at preserving what adherents call impoverished, slave-driving colonialism and white, heterosexual male preeminence.

In celebrating diversity, Christian students often are required to participate in activities that by nature violate their call to holiness and separatism. That "heathen have something to offer" opposes God's warning to "learn not the way of the heathen" or to "inquire after their gods" (John 15:19; Eph. 5:11; Jer. 10:2; Deut. 12:30).

EMPOWERMENT

The most fundamental skill that truly empowers—that is, literacy—has been in decline in this country for at least fifty years. Too many graduates lack ability to read diplomas they receive at the end of their high school careers. In the name of empowerment, students in reality are "deliberately dumbed down" (Phyllis Schlafly, Eagle Forum). According to Martin Gross, author of *The Conspiracy of Ignorance,* the bottom third of college students end up teachers in our public schools.

Incredibly, a high school in Prince George's County, Maryland, is now having police officers teach students how to behave safely when being arrested. So much for academia! It comes as no surprise to learn that fully 99 percent of our college seniors recognize cartoon characters Beavis and Butthead, but less than a quarter of them can identify James Madison as Father of our *Constitution* (William J. Bennett, former U.S. Secretary of Education).

The seeds for today's massive restructuring away from academics to behavior modification began in 1965 with the *Elementary and Secondary Education Act.* The ESEA made funds available through Title 1 to attack problems of the educationally disadvantaged, including handicapped children. With $118 billion of federal tax dollars spent through Title I programs of the ESEA, presently over one-third of public school students attend remedial classes. Additionally, the ESEA opened school doors to a flood of psychiatrists, psychologists, social workers, and the like to deal with any languishing self-esteem resulting from colossal failure of the system.

All the while Johnny still cannot read, Congress allocates tens of millions of dollars in public education for contraceptive-based sex education reflecting Kinseyan ideology and practice. Furthermore, systematic legal drugging of school-aged children serves education restructuring by turning millions into patients in apparent need of a village of professionals. From 1990 until 1997, there were reportedly 160 deaths and 569 hospitalizations (some life threatening) associated with Ritalin, which is known to cause the brain to shrink. Although no peer-reviewed scientific paper officially documents their existence, Attention Deficit Disorder (ADD) or Attention Deficit and Hyperactivity Disorder (ADHD) result in some 2.5 million school-aged children taking Ritalin.

Permissive Education

U.S. political leader Horace Mann of Massachusetts defined the Hegelian Unitarian period in America's education history. This father of permissive education believed in the perfectible nature of man. In 1850, Mann bamboozled America with false assurance that, in a century, secular education would eradicate crime and poverty. Years later, Dr. John Goodland of the National Education Association wrote a report entitled "Schooling for the Future" in which he similarly applauded behavioral change (re-socialization), not academic pursuit, as education's primary goal.

If 1996 is any indication of the success of secularization and re-socialization, America's public education system is in deep distress. It was then that a spree of uninterrupted shootings began, wiping out scores of students and teachers in Moses Lake, Washington; Bethel, Alaska; Pearl, Mississippi; West Paducah, Kentucky; Jonesboro, Arkansas; Edinboro, Pennsylvania; Springfield, Oregon; and Littleton, Colorado. It seems that, in following after the example of Eli, and not Elisha, Horace Mann missed the mark, with grave consequences following.

Consider this. In many cases, today's student may not be able to read, but he can position a condom on a banana. He cannot spell, but he expresses himself well in politically correct terms. He may not compute with skill, but he can and will recycle. He may never have read the classics, but he lacks no self-esteem. He hasn't a clue where Djibouti is, but he feels a certain sense of cosmic harmony with her citizens. He may be devoid of a personal relationship with the Savior, but does not hesitate to hug a tree.

ELI'S INDULGENCE; ELISHA'S DISCIPLINE

A judge and high priest, Eli and his sons lived at Shiloh in a dwelling adjoining the Tabernacle. Eli possessed spiritual perception, and yet was weak, indecisive, and unfaithful to stewardship; moreover, as a parent, he was indulgent. For this reason, Eli was reckoned as accomplice with his sons in their sins against God. As such, he was included in God's message of judgment (1 Sam. 1–4; 14:3; 1 Kings 2:27).

Having received a double portion of Elijah's spirit, Elisha was extraordinary in terms of his character and power ministry. Says Commentator Dr. J. Sidlow Baxter, Elisha was a man "normally shorn and clad," having "a gentle and sociable presence." Furthermore, he demonstrated filial affection and humility. Once, God used Elisha to bring a child back to life. However, when rebellious little children mocked him as he went up to Bethel, Elisha pronounced sobering judgment on them in the Name of his Lord (1 Kings 19:20; 2 Kings 2:23–24; 3:2; 4:8–37).

Dr. Spock's Folly

The late Dr. Benjamin Spock was a pediatrician, U.S. political activist, and writer. He, too, failed to take his cues from Bible models. In *Common Sense Book of Baby and Childcare* (1946), Spock urged less rigidity in bringing up children than had been advised previously. He claimed not to have rejected all parental discipline; but under his advisement, permissiveness ran its course.

ESSENTIALISM REVISITED

An educational theorist of the 1930s, Arthur Bestor gave birth to essentialism, which rightly heralds the academic standards, discipline, and personal accountability of traditional education. Bestor's theory was reborn in the back-to-basics trend of the 1970s. As a result, some two million home-schooled children are presently receiving an extraordinary traditional education.

Notwithstanding, Carnegie, Rockefeller, and Ford revolutionaries continually ravage American education by financing forced bussing, teacher unionization, textbook subversion, and school consolidation. Academically, educrats supplant true science with evolution, phonics with defunct whole-word approaches. Sex and global education (more accurately, indoctrination) flush "misguided" ideals of patriotism and love of God/family. Moreover, the lion's share of massive sums spent on public education never reaches America's classrooms, but is gobbled up by administrative jackals. Education author Samuel Blumenfeld criticizes the National Education Association for gaining increasing power and money for the educational establishment "without the foggiest concern for children."

While New York public education is controlled by a bureaucracy of thousands of administrators, Catholic schools, in contrast, need only twenty-nine administrators in addition to school principals. The former spends about eight thousand dollars per student, graduating less than half of its eighteen students per class. The latter spends only three thousand, graduating an impressive 98 percent of its thirty-six students per class. Progressivism is illusion only. The numbers simply don't add up.

Polytechnical Education

The socialistic German plan of education, containing elements of the Marxist-Leninist Soviet system, serves as basic model for polytechnical education behind today's education restructuring. Marc Tucker's report, "A Human Resources Development Plan for the U.S." outlines education restructuring as including the following:

Federal government's controlling curriculum to include understanding and appreciating others in the world community, self-esteem, ethical judgment (albeit situational and self-serving), change adaptation, and proper environmental attitudes—all of which upstage reading, writing, and arithmetic (which occupy only about one-quarter of the school day).

Engaging in behavior modification programs to change attitudes, values, and beliefs of children who fast become workers, not thinkers; followers, not leaders; group members, not individuals.

Implementing cradle-to-grave control over personal development. Incredibly, America's admittedly godless education system has presumed to take charge of our children's character development.

Re-educating parents and interfering with parental rights by means of sundry groups instituted to militate against the primary social importance of traditional family.

Building massive data banks on each child in what Steve Forbes calls our "transparent society," making it easy for government and private companies to track and monitor details of one's business, personal and financial.

Controlling employment and career choices for students through the *School-to-Work Opportunities Act* signed into law by Clinton (1994) in attempt to make Hillary's *Human Resource Development Plan* with its federal job placement program the law of the land. Career education does not necessarily prepare the student for a chosen profession. Instead, it fits that student to the workforce needs of the global community. Based on a student's profile, perhaps established by means of theosophist Alice Bailey's "seven-ray multiple intelligence," the student is funneled into a job or career classification to which (s)he is presumed suited to best serve.

Using schools to implement socialized medicine and to expand the welfare system. Systematic legal drugging serves education restructuring by turning millions of students into patients.

"Who's the Responsible?"

While living in the Middle East, I witnessed a visibly rattled Iraqi in search of official assistance. To my bemusement, he repeatedly demanded, "Who's the responsible?" This same question is not so funny when posed within a family or classroom setting where the answer is not obvious. I speak as a trained, experienced educator when I say, "The buck correctly stops with parents."

It has been told that, during the Civil War, Abe Lincoln heard of a soldier having been given a religious tract censuring the "sin of dancing." Ironically, both of his legs had been shot off. Clearly, moralizing was not what was needed. The same holds true in parenting effectively. Not moralizing, but rather parental guidance and corrective intervention work best. Dr. John B. Watson's "perfect parenting" popularized the notion of scientific mothering void of coddling, hugging, or kissing. Not surprisingly, his theory of behaviorism proved dismally ineffective. If for this reason alone, federal scientific childcare is untenable. The government has no call or right to raise children or to provide for their care. This responsibility belongs to parents alone.

Even *USA Today* agrees that a dad's attention coupled with a close emotional bond pay off in less delinquent behavior and more education by the time children reach their early twenties (22 August 1996). According to God's Word, a good father takes time to correct and discipline his children: "My son, do not despise the Lord's discipline, or be weary of His reproof, for the Lord reproves whom He loves, as a father the son in whom he delights" (Prov. 3:11–12).

School Choice

Any school to which one sends his child should affirm and reinforce that parent's values. With this in mind, many parents choose to home-school or to provide private, religious schooling for their children. In hopes of leaving no child behind, twenty-first-century parents and politicians alike call for school choice.

Charter Schools

Thirty-four states now serve in excess of one-half million public school students in more than two thousand charter schools that provide public education through private enterprise. Charter schools boast likeminded learning style/theory among its staff and parents. Some are traditional—some progressive.

Chris Whittle of the Edison Project believes that initial signs are very promising. In his words, "earning will follow learning." Created by partnership between the private sector and government, these public schools have no elected boards. Significantly, they come with strings attached. Therefore, many believe charter schools to be the Trojan Horse to attract holdouts to education restructuring.

Vouchers

Vouchers are intended to allow children in certified failing public schools to attend private schools with taxpayer money. Critics believe that they blindfold admissions offices so that "morally-challenged" students could, in time, overwhelm private schools. Supported by the foundations, the Counsel on Foreign Relations, and the Aspen Institute, vouchers likewise come with strings. For subsidy, independence is surrendered to government.

TUITION TAX CREDITS

Many believe a safer approach to be tuition tax credits combined with private scholarship programs. Under such a system, parents and schools are not beholden to the federal government. Even better, the federal Department of Education is not involved. Former senior associate with the U.S. Department of Education, Dr. Dennis Cuddy calls the DOE "one of the major transmission belts of world socialism." Its grand social engineering plans fly in the face of the Tenth Amendment, which precludes federal involvement in education.

In a very real sense, big government transfer of local, parental authority and values to a powerful state controlled by a godless Department of Education severely restricts our moral and constitutional right as believers to speak, teach, and live by Bible values we hold dear (Deut. 6:7).

The goal of American public education has increasingly become a society in which people can more comfortably live with economic and political change. Be warned that the design teams for the United Nations Global Education Project are activists for New Age globalism. *The Summary Report of the National Education Association Bicentennial Program* reveals its goal "to change the course of American education for the twenty-first century by embracing the ideals of global community and the equality and interdependence of all peoples and nations." To supplant America's Christian roots with New Age principles is to exchange truth for fables (2 Tim. 4:3–4).

Bible Truth

The Bible warns of teachers who go astray by forsaking the straight path of moral absolutism. Among these are change agents of values-neutral education who fail to acknowledge God's Word as the plumb line for truth. Given no real guidance or correction, their students are induced to call evil, "good"—and good, "evil." Take, for example, Sid Simon's provocative lifeboat scenario. The question is posed, "Whom [of a specified group] do we eliminate for the good of the whole?" No allowance is made for solutions to save; rather, the student's "free" choice has imposed upon it firm parameters with unmistakable message that some have less value, thus less right to live than others (2 Pet. 2:1, 2, 25; Isa. 5:20).

Simply put, world citizens-in-the-making are being groomed, wrongly so, to eliminate the one true God in exchange for the universal god-force, and to elevate the supposed good of the New World Order over God's unalterable moral code. Society is none the better for it. William Bennett suggests that values-neutral schools can (and often do) produce morally indifferent students. In the 1820s, gifted orator Daniel Webster issued somber warning: "If truth be not diffused, error will be." Webster's chilling words affirm Bible truth that, in these last days, the ungodly will continue to wax worse and worse, deceiving and being deceived (2 Tim. 3:13). What better place to carry out this froward agenda than America's "progressive" public education?

CHAPTER 18

Hamartia

Racism

> But if you show partiality, you are committing sin *[hamartia]* and are convicted by the law as transgressors (James 2:9 NASB).

Race and Ethnicity Defined

In anthropology, "race" applies to the variety of modern humans, with common clusters of distinctive physical characteristics. Three primary varieties are Caucasoid, Mongoloid, and Negroid; however, migrations and interbreeding have caused a range of variations. Put simply, race speaks to one's bloodline.

On the other hand, ethnicity is from the Greek word *ethnos,* meaning "a people." Social scientists use the term to indicate a shared sense of identity, which may or may not include skin color or common descent. It is a social term—overlapping such concepts as race, nation, class, and religion—often based on a common culture or language.

By definition, racism exalts the superiority of one's own race, or ethnicity, while at the same time it demeans another. In sum, it is partiality and, therefore, the Bible calls it *hamartia,* or sin.

Racism at Work

Racism may exist in an unconscious attitude based on preconceived notions, or negative stereotypes, about different groups, as could result with some forms of racial profiling. Impulsive reactions to stereotypes can be tragic, prompting unsavory practices of name-calling, discrimination, and (in the most severe cases) infliction of physical harm. For example, in the aftermath of the Oklahoma City bombing (April 1995), and the attack on America (September 2001), Muslims across America were targeted—their mosques desecrated, car windows broken, and veiled women harassed. Recent economic turmoil in Indonesia prompted comparable eruptions of what Professor of History Donald Holsinger calls "cultural chauvinism"—this time Muslims against Christians.

As a young child living below the Mason-Dixon Line, I recall being whisked away lest unwittingly I should enter the women's restroom clearly labeled "Colored Women Only." The back of the bus was likewise reserved for those considered of lesser racial value than white counterparts. A few years later, in the early days of integration, our high school suspended what would have been my senior prom for fear that a black boy might ask a white girl for a dance.

Years later, while living along the Persian Gulf, I once again witnessed disdain of one race against another—i.e., Kuwaiti Arabs toward Indians and Pakistanis, whose designated role, albeit unspoken, was limited to keeping villas clean, driving limousines, and/or cooking meals. Even the highly educated and wealthy were treated as second-class citizens. Grievous as these examples are, they tell the sad story of racism, as experienced throughout the world, even in so-called enlightened contemporary times.

Racism in History

Racism is not new. Take Ruth, for example. A Moabitess, she descended from the grandson of Lot by incest with his elder daughter. Though her race was denounced by prophets of old, and disdained by contemporaries, Ruth bore distinction as progenitor of the Messiah. Once again we see that God is no respecter of persons

(Ruth 1:4; Gen. 19:30–38; Isa. 15:1–9; Jer. 9:26; Ezek. 25:8–11; Amos 2:1; Zeph. 2:8–11; Matt. 1:5; Acts 10:34).

While Samaritans represented a religious tradition, or sect, as opposed to bloodline, their stigma was no less felt, for many Jews in Christ's day used "Samaria" as a term of contempt. With regard to the New Covenant, all in Christ are one, yet it has been said that there is no more racial hour than that of the Sunday church service. Thankfully, circumstances are changing; but, in some areas, the problem persists to the shame of those who promulgate it.

At a National Association for the Advancement of Colored People (NAACP) convention in Baltimore, presidential candidate Governor George Bush acknowledged the existence of racism in America. He bemoaned the fact that "the party of Lincoln has not always carried the mantle of Lincoln." Racism characterizes a number of contemporary movements as neo-Nazism, extreme Islamic fundamentalism, ethnic cleansing, the new eugenics, hate-crimes legislation, and the political correctness movement (Col. 3:11; Gal. 3:28; John 8:48).

Neo-Nazism

Parties with Nazi or neo-Nazi ideologies still exist in Germany and many other countries for that matter. While touring Berlin in 1992, my husband and I were confined to our hotel room while scores of neo-Nazis flooded the streets vociferously demonstrating in favor of racism, nationalism, and supremacy of the state over individuals.

Modern humanists join neo-Nazis in search of a super-master race. "One world—one species" is their shared motto. While the neo-Nazi purposes to "accentuate the positive—eliminate the negative," the mystical humanist seeks an altogether new species resulting from an anticipated planetary quantum leap to "christhood." In contrast, the secular humanist hopes to control evolution and to improve hereditary qualities by means of genetic manipulation.

Islamic Fundamentalism/Ethnic Cleansing

It has been reported that more Christians were martyred in the twentieth-century than throughout the past nineteen combined. For their collective association (i.e., ethnicity), contemporary

Christians suffer as victims of persecution in over seventy countries under the heavy hand of communists, Hindu extremists, and radical Islamic fundamentalists.

Bethann Toupin of Amnesty International reports arrests of whole groups of Christians, subsequently tortured and beaten by Muslim zealots. Muslims converted to Christ, as Robert Hussein of Kuwait, fear death, especially during *Ramadan*, a time when Christians face intensified persecution for their supposed apostasy. While the Kuwaiti *Constitution* guarantees religious freedom, no lawyer would defend Hussein. Furthermore, Hussein's request to try his case in a Kuwaiti constitutional court was denied.

The government of Afghanistan broadens the tent pegs of its persecution to include women in general. Once the *Taliban* took power in 1996, women had to wear *burquas*. Many were beaten and even stoned publicly for failing to do so. It is alleged that one woman was beaten to death by an angry mob for accidentally exposing her arm. In such cases, right-wing fundamentalist Muslims, as these, deny their women a tolerable human existence. This blatant discrimination is based on Sura 4:34, a passage from the *Koran* giving men authority over women because "Allah has made the one superior to the other."

The son of a former vice president of Sudan expresses a black viewpoint regarding Arab racism: To the Arab, the African is born to be his slave. In Sudan, human rights abuses continue to be aggravated by a number of issues, racial enmity being one. As a result, Christians suffer widespread abuses, including massacres, rape, and torture committed by government security and armed forces. Since the 1980s, Arab tribal militias have kidnapped women and children, forcing them into household and farm labor. A thirteen-year-old rape victim testifies to having been called a "black donkey."

The New Eugenics

Racial superiority is a theme familiar to Cecil Rhodes, who believed the British to be a superior race. His global goal was to make the Anglo-Saxon race "one Empire." Today, the Rhodes Scholastic Fund is awarded to the well bred recommended for special training in internationalism. These promote the notion of a ruling elite in the world community. Nominees dominate the State Department and, from time to time, even grace the White House.

Following Rhodes, the Rockefeller Foundation, Carnegie Institution, and Carnegie Foundation championed his cause by supporting Hitler's effort to purify the human race. Those who orchestrated the Holocaust embraced eugenics (Greek, "well born"). Their elimination of Jews and Gypsies promised to purify the European gene pool. Nobel Prize winner Elie Wiesel calls theirs a "science of murder." Murderous participants held degrees in biology, general medicine, law, and, yes, even theology.

Today's "new eugenics" is birthed out of the *Roe v. Wade* legacy. Now a Christian, Norma McCorvey (Jane Roe) regrets her part in the court's landmark ruling, for it opened the floodgates to partial- and live-birth abortion, infanticide, selling baby parts in the name of science, and approval of the baby pesticide RU-486. In the words of the late French oceanographer Jacques-Yves Cousteau, "It's terrible to have to say this. World population must be stabilized, and to do that we must eliminate 350,000 people per day. This is so horrible to contemplate that we shouldn't even say it. But the general situation in which we are involved is lamentable" (Cousteau 1991).

Today's cutting-edge trend is to help women give artificially inseminated birth to smart and/or beautiful designer babies, and to eliminate inferior ones. Some perceive prenatal genetics screenings as a component of modern eugenics. Founder of Planned Parenthood, Margaret Sanger believed that the unfit should not be allowed to reproduce. In 1939, she dubbed blacks "inferior"—and people of faith (inclusive of fundamentalists and Catholics) "expendable." Nonetheless, Sanger is lauded today as a health and birth control heroine. In the Sanger tradition, Singapore became the first democratic country to adopt an openly eugenic policy by granting favors to mothers with university degrees, and to women who submit to sterilization following birth of their first or second child.

Even people of faith support the so-called new eugenics. Take, for example, Jewish Senator Leiberman from Connecticut. The Gore 2000 vice-presidential running mate allegedly follows the tenets of

Orthodox Judaism. If, for instance, the Senate votes on the Sabbath, Senator Leiberman refuses to drive. Instead, he walks three miles to Capitol Hill. Fellow Orthodox Jew, columnist and movie critic Michael Medved accuses Leiberman of violating orthodoxy's uncompromising strictures against even weightier matters. Incredibly, Leiberman endorses the horrific practice of partial-birth abortion. This medical procedure allows a baby to be almost entirely delivered before its skull is punctured and its brains suctioned out.

Hate-crimes Legislation

The Bible makes it abundantly clear that godly men are not to succumb to sexual misuse of their bodies. Furthermore, they are not to demonstrate "soft" or "delicate" tendencies (i.e., effeminacy, 1 Cor. 6:9). Alternative lifestyles are denounced by clear text of Scripture from both Old and New Testaments. Nonetheless, the highest court of America's Presbyterian Church ruled in June of 2000 that its ministers may instigate holy unions, if not homosexual marriages. The General Theological Seminary of the Episcopal Church has revised its housing policy to allow committed same-sex couples. Reformed Judaism was the first major U.S. religion to adopt a national policy sanctioning homosexuality (Lev. 18:22; Rom. 1:24–27; 1 Cor. 6:9–10).

Postmodern thought forbids biblically correct thinking. To counter moral absolutism, the charge of "hate-monger" is leveled against believers, unfairly so, when they align with biblical mandate regarding gender preference and sexuality. This represents yet a new form of racism emerging today. Ask talk-radio hostess, Dr. Laura Schlessinger, who morally criticizes homosexual special rights and parenting. In the fall of 2000, Dr. Laura experienced discrimination first-hand when gay activists demanded that Paramount drop her television show, and Procter and Gamble refused to sponsor it. Excluding even the possibility of good-faith dissent, these radicals demonstrated "liberal monism," a term coined by Jean Bethke Elshtain of the University of Chicago. They unjustly maligned Dr. Laura as a "hate-monger."

According to the *Wall Street Journal*, even members of the American Psychological Association gathered in Washington, D.C.

to vilify Dr. Laura as a homophobe. Some pedophile-friendly mental health experts of the APA suggest that Americans have an inordinate fear of child sexual molestation by adults. Incredibly, these specialists blame homophobe parents, not pedophiles themselves.

According to a Coral Ridge Ministries survey—results of which were sent to Congress, the national media, and the White House—96 percent of the responders strongly disagree with the claim that homosexuals qualify as an oppressed minority and therefore deserve special consideration under the law. To protect one group by trampling on fundamental rights of others is partiality, which the Bible calls *hamartia,* or sin. Despite objection by millions of devout Jews and Christians, politicians applaud expansion of federal hate-crimes legislation to include sexual orientation, thus sending the erroneous message that biblical morality regarding homosexual behavior, even pedophilia, is comparable to prejudice toward African-Americans or the disabled.

Proposed hate-crimes legislation renders certain victims more deserving of legal protection than others. Under the *Local Law Enforcement Enhancement Act* of 2000, to attack a man because he is gay invites a longer prison sentence than if his motive were simply cruel greed. Says policy analyst for the Family Research Counsel, Yvette Cantu Schneider, this is preferential treatment. A former lesbian, Schneider poses the provocative question, "Was my well-being worth more seven years ago [when I was gay] than it is today [when I am straight]?" Given hate-crimes legislation, the answer is "apparently so." This is partiality, and once again partiality is *hamartia.*

The Political Correctness Movement

A proponent of social-democratic liberalism, Arthur M. Schlesinger, Jr. wrote a national bestseller, *The Disuniting of America: Reflections on a Multicultural Society.* While his arguments against extreme multiculturalism may well be based on several false premises, Schlesinger rightly identifies what he calls a "cult of ethnicity," which adamantly protests the Anglo-centric culture. While his book is helpful in exposing certain error, Schlesinger nonetheless gives hearty approval to another damaging cult, that of "white guilt."

Today's Afrocentrism is a politically correct theme which applauds indiscriminately all that comes out of Africa while at the same time condemning the Euro-American culture with its strong Judeo-Christian leanings. According to Charles Crismier of Save America Ministries, racism may have started with whites—hence, the feeling of guilt—but now, surprisingly, even black pastors across America call for segregation and black separation.

In the Eschatological Discourse (Matt. 24), Jesus warns that in these last days, *ethnos* (race) will rise up against *ethnos* (verse 7). Nevertheless, in Christ, there is neither Jew nor Greek, bond nor free—black nor white. Since it is not acceptable to do evil that somehow good may come, reverse discrimination cannot possibly solve the sin of bigotry (Gal. 3:28; Ps. 34:14; Acts 10:28).

Still, postmodern Afrocentrists blame Christians for keeping African-American minds in bondage. To the contrary, it is the flesh nature, not its color that yields bondage. Sanctified Christians, black or white, are not subject to the yoke of bondage. Theirs is the promise of glorious liberty (Gal. 5:1, 19–21; Rom. 8:21).

According to adherents of Afrocentric thought, opponents are racists, seeking to preserve white, heterosexual male supremacy. Director of Harvard's African-American studies program, and arguably the most distinguished black scholar in the world, Professor Henry Louis Gates, Jr., rightly opposes this sort of Afrocentric scapegoating. It simply fuels the hatred.

While opponents are labeled "racist," adherents insist that they themselves cannot be racist because somehow they lack power. Advocates of black reparations believe that blacks do not prosper in the U.S. today because their ancestors were enslaved over one hundred years ago. Never mind that there are no living victims, nor perpetrators of American slavery. Somehow, a check issued promises to balance the score. Black author Professor Glenn C. Loury urges fellow blacks to reject victim status by adopting a renewed sense of accountability.

Through race-based admissions and racial quotas to reengineer society, racial preference programs decide on the basis of skin color who succeeds and who fails. For example, the Center for Individual Rights is working to stop the University of Michigan Law School and undergraduate college from illegal use of racial preferences. At Alabama State University, a black man, Jessie Tompkins, discovered that he did not qualify for a lucrative whites-only scholarship in the traditionally black college.

Conclusion

In today's enlightened culture, special regard for an individual over the group is considered racist, wrongly so, because it presupposes that individual to be of a dominant and/or superior persuasion. Postmodern collaborative consensus requires sacrifice of the individual and of moral absolutes. It is believed that only then can social and ecumenical harmony be ensured.

To the postmodernist, desired ends justify even ungodly means. For example, Dr. George Carey heads the Anglican Church as Britain's Archbishop of Canterbury. While worshipping at the largest Hindu temple outside of India in December of 1996, he urged Christians and Hindus to join forces against racism. With this mission in view, Dr. Carey freely worships in scores of mosques, synagogues, and shrines. His vision is to promote religious pluralism.

Notwithstanding, light cannot possibly fellowship with darkness and still maintain the attribute of light. For this reason, God commands believers to withdraw from religionists, idolaters, and others who walk out of the ranks of the straight and narrow. Christians are to eschew the spirit of error characterizing this present age. They must not join it (2 Thess. 3:6, 14; 1 Cor. 5:11; Rom. 1:25; 1 John 4:6).

In summary, racism plays off of bloodline or social association. It may be a conscious or unconscious state of mind with mild, moderate, or severe outcomes. In any case, racism is partiality; and partiality is bias, prejudice, or favoritism—all of which are unjust. As we have seen, the Bible calls this sin.

CHAPTER 19

Hamartia Rationalism

When the Comforter is come, he will reprove the world of sin *[hamartia]* . . . because they believe not on me (John 16:7–9).

Epistemological Rationalism

Simply put, epistemology is a branch of philosophy that examines the nature of knowledge. In basic form, rationalism is an epistemological doctrine in which sense experiences are deemed unnecessary to attain truth. That is to say, rationalists presume knowledge to be innate and derived from reason, not experience. In contrast, the apostle Paul attributes right knowledge to God alone. Paul further exposes the limitations and temporal nature of carnal knowledge (Rom. 11:33; Eph. 3:19; 1 Cor. 13:8; Col. 2:3). According to 2 Peter 1:2, Jesus our Lord is the *epignosis*, or "full knowledge" of God Himself.

Nonetheless, rationalism asserts that human reason apart from divine revelation is able to attain objective truth and, in turn, regulate human behavior. According to the Bible, however, human thinking and behaviors are found wanting. Independent of God, the mortal heart produces wrong thinking, murder, adultery, fornication, thefts, false witness, and blasphemy (Ps. 94:11; John 15:5; Matt. 15:19).

When the Supreme Court turned a fateful corner in 1962 by banning school prayer, a stunning decline of public and personal morality ensued, particularly among America's young people. Today, one-fifth of all students will have had at least four sex partners before they graduate from high school. In April 2002, NBC aired an Oprah talk show on how young women today view sex. Disturbingly, those interviewed equated oral sex with "a kiss on the cheek" in casual dating, one-night stands included. "It's only physical," one misled youngster quipped.

Government statistics reveal a frightful 106 percent increase in substance abuse among teenagers since 1992—with a 33 percent increase between 1994 and 1995 alone (Preliminary Estimates 1995).

Between 1965 and 1996, the juvenile violent crime arrest rate increased 215 percent, teenage suicides increased about 155 percent, and teenage girls engaging in sexual intercourse and out-of-wedlock births increased dramatically. Concurrently, before artificially boosted scores (1996), average SAT scores plunged nearly sixty points (Kennedy 2000).

Today's rationalism contends that knowledge is derived from the senses. While this may well depict carnal knowledge, it does not ring true of "the depths of the riches both of the wisdom and knowledge of God," which requires exercise of the "spirit of revelation" (Rom. 11:33; Eph. 1:17).

Plato

Plato first formulated epistemological rationalism as a system of eternal necessary truths accessible to human reason apart from sense-experience (*Republic*, *vi* and *vii*). Plato's philosophy influenced Christianity through Augustine and countless others.

Epistemological rationalism reached its zenith in the seventeenth century with the revival of Platoism and with development of mathematical physics by Copernicus, Galileo, as well as Kepler and Descartes. While most of these were said to have been Christians, René Descartes demoted God to mere "initial impulse." His famous premise, "I think; therefore, I am," ignored Bible truth that all things are out of *(ek)*, through *(dia)*, and unto *(eis)* Jesus Christ (Rom. 11:36).

LEIBNIZ

Gottfried Leibniz's system is celebrated as the crowning achievement of epistemological rationalism. Leibniz suggests that the life of a soul or metaphysical unit is self-contained. The universe, he believes, consists of an infinite number of spiritual substances, called monads. Although monads are coordinated by a pre-established harmony, each monad regards the whole from a distinct viewpoint. Human thinking occupies an intermediate position in the hierarchy of monads. While clear in comparison with animals, mortal perceptions involve confusion nonetheless. Therefore, human science, at best, orders knowledge so that it approximates as much as possible the ideal deductive system.

Leibniz's foundation inspired Bertrand Russell, English philosopher and mathematician. Russell was a liberal pacifist and moralist who wrote *Impact of Science on Society*, in which he asserted that "a scientific world society cannot be stable unless there is a world government." Russell advocated population control by means of birth control and even bacteriological warfare. With his wife, Russell ran a progressive school in the late 1920s and early 1930s.

KANT

Immanuel Kant attempted to combine rationalism and empiricism into a single system, called "critical philosophy." In the view of this eighteenth-century German philosopher, knowledge is not derived from experience; however, it is dependent on human understanding. To Kant, rationalism provides basis for science only if one adopts skepticism regarding metaphysics, branch of philosophy that systematically investigates first causes. Kant argued that God's existence could not be proved theoretically. Truly, the Lord knows the thoughts of man, and they are but vanity (Ps. 94:11).

Kant reasoned that law given by reason—i.e., the so-called categorical imperative—prompts right actions. Paul presents the more accurate reality. Though his "inner man" favored God's law, Paul bemoaned the fact that he was taken captive by the law of sin. As a result, his actions violated his own desire to produce good works.

And so it is with each of us, for apart from divine empowerment, all fail in pursuit of the ideal (Rom. 7: 22–24; Ps. 13:3).

Hegel

Though contrary to the mathematical method, and inspiration typical of classical rationalism, Hegelianism nevertheless represents an apparent return to rationalism. George Hegel was an idealist who believed that man is best when serving the State. This German philosopher effectively undermined the notion of fixed rights and wrongs. Leftist followers, as Karl Marx, used Hegel's dialectic to show the inevitability of radical change and to attack religion and the social order of the European Industrial Revolution. In Hegel's dialectic process, ends justify means.

Today's Outcome-Based Education (OBE), otherwise known as "mastery learning," resurrects Hegelian dialectics as a behavior modification technique of group consensus under peer pressure. Collaborative learning involves collective thinking, prodding participants beyond old truths and moral absolutes into the ambiguous realm of evolving truth. Ground rules disallow adversarial processes; instead, participants find common ground. Cooperative learning gives the faulty impression that all students are succeeding when, in fact, participants rest on efforts and leadership of the group's brightest members.

Briefly, group think is collaborative consensus sacrificing absolutes to ensure social harmony. This is key to the global citizenship agenda toward creating what Chester Pierce of Harvard University dubs "the international child of the future." The idea is to supplant individualism and America's natural competitive nature with illumined, politically correct eco-indoctrination using the Marxist decision-making process of dialectics featuring fact-based "thesis," feeling-based "antithesis," and compromise "synthesis."

Age of Group Consciousness

The New Age adept is a highly evolved enlightened one, having purportedly undergone repeated reincarnations toward earning successful egoic advancement. Previously an embryo-god, the adept allegedly has shifted consciousness from self to the group as qualification for lording over less accomplished counterparts. Anticipating a forthcoming golden era of pseudo-peace and brotherhood, illumined Freemasons hope to possess the divine self in recovering the Lost Word. New Age occultists similarly achieve the higher self, or christhood, through a series of upward mobility reincarnations.

Ethical Rationalism

First developed by Plato, ethical rationalism applies epistemological rationalism to morality. Primary morals are held to be innate and the Golden Rule, motivated by reason; however, God's Word warns that mortal minds and seared consciences are corrupt. Furthermore, "precepts of men" fail to produce objective truth and right behavior, as rationalists assert. Instead, carnal mindedness undermines wisdom and ultimately leads to ruin (Titus 1:15; Isa. 13–14; Rom. 8:6).

According to pollster George Barna, nearly three-quarters of all Americans reject the very concept of absolute truth. Although the Word of God would have us to "buy the truth and sell it not," less than half of those who call themselves born again Christians believe that anything is absolutely true—this, according to Mark Hatch in *Boiling Point*. Sadly, America's evolving ethics relinquish traditional values as loyalty, purity, accountability, and self-sacrifice. All too often, today's spirituality is driven, not by truth, but rather by what feels good and proves to be convenient (Prov. 23:23).

You recall that Horace Mann was the mid-nineteenth-century American political leader who somehow sold Americans on the misguided idea that one hundred years of secular education would eradicate crime and poverty. To the contrary, one of the students responsible for the Columbine massacre in 1999 allegedly stated on his Internet site, "I am the law. If you don't like it, you die. . . . If I don't like you or what you do, you die." The same student wrote in a classmate's yearbook, "*Ich bin Gott*"—German for "I am God." It seems that primary morals are not necessarily innate, as ethical rationalists would have us to believe.

Stoicism

Among philosophers of the ancient world, stoics developed a form of ethical rationalism popularized by Cicero—Roman orator, writer, and politician (106–43 BC). Stoics held that a spark of divine reason inhabits every man, and happiness lay in accepting the law of the universe. As pantheistic materialists, stoics believed in the human brotherhood, defining characteristic of the emerging New World Order.

Materialism is the philosophical theory that nothing exists above matter and matter in motion. The theory altogether excludes the possibility of God. On the other hand, pantheism is belief that all life is god or part of god, considered to be the sum total of all that exists. So pervasive is pantheistic error that it gives form to all ancient mystery religions, modern witchcraft, mystical humanism, the holistic movement, illumined Freemasonry, Eastern mysticism, and New Age occultism. Today, its tentacles encircle education restructuring efforts and radical environmentalism.

Theological Rationalism

Favoring natural as opposed to revealed religion, theological rationalism developed rapidly after the Reformation. At the same time it trivializes revelation and divine authority, it affirms reason, which is unable to grasp religious truth. But the apostle Paul assures us that believers can, in fact, have the mind of Christ Jesus. The skeptical, anti-religious attitude of theological rationalism allies with liberalism (Phil. 2:5–6).

In the eighteenth century, English deists, French *philosophes,* and German theologians further developed theological rationalism. French writer, deist, and philosopher Voltaire embraced belief in a rational religion of nature as opposed to the orthodox beliefs of Christianity. Deists believe that God may be source for natural law, but He does not intervene directly in the affairs of the world. Man's only religious duty is to be virtuous—but by what standard?

Conclusion

Author-publisher Ted Flynn laments that "rationalism has been the death of our culture." This is exemplified in a story that has made its rounds on the Internet:

> Some day, a long time from now, a well-known soul finishes his time on earth and approaches the pearly gates of heaven. He identifies himself to St. Peter as former Leader of the Free World. Before entering, however, he must first confess all of his sins.
>
> Biting his lips, he answers, "Well, I tried marijuana, but you can't call that 'dope-smoking' because I didn't inhale. There were extra-marital relationships, but you can't call them 'adultery' because I didn't have full sexual relations. And, yes, I made some misleading, but legally accurate statements. You can't call it 'bearing false witness' because it didn't meet the legal standard of perjury."
>
> With that, St. Peter consults the Book of Life and declares, "OK, here's the deal. We'll send you somewhere hot, but we won't call it 'hell.' You'll be there indefinitely, but we won't call it 'eternity,' and when you enter, you don't have to abandon hope. Just don't hold your breath waiting for it to freeze over!"

No matter personal notoriety or one's bogus sense of self-righteousness, human reasoning apart from God's immutable law is *hamartia.* It never fails to miss the mark with grave consequences following.

The apostle Paul admonishes us to "let this mind be in you, which was also in Christ Jesus." Christ humbled Himself, forfeited self-interest, and deferred to the will of His Father. In doing the same, we surrender our faulty human rationale to His wisdom. Better to fall voluntarily on the Rock of Christ Jesus, and thus be broken, than to suffer the stone of God's righteous judgment to fall on us (Phil. 2:5–8; John 14:24; Matt. 21:42–44).

CHAPTER 20

Hamartia Syncretism

> For all nations have drunk the wine of her passionate unchastity, and the rulers and leaders of the earth have joined with her in committing fornication (idolatry), and the businessmen of the earth have become rich with the wealth of her excessive luxury and wantonness. I then heard another voice from heaven saying, "Come out from her, my people, so that you may not share in her sins *[hamartia]*, neither participate in her plagues, for her iniquities *[hamartia]* are piled up as high as heaven" (Rev. 18:3–5a, AMP).

Neo-pantheistic Syncretism Prophesied

Today's forthcoming transnational government commands a collective system of global economics, which in time may be accessed only by those who receive Antichrist's mark, or stamp, indicating ownership and subservience. Likely to be an embedded transponder, using radio waves to identify its bearer, this mark will authorize world citizens to buy or sell in the New World Order (Rev. 13:16–17; 14:9–11).

The Bible indicates further that a False Prophet will cause all world citizens to receive this mark in their right hands or foreheads. According to Revelation 13:14–18, he will speak as the Dragon, Satan, and come alongside Antichrist to perform deceiving miracles. In the not-too-distant future, this False Prophet will function as head of the one-world false religious system, that of neo-pantheistic syncretism (Rev. 17:5). His unseemly character is concealed in the ominous biblical phrase, "Mystery, Babylon the Great, the mother of harlots and abominations of the Earth." The False Prophet will make an image of Antichrist and then force its worship under penalty of death (Rev. 16:13–14; 19:20).

Neo-pantheistic Syncretism Acclaimed

By Wiccans

Practices of ancient mystery religions to be resurrected in the end times are replicated through wicca, old-English term from which we get the word, "witch." On 3 March 2000, NBC aired a special program on Northwest wiccans. While young women are especially attracted to this branch of paganism, young men are involved as well.

Pagan earth witches total an astonishing quarter-of-a-million in "Christian" America alone. Now, wiccans qualify as military chaplains. Many more are politically active in saving Mother Earth, viewed as a living organism deserving worship and in need of global oversight. For global interests to prevail, Christianity must be undermined. Modern witches call this their "Great Work." Toward this end, their relationship with the one-world conglomerate is symbiotic.

An association of 188 nation-states joining more than 126 organizations and agencies worldwide, the United Nations convenes at the highest levels and stands poised at the center of the New World Order. Already it represents a limited form of world government. Astonishingly, the United Nations infrastructure includes the World Health Organization, which recommends integration of witch doctors into health teams of African states.

Originally, Halloween was a druidic festival. A pagan priesthood of ancient France and Britain, the druids drenched their altars with blood of human burnt sacrifices. It was believed that on the eve of their new year, the Lord of Death permitted wicked souls under his dominion to return to their earthly homes. The living offered sacrifices to appease these wicked dead and, thus, avert any pranks they might play. Despite these facts, more often than not, witches today are associated with the apple-bobbing, taffy-pulling children's holiday of Halloween, which even Christians celebrate.

One of eight major festivals of witches, Halloween is considered to be the day of the year most suitable for demonic activity. Most assuredly, witches do not view Halloween as a harmless harvest festival. Nor should Christians. The apostle Paul saw to it at Ephesus, that, for the believers' sake, even witches' books were burned. Christians are called to restrain the "sacred secret of lawlessness." Taking a godly stand regarding this November Eve/October 31st witches' holiday is a good place to start (Acts 19:18–19).

BY SECRET SOCIETIES, MYSTICAL HUMANISTS, AND NEW AGE OCCULTISTS

A pillar of Freemasonry is infinite wisdom of the Great Architect of the Universe. Illumined Masons recognize the "knowledge of the universe" through their "own inward nature." They need no faith in supernatural forces except to know that the "All-seeing Eye" keeps each one in view (Van Cott 1959).

The Greek word for knowledge is *gnosis*. Gnosticism is an esoteric cult of divine enlightenment that synthesizes Christianity, Eastern religions, and ancient mysteries. Passed on through twelfth-century Knights Templars, the gnostic belief system continues today in Freemasonry; moreover, mystical humanists present themselves as contemporary gnostics. Says Gary Kah of Hope for the World ministries, gnostic experiences take the place of God and become an end in itself. Both Peter and Paul issued warnings regarding arcane seduction of cults, as gnosticism (2 Pet. 3:17; 2 Thess. 2: 4, 7, 11).

As neo-gnostics, New Age occultists openly and actively work for world peace and harmony. Take, for example, "72 Hours" (31 December 1999–2 January 2000), an interfaith bridge-building project of the UN-associated United Religions Initiative (URI). Throughout those three days, groups of mystics from around the world engaged in interfaith peace and unity initiatives that counterfeit the peace from above that passes all human understanding (Phil. 4:7).

Massive Millennium Celebrations at the Great Pyramids of Giza featured a spectacular multimedia sound and light show designed to welcome the golden age of the new millennium. Symbolizing the dawn of a new occult order, one of neo-pantheistic syncretism, a gold-covered capstone was air lifted and placed atop the Great Pyramid of Cheops. This event kicked off the Millennium Symposium, three-day event sponsored by the United Nations Educational, Science, and Cultural Organization (UNESCO) and produced by the Millennium Project of the American Council for the United Nations University.

Neo-pantheistic Syncretism Defined

Simply put, syncretism is doctrinal mix and compromise. Neo-pantheistic syncretism melds ancient belief systems with traditional Christian dogma, and therefore misses the mark of pure doctrine. Three principles of paganism include animism (concept of spirits residing in all natural objects—animals, too), polytheism (belief in many gods), and pantheism. The latter proclaims all life to be god or part of god, defined as the sum total of all that exists. Not only is pantheism at the root of all ancient mysteries, it also gives form to modern witchcraft, mystical humanism, the holistic movement, Eastern mysticism, and New Age occultism.

Neo-pantheistic Syncretism Steered

In the Political Sphere

In marrying spiritual elements of the East with biblical concepts of the West, neo-pantheistic syncretism employs biblical phrases, but with meanings and agendas that God never intended. Among its leaders are Maurice Strong, former secretary-general of the Rio Earth Summit and director of the International Union for the Conservation of Nature. Second in command at the United Nations, Strong owns a Colorado ranch, *Baca Grande*, which serves as a veritable Mecca for New Age mystics. Strong advocates its becoming the "Vatican City" of the New World Order.

IN THE EDUCATION SPHERE

Robert Muller is the former UN secretary-general and Chancellor of the University of Peace, Costa Rica. Author of *New Genesis, Shaping a Global Spirituality* (1984), Muller sustains eleven Schools of Ageless Wisdom. His self-proclaimed title is Father of United Religions, and his UNESCO prize-winning World Core Curriculum is at the root of today's education restructuring efforts.

Muller calls for cosmic education shaping global spirituality, which embraces cosmic laws common to every faith. All members of the design teams for the Global Education Project embrace Muller's brand of universe-worshipping cosmolatry. New Age activist Dorothy J. Maver serves on the steering committee of possibly the most significant group behind education restructuring—namely, the Global Alliance for Transforming Education. Cosmolatrists, as Maver, fancy that humans act as Mother Earth's consciousness.

IN THE RELIGIOUS SPHERE

Unbelievably, Muller credits creation of his World Core Curriculum to the Tibetan, spirit guide of English Theosophist Alice Bailey. Bailey claimed that "the concept of a world religion and need for its emergence are widely desired and worked for. The fusion of faiths is now a field for discussion. Workers in the field of religion will formulate the universal platform of the new-world religion" (Bailey 1948).

Says Merwin-Marie Snell, "The religion of the future will be universal in every sense. It will embody all the thought and aspiration and virtue and emotion of all humanity; it will draw together all lands and peoples and kindred and tongues into an universal brotherhood of love and service; it will establish upon earth a heavenly order" (Snell 1993).

"The new mingling of faiths will cause a fresh interpenetration of ideas and customs. Out of the encounter some paring of outmoded encrustations will perhaps take place. The new intercourse will fructify in more inclusive, universal faiths, perhaps even a new-world faith as a basis for the coming world civilization" (Casper 1980).

A member of the Council of Religious Leaders, Bishop C. Joseph Sprague heads 425 churches in the Northern Illinois Conference of the United Methodist Church. Having founded Communities of *Shalom*, Sprague also chairs the National *Shalom* Committee. Working for "systemic change," *Shalom* sites across the country collaborate with the communities they serve. Unfortunately, Sprague's brand of *shalom* encourages neo-pantheistic oneness with nature. His spiritual renewal bypasses God's plan to yoke with the Son and to learn of Him (Matt. 11:28–30).

Neo-pantheistic Syncretism Exposed

Esoteric philosophy refers to exclusive truth for an enlightened inner circle of initiates. The Greek root means "private" or "confidential." While its underlying agenda is secretive, the earmarks of neo-pantheistic syncretism are manifest. For lack of maturity in the Word, many Christians are tossed off center by every wind of doctrine. As a result, they fall prey to religious error discernable on a number of fronts—animal rights, entertainment, and false theology, to name three (Eph. 4:14).

In the Animal "Rights" Movement

PeTA stands for People for the Ethical Treatment of Animals. Its motto pronounces that "animals are not ours to eat, wear, experiment with, or use for entertainment." The notion that animals deserve to become a protected societal class is the myth commonly promulgated by advocates. By preying on people's honest and proper concern for animals, PeTA takes in millions of dollars every year; however, the *Detroit Free Press* reports that PeTA uses only about fifteen to twenty percent of its income for animal welfare.

One chilly, wet evening, I witnessed young activists yelling obscenities at silver-haired seniors huddled arm in arm as they scurried out of the cold and into the Seattle Opera House. To these angry youths, fur jackets deserved more respect than law-abiding grandmas, attempting, under rude protest, to stay warm and dry. While a person properly may choose not to use animal fur, that one errs in failing to honor the very crown of God's creation while foisting personal views on others whose consciences remain clear (Matt. 10:31; Rom. 12:10).

In the last two decades, sabotage in the name of the environment, called ecotage, has swept the American West. With fewer than one-fourth of these cases solved, many more threats to property and humans have yet to be acted upon. Evidently, PeTA joins radical environmentalists in assigning more value to animals than to humans for whom Jesus died. So strong are animal activist beliefs that PeTA's co-founder and national director once announced, "a rat is a pig is a dog is a boy."

A liberal Australian philosopher who refuses to wear leather shoes or to eat meat, Peter Singer represents Animal Liberation, animal rights organization based on a neo-pantheistic belief system. Singer believes that primates should be recognized as "nonhuman persons." So extreme is the animal-rights position that a Montana rancher was fined four thousand dollars for killing a grizzly bear that charged him on his own property.

The heavenly Father made garments of animal skin for Adam and Eve to wear, and Christ Himself ate broiled fish. Similarly, as a tent-maker, the great apostle to Gentiles, Paul, was no animal-rights activist. Keep in mind he fabricated tents from strong goat's-hair cloth stretched over poles and held in place by cords that reached out to stakes driven into the ground. Even so, some believers judge others for their proper liberty in "taking dominion," as God has commanded (Gen. 3:21; Luke 24:42–43).

In the Entertainment Industry

Omega Code. I applaud and support fellow believers in their artistic attempts at reaching the lost who might otherwise not be open to a religious message. This is true whether or not those efforts suit my personal taste. With this given, I welcomed the premiere of Trinity Broadcasting Network's 1999 full-length, big-screen film, *Omega Code*.

However, careful viewing of the *Omega Code* and its 2001 sequel, *Megiddo*, raised red flags worth exploring. Main characters portrayed Bible villains (Antichrist, his False Prophet, their dupes) and the good guy, Dr. Lane. Lane failed to repent for his sins, but simply evolved from author-teacher guru of faddish New Age doctrine to would-be believer. Significantly, the target audience heard no clear salvation message. On one occasion, Dr. Lane cried, "Jesus, save me"—specifically, from a tight spot—but intercessory prayer seasoned none of Dr. Lane's efforts, nor did he display clear-cut connection with the remnant Body of Christ.

The Apocalypse unveils or reveals Jesus Christ; but throughout the entire film, this Name above all names was named only once. While symbolized by light, the Second Coming and onset of Millennium were portrayed as virtually Christ-free. Yes, God is the true light, but the chief god of Babylon and Ninevah likewise represented light. In Latin, Lucifer means "Bearer of Light"; and planetary light-bearers are destined to usher in New Age mass planetary Luciferic Initiation. Light's substituting for a clear depiction of events surrounding the advent of Jesus Christ seriously muddied Bible truth (1 John 1:5).

Unfortunately, apocalyptic events depicted in the *Omega Code* appeared to transpire, not at the hand of God, but rather by human effort. Furthermore, New Age and Bible terms were indiscriminately intermingled—e.g., "higher power" and "ten horns of power"; "global work" and "Millennium"; "new peace" and "Prince of Peace." Although the plot paralleled the biblical account of the nature and mission of Antichrist, a mishmash of eschatology threatened to baffle even biblically grounded Christians. The non-discriminating viewer was confused at best, misguided at worst.

At first an oral tradition from which gnosticism emerged, Kabbalism is an ancient esoteric tradition containing strong elements of pantheism. Based on the assumption that the Torah ("Law") contains the genetic code of the universe, the *Omega Code* started with an astonishing discovery by a Jewish Kabbalist, who unlocked a holographic computer program of the Bible. Hidden messages promised to recapture the whole of human history.

The *Bible Code* used the *gematria*, numerical value assigned to each Hebrew alphabet letter and applied in highly complex formulas that mirror Egyptian and Tibetan *Books of the Dead*. Its use alleges to decipher secret names of God, angels, and future events. Provocative, yes, but Kabbalism is medieval occultism that presents a mystical, magical interpretation of the Bible. According to Bible Answer Man Craig Bluemel, use of the *gematria* detracts from plain text of Scripture. What's more, its use overly emphasizes emotionally charged contemporary issues.

The Christian's source of truth is not esoteric hieroglyphics, but rather "the more sure Word." Not codes, but the Spirit guides believers into all truth. Even a child can grasp Bible principles. Hundreds of years before Christ, the prophet Jeremiah warned of a mighty, ancient nation of obscured language that would come from afar to destroy Israel. That the "obscured tongue" of computer technology is necessary to explore the depths of the riches both of the wisdom and knowledge of God is untenable. The *Omega Code* left an altogether different impression (2 Pet. 1:19; Rom. 11:33; John 16:13).

Spirit of Olympics. Ostensibly lauding character of model athletes, the Olympics likewise herald global harmony. Its symbol of five interlocking rings represents the five continents in unity. The fact remains, however, that ancient games were decidedly brutal. For example, the sport of *pankration* allowed kicking, and contestants broke fingers of their opponents.

Down play of religious distinctions (e.g., Jesus, the only Way, John 14:6) is a guiding principle of the Olympic Committee, yet even good people of faith embrace Olympic ideals. Riveted to the power of the Olympic dream, over three billion viewers around the world sat glued before their television screens for the 1996 Atlanta Olympics. The 2002 Salt Lake City Olympics drew a crowd of 52,000, welcoming some 2,318 athletes from seventy-seven nations.

As was the case with Greek society, politically correct, albeit biblically incorrect homosexuality enjoys full backing of the international Olympic movement. Moreover, Olympic games are sprinkled with oath taking, similarly forbidden by Scripture. An United Nations declaration (1996) entreats all nations to observe "the Olympic Truce" (Matt. 5:34–37).

The revivalist of modern Olympics (1896), Frenchman Pierre de Coubertin was characterized as "the Olympic Humanist." Not to be confused with humanitarianism, humanism is a doctrine, attitude, or way of life centered on relativistic human values that exalt humankind's dignity and worth based on self-determination through reason. Notwithstanding the movement is a religious potluck strongly seasoned with New Age religious imagery. Olympians use religious metaphors as “enlightenment,” “bowing down,” and “sacred duty/trust.”

As exemplified in Norway’s winter Olympics of 1994, contemporary Olympic ceremonies extol the goddess of Mother Earth, *Gaia*. Zeus was the ancient god of the Olympics. Back in 776 BC, Nike was the Goddess of Victory, not a trademark for shoes! To the Olympian, winning became everything; and man was divine. In ancient times, even the sweat of competitors was considered sacred. In contrast, the Bible forbids worship of alternative gods or goddesses (Ex. 20:3).

Furthermore, Christians are to abstain from every form of evil. The Greek middle voice in 1 Thessalonians 5:22 indicates that to do so is for self-interest. If only inadvertently, those who light and bear the famed Olympic torch align with Nazism, racism, and supremacy of the State over individuals. This is true because Nazi propagandists instituted the practice in the Berlin Olympics of 1936.

For good reason, the Roman Emperor Theodosius banned the games in AD 394. Having become a Christian, he no longer could condone its pagan celebrations. While attending or participating in the Olympics may not represent *hamartia,* embracing its spirit is unwise and inappropriate for Christians whose call is to be categorically separate from the world and its godless ways (2 Cor. 6:17).

In Its False Theology: “All is Energy”

To the neo-pantheist, the god-force flows through all; therefore, it stands to reason that humans, too, are gods, or part of god. Discovering one’s christhood, or higher self, is achieved by means of transformation, code word for demon possession. Furthermore, the neo-pantheist seeks to steer the primal energy force, as do Zen Buddhists in practicing what they call divine breathing. With this purpose in mind, New Age mystics wear crystals to send out energy used for psychic healing. Others submit to therapeutic touch, in which the therapist’s hands sweep along the body of a patient without touching it. With the flick of a wrist, bad forces are eliminated so as to balance energies therein.

A three-thousand-year-old Chinese practice, *feng shui* concerns itself with vital energy, *qi*. Proponents believe that household ornamentation, furniture arrangement, and the direction of rooms affect *qi* and, therefore, make the difference between success and failure in life. According to the *Los Angeles Times*, homebuyers are increasingly hiring *feng shui* consultants to examine homes they hope to purchase. Sales contracts are sometimes contingent on *feng shui* inspection.

Many healing techniques of Eastern medicine are becoming familiar to a growing number of American physicians and patients. Energy medicine features the mapping out of "meridians," comparable to magnetic fields. In circulating energy throughout the body, these energy channels supposedly balance the flow of energy therein. Today, magnetic field therapy is used widely all over the world to treat everything from ulcers to severe burns. Bio-magnetism promises relief from pain and renewed vigor, despite one's age. Therapeutic magnets operate similarly to acupuncture, but without needles. Acupuncturists use hair-thin needles, or variants, to stimulate designated points along the body through which *qi* energy flows. Each point is believed to connect with a specific organ and body function. Over twenty U.S. states license acupuncturists, and a growing number of insurance companies cover its use.

Magnet pads function in the same way. They come in diverse sizes, shapes, and strengths for use on different parts of the body, depending on the malady being treated. Significantly, these are said to operate against the backdrop of Mother Earth's magnetism, which supports biorhythmic balance of all living things. This pantheistic theory promises effective relief in a low-cost, non-invasive manner while at the same time reducing dependence on chemical cures and their negative side effects. For these reasons, magnetic therapy has gained popularity among Christians.

On a recent trip to Singapore, my husband and I enjoyed an hour of foot reflexology, which operates on similar principle. For us, this experience consisted of nothing more than vigorous massage—this, after a long day on our feet. In like manner, Christians who use magnets, or employ acupuncture, likely do not embrace Eastern mysticism's "all is energy," self-god lie any more than their Christmas traditions align with the pagan practice of tree adornment, as condemned in the Old Testament (Jer. 10:2–4).

Nevertheless, once the spiritual principle of neo-pantheistic syncretism is imbibed, the line has been crossed. Its outcome is *hamartia*. For discerning Christians, erring on the side of carefulness is preferable to dabbling in ancient practices, despite any favorable medicinal claim.

Neo-pantheistic Syncretism in the New World Order

America has become the most religiously diverse country in the world. The 21 August 2001 Editorial Page of *USA Today* ran an article targeting a new study by the Pluralism Project at Harvard University. It read, "In [our] nation founded in part by people desperately seeking a place to practice their own beliefs, there are now as many Muslims as Jews, more Buddhists than Episcopalians, and more Hindus than Disciples of Christ."

With escalating fervency, a clarion call for religious tolerance trailed synchronized terrorist attacks on America (11 September 2001). Thereafter, presenting Jesus as the only way met with unprecedented disapproval. Political correctness mandated instead an all-inclusive, milk-toast spirituality that everyone could affirm. Goaded by the world's political and religious leaders, peace loving Muslims and Christians linked arms as "brothers." Living peaceably with all men may indeed be scriptural, but sharing in the *hamartia* of syncretism is not. Better for God's people to "come out" than to linger at the wide gate, or saunter down the broad way to destruction (Rom. 12:18; Rev. 18:3–5a; Matt. 7:13).

CHAPTER 21

Hamartia
Terrorism

> Neither yield . . . your members as instruments [weapons] of unrighteousness unto sin *[hamartia]*; but yield yourselves unto God, as those that are alive from the dead, and your members as instruments of righteousness unto God (Rom. 6:13).

Abounding lawlessness, fierceness, and lack of natural affection characterize the last days. Nowhere are these traits more evident than in barbarous conduct of radical Islamic fundamentalists. Curiously, the word "Arab" comes from the primary root "to lie in wait" or "to engage or meddle with." With a mind to fight, faithful Muslims are commanded to lie in wait for unbelievers and then slay them. In fact, the *Koran* (Yusif Ali translation) declares that "fighting is prescribed for [the House of Islam]." Indeed, Muslims are to "smite [unbelievers] above their necks and [then] smite all their finger-tips off them." They are commanded further to slay transgressors wherever they are found. It is understandable why the Bible calls the representative of today's Arab world, Ishmael, a "wild ass of a man" whose hand is against every man (2 Tim. 3:1–7; Gen. 16:12; Surah 2:190–191, 216; 8:12; 9:5 of the *Koran*).

Whole nations in the Middle East, Asia Minor, the Orient, and Africa embrace and enforce Islamic fundamentalism; and no less than 10 to 15 percent of Muslims worldwide are of the militant strain. In its mission to impose cultural imperialism, Islam is an angry religion in search of a fight. By no means is it peaceful and friendly, as some would have us to believe. Indeed, of thirty sporadic or sustained military conflicts today, twenty-eight of them involve the House of Islam.

For years, my husband and I have befriended and prayed for a Muslim family that we count as dear. Secular Muslims, as these, are comparable to nominal Christians. While all of them endeavor to live uprightly, none accept authenticity of their respective holy books. Recent rhetoric invites Americans to embrace Muslims, but the *Koran* fails to reciprocate. In contrast, it commands Muslims to "take not the Jews and the Christians for friends and protectors." In no uncertain terms, the *Koran* "estranges" Christians "with enmity and hatred" and calls Jews "despised and rejected apes" (Surah 5:14, 51; 7:166).

When God called Abram, He promised to bless supporters and curse opponents of Israel. Notwithstanding, experts agree that Muslim rage over U.S. support of Israel virtually guarantees continued worldwide terrorism. The *Hezbollah* ("party of God") are hyper-fundamentalist Muslim warriors headed by Imad Mughniyeh, thought to have participated in the Twin Towers attack on America (11 September 2001). According to the *Hezbollah*, "the war is open until Israel ceases to exist and . . . the last Jew in the world is eliminated" (Gen. 12:3).

Osama Bin Laden

A criminal in flight, Saudi-born Osama Bin Laden is a terrorist-financier whose family in Saudi Arabia manages a world-class construction business worth billions. With up to twenty thousand followers, Bin Laden has declared *jihad* on thousands more. *Jihad* or "struggle" is holy war undertaken by Muslims against the House of Infidels. Death in *jihad* assures the devout Muslim instant access to heaven, where he is encircled by a bevy of beautiful virgins. It is no wonder that a recent survey identified fully 70 percent of Palestinian men willing to die as suicide bombers!

In the 1981 *Mecca Declaration*, Islamic powers pledged a *jihad* against Israel, which, according to Scripture, is destined to culminate in a future, final world war called Armageddon. Scripture prophesies escalating warfare leading up to Armageddon when allied forces of evil will attack Israel, both national and spiritual. While "national Israel" speaks to Hebrew princes with God (the *blood offspring* of Abraham), "spiritual Israel" identifies New Covenant, Spirit-filled believers (Abraham's *spiritual offspring*, Gal. 4:26, 28, 31; Rev. 16:12–16; Eph. 6:12).

In 1988 Bin Laden and another suspect allegedly issued a religious edict *(fatwa)* calling on Muslims to kill Americans "anywhere in the world where they can be found." Subsequently, he was indicted for embassy bombings in East Africa (1998). In December of 1999, three Algerian would-be terrorists were arrested in Seattle and New York. These, too, were linked with Bin Laden, as were Chechens and rebel groups who bombed a series of Moscow apartments in the summer of that same year.

East African embassy bombings involved e-mail messages. The same is true of the 1993 attack on the World Trade Organization. By means of plain text on bulletin boards, the Internet provides Bin Laden's henchmen with a relatively secure and anonymous method of communication. Through the Internet, fierce terrorists relay operational information, raise needed funds, and engage in deceptive perception management. Espionage techniques allow terrorists to hide message traffic in images, as on porn or sports sites. Remarkably, Bin Laden's telecommunications industry is worth in excess of three trillion dollars.

Saddam Hussein

"Devil" *[diabolos]* means literally "to riddle through" [as with accusation, the Devil's primary business]; and "Satan" means "adversary." The Devil and Satan are one and the same. Following the Gulf War, Iraqi fundamentalists first applied the derogatory term of "Great Satan" to America. If anything, Iraq is the true riddler and Great Satan. After all, her womb gave birth to ancient mysteries embedded in satanic secret societies collectively known as the Brotherhood of Darkness. Furthermore, it is Babylon in Iraq (not America) that Jeremiah calls "the hammer of the whole earth [to be cut asunder]" (Jer. 50:23).

Known as the "Butcher of Baghdad," Saddam Hussein is an Iraqi left-wing politician in power from 1968 and President from 1979. Having joined the Arab Ba'th Socialist Party as a youth, he soon became involved in revolutionary activities. Imagining himself as a sort of Nebuchadnezzar reborn, Hussein offers a contemporary portrait of Antichrist-to-come. The red horse of warfare, the black horse of famine, and the pale horse of death accompany Nebuchadnezzar, Hussein, and Antichrist—all three (Rev. 6:2–8).

Hussein joins Bin Laden in demonstrating abounding lawlessness, fierceness, and lack of natural affection to which Scripture alludes. A literal, amplified translation of Galatians 5:16 reads: "Let us, as our example Isaac, and our model Jesus, conduct ourselves in spiritual spheres that we should no, never fulfill the strong cravings of 'the lower, Ishmael nature.'" In God's economy, Ishmael is a type of carnality and self-life, producing works of the flesh, as expounded in Galatians 5:19–21. Throughout the Gulf War and its aftermath, Hussein exemplified this lower, Ishmael nature. Many recall his being photographed patting the head of his young guest, a wide-eyed Western boy. What many failed to notice was that Hussein used his left hand, reserved exclusively in the East for toileting purposes. What appeared to be a fatherly gesture was, in reality, a scornful insult.

Scripture characterizes evil men as "waxing worse and worse, deceiving and being deceived" (2 Tim. 3:13). Even former President Clinton, a pro-Palestinian, admits strong likelihood that within the next few years terrorist groups associated with the likes of Bin Laden, Hussein, and counterparts will launch unprecedented germ or chemical attacks on American soil. Moreover, Clinton acknowledges that America's defenses are not up to the challenge.

For just a few thousand dollars, a terrorist group can develop a biological weapon equal in its devastation to a small nuclear bomb. Britain's *Observer* newspaper quotes UN inspectors as revealing Iraq's secret stocks of nerve gas that, in very small quantities, could kill millions. Iran, too, is purchasing conventional, biological, and nuclear weapon components on open and black markets. A chemical safety group, the Stockholm International Peace Research Institute (SIPRI), fears that regulations on control of such materials are "quite loose." With air travel so convenient, infectious agents can leap continents with relative ease.

Great Arsenal of Weapons

Revelation 6:4 alludes to a great sword in reference to an extraordinary arsenal of weapons to be employed at the future, final world war called Armageddon. This arsenal likely will include cyberspace sabotage, living bombs, high-powered land mines, and modern nuclear missiles/warheads. Anthrax is one of the deadliest toxins known to humanity. If dispersed in the air above a large city, it could feasibly kill millions by pneumonia and suffocation. Sound evidence indicates that renegade Soviet scientists have developed yet another terrifying new nerve agent. VX gas is ten times more lethal than sarin gas, developed by Nazi scientists and deployed in a Tokyo subway by a Japanese doomsday cult (March of 1995). The Pentagon's proliferation report claims that more than twenty-five countries have developed, or may be developing, nuclear, biological, and chemical (NBC) weapons along with the means to deliver them.

These days, all too many willingly yield their members as weapons of unrighteousness. In the last two decades, ecotage has swept the American West causing at least one hundred major acts of vandalism, arson, and bombings since 1980. Resulting damage has been in the tens of millions of dollars. Agro-terrorism threatens to destroy corn, rye, rice, and wheat. Using thermo-generator guns that raise temperatures, weather-war strategists purpose to drop large groups of people dead in their tracks; and global magnetic warriors propose inciting large populations to unstable behavior, electronically. Despite escalating threats as these, America's military was asleep at the wheel under the Clinton/Gore watch at which time ammunition forfeited ballistic superiority when made out of environmentally friendly, lead-free tungsten.

Real or imagined threats convince the masses of need for absolute control. New diseases, an imploding social system, rising crime, moral decay, and even a failing education system also apply. The Education Department report, *A Nation at Risk* (1983), issued the stunning declaration that "if an unfriendly foreign power had attempted to impose on America the mediocre educational performance that exists today, we might well have viewed it as an act of war."

Chaos, Societal Transformation, and Control

Former Defense Secretary William Cohen is quoted as having said, "The scenario of nuclear, biological, or chemical weapons in the hands of a terrorist or rogue nation is not only plausible—it's quite real." In *The Islamic Invasion,* Dr. Robert Morey warns that Islamic fundamentalism is both organized and well funded. Radical Muslims are in the process of buying the U.S. Congress, and already they own vital news media outlets. By the year 2020, over twenty-five million Muslims in the U.S. are likely to declare Islamic law. All the while Bin Laden is gathering weapons to complete his reign of terror against the U.S., black Muslims are looking to revolt. It seems Chicken Little really *does* have something to cluck about!

Everything from terrorism to out-and-out warfare—socially and conventionally—hikes "the sky is falling!" rhetoric among the world's distraught citizens. Given this exceedingly bleak scenario, it stands to reason that outside restraint and control are all the more warranted. But be forewarned. Many in positions of power would exploit crises to facilitate centralized world government. The widespread notion that "they" should *do* something about escalating crises opens the door to an oligarchy poised to offer "real" solutions for "real" problems (Rev. 13:1,7).

Formerly a consultant for the Defense Department, Barbara Marx Hubbard proposed one such solution in her book, *The Book of Co-Creation.* Hubbard classifies one-fourth of the human population as "defective seeds" to be eliminated from the social body. For the sake of the world, "riders of the pale horse, Death," must destroy whom god selects. Weird, yes; but, after all, Hubbard credits her manuscript to the spirit who allegedly channeled it—namely, the Christ Light. Channeling is the ancient practice of necromancy, calling back the dead (actually demons). A form of witchcraft, channeling is sternly forbidden in Mosaic Law (Deut. 18:10–11).

To internationalists, chaos is self-serving; therefore, helpful. Domination-intent secret societies join New Age guru Barbara Marx Hubbard in implementing the principle that, for the sake of the world, chaos is needed to ease change. Global elitists parrot the *mantra* "out of chaos will come order." Theirs is a New World Order. Canadian billionaire Maurice Strong likewise calls for chaos in his campaign to halt technology and modern industrialism. A rabid environmentalist, Strong is the powerful director of the World Future Society, a kind of clearing house for all global conglomerates.

A biology professor at California State University, Dr. Stan Metzenberg has exposed National Science Education Standards as being "based on the flimsiest excuse for research"; moreover, less than half the science is peer reviewed. But, then, counterfeit science serves well the cry for global regulations and control. Although the scientific community has reached no consensus to warrant need for the nearly three hundred UN environmental treaties already administered, would-be environmentalist Mikhail Gorbachev champions enforcement of additional eco-regulations to be enforced worldwide. The very big business of radical environmentalism unites over twelve thousand groups under a political platform that outweighs any ostensible campaign for breathable air and drinkable water.

Co-founded by self-proclaimed eco-warrior Dave Foreman, *Earth First!* is a radical environmental group that openly calls for death of American citizens. In a 1995 edition of *Earth First! Journal,* Greenpeace board member Mike Roselle declared *jihad* even on bystanders because, he claimed, "in these desperate hours, bystanders are not innocent." Perhaps not surprisingly, Theodore Kaczynski was a member of *Earth First!* A recluse living in a remote Montana cabin, this Harvard-trained "Unabomber" abandoned his career as a mathematics professor at the University of California, Berkeley, in the late 1970s. Subsequently, in 1997, Kaczynski was convicted of sending out sixteen package bombs, which killed three people and injured twenty-nine others from 1978–1995.

Attack on America

These grievous acts pale when compared with the monstrous attack on freedom itself on 11 September 2001. The entire world reeled in incredulity when four concurrent aircraft hijackings ended in brutal annihilation of the once-majestic twin towers of New York City's World Trade Center. Just hours before, these 110-story towers distinguished the awesome skyline of Lower Manhattan, but in a blizzard of debris, the world's largest commercial complex crumbled helplessly before astonished onlookers. The nerve center of the nation's military, the Pentagon was similarly attacked. Not long thereafter, an United aircraft crashed in Shanksville, south of Pittsburgh.

The very month America commemorated Islam by unveiling the *EID* 34-cent postage stamp, Islamic extremists permanently altered the landscape of liberty throughout America and, indeed, the world—this, in the name of the nefarious "moon god" Allah. The fingerprint of Islamic extremist Osama Bin Laden marked this unprecedented and heinous wave of coordinated terrorist attacks. Astonishingly, in the wake of unspeakable devastation, Palestinian backers rejoiced, dancing and distributing cakes and candy in gleeful celebration of the carnage.

The Christian Perspective

You recall that Gideon's mighty soldiers drank water by putting their hands to their mouths while remaining upright with a single eye for battle. Unlike most of their peers, they did not lap up water on all fours like dogs. With their vigilance in view, God counted them fit for battle. As George Washington once said, "If we desire to secure peace, it must be known that we are at all times ready for war." Truth is, all believers are already at war. Theirs is a spiritual battle with spiritual armor. Vigilance and preparedness are of the utmost importance; however, in this case, the weapons of warfare are not carnal, but mighty through God to the tearing down of strongholds (Judges 7:5–6; Eph. 6:12–18; 2 Cor. 10:4).

To run for the hills and hide one's head in the sand are not biblically endorsed reactions. Similarly, fear mongering fails to produce desired results. Instead, compliant believers focus on things that are true, honest, just, pure, lovely, praiseworthy, virtuous, and of good report. Unfortunately, many misguided Christians choose instead to obsess about global governance, Armageddon, the Day of the Lord, Antichrist, False Prophet, Mark of the Beast, Tribulation, plagues, persecution, and the Lake of Fire. While these are based on true and honest Bible prophecies, be assured that dwelling on them issues no "good report." There is no need to toss and turn nightly with the weight of the world on one's shoulders. Chicken Little Christians unnecessarily "eat the bread of sorrows" when instead they should be shouting the victory (Isa. 41:10; Jonah 1:3; Phil. 4:8; Ps. 127:2).

God summarizes His requirement of believers as simply "to do justly, love mercy, and walk humbly with God"—not to manipulate others for self-interest, eliminate the unworthy, and walk arrogantly with a mind for confrontation. Believers are to hurl the whole of their cares on Him, stressing over nothing (Micah 6:8; 1 Pet. 5:7; Phil. 4:6).

All the while maintaining sobriety and vigilance, obedient Christians cede to the battle's being the Lord's. They understand, rightly so, that human effort fails to withstand what the Bible calls "forces of darkness" and what George W. calls the "axis of evil." While one's mortal body is vulnerable to injury, even death, the believer's ultimate protection is soundly ensured. With this truth firmly embossed on hearts, believers can yield freely to God. Their members, then, become instruments (yes, weapons) of righteousness. In all circumstances, the Lord Jesus Christ remains the world's only true hope (1 Pet. 5:8; 1 Sam. 17:45–47; Ps. 34:7; 44:3; 125:2; Zech. 2:5; Rom. 6:13; 1 Tim. 1:1).

CHAPTER 22

Hamartia
A-Traditionalism

> See to it that no one takes you captive through philosophy and empty deception, according to the tradition of men . . . rather than according to Christ. . . . In Him you were also circumcised with a circumcision made without hands, in the removal of the body [of the sins *(hamartia)*] of the flesh . . . (Col. 2:8, 11 NASB).

For many, the term "tradition" prompts recall of a popular musical score from *Fiddler on the Roof*. However engaging the character of Tevye is, this family patriarch demonstrates that even time-honored religious traditions can miss the mark and result in bondage. You see, apart from God's direction and empowerment, human effort remains fruitless. To insure that our lives, as believers, produce spiritual fruit, the heavenly husbandman diligently prunes back the deadwood of worldliness (John 15:1).

In yet another picture, circumcision cuts off the male foreskin as a right instituted by God to signal His covenant with Abraham and his descendants. In the New Covenant, the apostle Paul speaks of spiritual circumcision—that being, the circumcision of Christ. The latter involves no medical procedure. Instead, this cutting removes "the flesh" in reference to one's sin nature. To eliminate the dead branches of self-effort and "tradition of men" is to prepare for abundant blessing, spiritually speaking; however, many traditions pass worthwhile cultural mores from one generation to the next. Be assured that godly practices and beliefs, as these, enhance life and, therefore, are properly embraced, celebrated, and handed down. Contemporary secularists, nominal Christians, and New Age mystics are all too quick to lay aside godly traditions. For this reason, believers must uncover and then discard misguided tenets of godless a-traditionalism that denigrate the *U.S. Constitution*, godly principles of free enterprise, biblical Christianity, and the traditional family (Gen. 17:10; Col. 2:8, 11; Matt. 7:17).

U.S. Constitution Undermined

The *Constitution* Redrawn

Having served as supreme law of the federal government since its adoption in 1787, the *U.S. Constitution* compiles fundamental laws that define relations of the legislative, executive, and judiciary branches. Strict Constitutionalism interprets the *Constitution*—not by political whims—but rather according to the founders' intent. Most of the delegates who attended the original Constitutional Convention relied on the wisdom of Christian philosophers who had studied economics and government. For good reason, traditionalists oppose all efforts to call a new Constitutional Convention (Danford 2000).

The Establishment Clause of the First Amendment was intended, first, to ban a national religion and, next, to bar the state from favoring one religious view over another. Having scrutinized Jefferson's letter to the Danbury Baptists, the Federal Bureau of Investigation (FBI) affirmed this position. Nevertheless, modernists call for a new "living" *Constitution*, rendering America's supreme law up for grabs. Founding fathers never purposed to bar school children from having a Christmas program, or from singing, "O Little Town of Bethlehem," as liberal justices today would have us to believe. Supreme Court justices, not the nation's founding fathers, erected a so-called "wall of separation."

The *Constitution* Eclipsed

Founding fathers sought to limit governmental power despite demands of foreign policy. According to Alexander Hamilton, treaties should be agreements between "sovereign and sovereign," wielding no power to eclipse the *Constitution*. Unfortunately, treaties and international agreements are used increasingly to control domestic matters. At times, employing words of an international treaty invalidates state law. According to law professor James Hirsen, this judicially renders the *UN Charter* the supreme law of the land.

Many fail to recognize that it was a convicted spy for the USSR, Alger Hiss, who wrote this *Charter.* Even more alarmingly, an updated version of the *UN Charter* was proposed at the fifty-fifth annual meeting of the UN General Assembly (2000). Simply put, this *Charter for Global Democracy* redefines the *U.S. Constitution.* While the *Constitution* guarantees representative government, the *Charter*, in contrast, appoints leaders who are unaccountable to the people. For example, under the *Charter*, elected representatives do not decide taxes exacted by the UN's global IRS, nor does the UN Criminal Court guarantee citizens' right to trial by jury. Only the *U.S. Constitution*—not the *Charter*—guarantees the right to keep and bear arms.

Criticized for believing politics to be a tool of evangelism, D.L. Moody quipped, "It is true, I am a citizen of another kingdom, but I own property in Cook County!" Moody no doubt understood America's greatness as being fortified by the right to own and control private property. Both the *Communist Manifesto* and the *UN Charter* undermine constitutional rights regarding private property. When it comes to land use under jurisdiction of the United Nations, there is no distinction between federal and privately owned land.

Template for implementing the *Biodiversity Treaty*, first introduced at the 1992 Rio Earth Summit, the Wildlands Project declares as wilderness half of America's land. Zones of cooperation around so-called biosphere reserves enable private land to be taken without appropriate compensation, as required by the Fifth Amendment. While the treaty has not been ratified, it is nonetheless being implemented—this, by decree and degree. Through the *Desertification Treaty*, federal government tells Americans how they may or may not use private property. Claiming jurisdiction over 70 percent of the entire earth's land area, this global convention slipped through the 106th Congress without adequate review (October 2000).

The *Constitution* Eroded

Our nation was founded on the Christian premise that the Creator, not the state, endows individual rights. In *Zorach v. Clauson* (1952), the U.S. Supreme Court ruled that "we are a religious people whose institutions presuppose a Supreme Being," adding further that one cannot read hostility to religion into the *Bill of Rights*. Nonetheless, a step by step erosion of constitutional principles by Congress and the courts has resulted in banning God from classrooms and prayers from high school football games.

Free Enterprise Undermined

Former Prime Minister of Great Britain Mrs. Margaret Thatcher believes, rightly so, that the triumph of America's economic prosperity is her free market system based on respect for rule of law, individual effort, and fair dealing—all Judeo-Christian principles. Free enterprise maintains prosperity by keeping the economy and jobs going so that ordinary people profit from their own talents and abilities (Heb. 13:17; Prov. 6:6; Micah 6:8; Jer. 22:13; 1 Tim. 5:18).

To rejoice in the fruit of one's labor is the gift of God, not to be denied. Top-notch university research demonstrates the value of market-based principles; nevertheless, trendy eco-socialists work to supplant rightful private ownership with public ownership of the means of production, distribution, and exchange (Eccles. 5:19).

Managed in Geneva by a supra-national body that establishes, administers, and enforces regulations, the World Trade Organization (WTO) often rules against the United States. While feigning "free trade," the WTO pushes an agenda for central control of world markets. In so doing, the WTO locks nations into regulations that exceed authority of their own constitutions. This threatens to kill the goose that laid the golden egg—namely, America's free enterprise system.

Judeo-Christian Faith Undermined

Just before Christmas 2000, President-elect George W. Bush appointed as attorney general the evangelical Christian Senator John Ashcroft (R-Missouri). In his acceptance speech, the Senator quoted Micah 6:8: "He hath shewed thee, O man, what is good; and what doth the Lord require of thee, but to do justly, and to love mercy, and to walk humbly with thy God." This met with a flurry of protest.

Although over seventy million Christians attend America's churches, Christian speech is just about the only expression banned today. In years past, godly speech and deportment characterized the accepted norm. Gentlemen tipped their hats to ladies, and, for the most part, all honored the clergy. Everyday idioms were plucked from pages of Holy Writ. Moreover, it was common for prayer to precede school lessons, family meals, public forums and functions; and children were permitted their innocence. While chastity and marital fidelity drew praise—not ridicule—vulgarity and sexual immodesty aroused indignation. Love of God, family, country, and apple pie typified America at her best.

Ungodly Deportment, Speech, and Mindset

In contrast, we see evidence today of a national campaign to purge God from public life and government buildings. In 1995, the American Civil Liberties Union (ACLU) filed a lawsuit against a Baptist judge, the Honorable Roy Moore. Why? Because he displayed the Ten Commandments in his courtroom—ironically, the *same* Ten Commandments engraved on the walls of the Supreme Court in Washington, D.C.!

Many Americans are unchurched and consequently unaware of the biblical origin of broadly used phrases as "reaping the whirlwind," or "casting one's bread upon the waters." So as not to offend, no mention is made of the one true God if indeed public prayers are offered at all (Hosea 8:7; Eccles. 11:1).

The contemporary mindset is foreign to Bible-believing traditionalists, but aligns nonetheless with 2 Timothy 3:1–5. According to this powerful passage, people in these last days will increasingly exercise misplaced love of self, money, and pleasures. Theirs is an improper self-image, devoid of loyalties and godliness.

Skewed Portrayal of Women and Clergy

Despite the arrogant radical feminist presumption of gender superiority, women all too often are devalued as mere love toys. For example, on national television, Darva Conger married a stranger, purportedly a multi-millionaire. After the "relationship" didn't work out, she was induced into posing nude for a girlie magazine. By and large, her grievous behavior was met, not with shamefaced incredulity, but rather with grins and winks of the eye. Women are not alone in being denigrated. While it is true that there are wayward ministers whose behaviors fall dismally short of their calling, today's entertainment industry routinely portrays men of the cloth as being irrational, hypocritical, indulgent, and even criminally insane. As a result, Christian testimony suffers great harm (Isa. 56:11; Jer. 6:13).

Family Undermined

In the words of Oklahoma Governor Frank Keating, "It's easier to get out of a marriage than a Tupperware contract." So trivialized is the traditional family that the United States Census Bureau recently announced, for the first time ever, it will not collect data on marriage, divorce, and related matters. Then there is the UN *Convention on the Elimination of All Forms of Discrimination against Women*. Appallingly, this international Bill of Rights for women encourages legalized voluntary prostitution. Furthermore, CEDAW uses overly broad language that interferes with domestic law concerning adoption, marriage, divorce, child custody, and the like.

According to Beverly LaHaye, founding president of Concerned Women for America, the Healthy Families America plan is a dangerous, privacy-invading scheme sending government monitors into homes of all first-time parents across America. Such professionals no doubt target traditional parenting practices deemed unsavory. Radicals believe that, to protect children, families must be regulated and limited in size.

Families Regulated

On the *Today* show (24 March 2000), Maria Shriver parroted a slogan of the United Nations International Children's Emergency Fund (UNICEF) when she asserted that "everybody's children are all of our children." This misleading slogan suggests that the job of parenting mandates partnership with the ever-present state that, incidentally, never accepts responsibility for its own failed child-rearing policies.

Families Limited in Size

Thomas Malthus was the English economist and cleric whose *Essay on the Principle of Population* (revised 1803) first advocated population control. A Marxist-Leninist principle, Malthusian sustainability is described in the 1997 *USSR Constitution*. With his *Commission on Population Growth and the American Future*, John D. Rockefeller re-ignited the three-decades-old myth of global over-population. Sustainable communities require producers, not depleters (as infants, retirees, stay-at-home moms), as well as middle-class consumption pattern adjustment, called for in the *Kyoto Protocol* (November 2000).

Esteemed founder of Planned Parenthood, Margaret Sanger believed that the unfit should not be allowed to reproduce. Stanford's population guru Paul Ehrlich linked with Sanger in heralding modern Malthusianism. Upholding the UN concept of sustainable development, his flawed premise was this: While populations increase in geometric ratio, food supplies increase only in arithmetic ratio. Accordingly, to insure adequate food supplies for all, the earth's population must be curbed—severely and selectively.

About one hundred members of the Club of Rome, from which most planning directives for world government come, expressly purpose to reduce earth's population of six billion down to two billion. Toward this end, Dr. Rebecca Gompers is raising money to equip a 150-foot, sea-going abortion clinic to offer free abortions off the coast of any country that prohibits the practice.

Right to Life Undermined

The Bible teaches that God makes the barren woman a joyful mother of children. An "heritage of the Lord," children are "graciously given." As such, they are to be blessed. Indeed, the fruit of the womb is "*His* reward"; furthermore, children are as arrows in the hand of a mighty man. Happy is the man with a quiver full of them. The very crown of old men are grandchildren, whom Jesus characterizes as befitting the kingdom of heaven. No child, at whatever age, is a "non-person," or in any way is expendable (Ps. 113:9; Gen. 33:5; 48:9; Ps. 127:3–5; Prov. 17:6; Matt. 19:14).

Nevertheless, in 1973, *Roe v. Wade* opened the floodgates to today's new eugenics demeaning unborn children as non-persons with no constitutionally guaranteed rights. Astonishingly, a philosophy professor at the American University claims that "infants do not possess in their own right a property that makes it wrong to kill them." China takes the lead by forcing practices of abortion and sterilization and by trafficking in human organs. There is a lucrative global market for body parts of babies, especially those aborted at partial birth. The collection, processing, and distribution of human tissues (bones, tendons, skin, body parts) is a near billion-dollar national business.

Princeton's bio-ethicist Peter Singer advocates killing up to twenty-eight days post birth. Equally egregious, partial birth abortion is a medical procedure whereby the abortionist allows the baby to be almost entirely delivered. Then, he punctures the baby's skull, suctions out the brain, and delivers the dead baby otherwise in tact. In 2000, the U.S. Supreme Court ruled in favor of this barbarous procedure.

While suffragette Susan B. Anthony was an outspoken critic of abortion, calling it "child murder," many today herald abortion as being all about choice and personal empowerment. With this in view, the 1994 UN Cairo Conference demoted people to mere resources whose numbers must be managed by international overseers; thereafter, the 1995 UN Fourth World Conference on Women in Beijing promoted abortion on demand.

All the while the UN spreads hysteria of the myth of overpopulation, statistics clearly show, to the contrary, that the current population is slowing. The U.S. Census Bureau's *Special Compendium for the Millennium* notes a prosperous past one hundred years, but raises concern because of America's rapidly *falling* birthrate. Nonetheless, founding director of the Better World Society, television titan Ted Turner supports belief that action must be taken to keep the population in check. Indeed, millions of dollars from the Bill and Melinda Gates Foundation continue to feed the UN Population Fund as well as population control studies at Johns Hopkins University.

Traditional- Undermined by Alternative- Lifestyles

Although modern liberals believe that gender roles are artificial, but being gay is neutral, God's Word describes homosexuality as the abominable fruit of a "reprobate mind." These are God's words, not mine. Nevertheless, politically correct modernists brazenly promulgate their own brand of intolerance in response to God's supposed intolerance (Lev. 18:22; Rom. 1:24–27).

The Gay Rights movement purportedly advances sentiments of "choice," "freedom from discrimination," "respect," and "education"; but each was violated at Seattle's Whitman Middle School. On 13 February 1997, unsuspecting students were ushered into an assembly to watch a politically charged play lauding the gay lifestyle. Offended students were compelled to endure heavy-handed homosexual propaganda. Worse yet, seventh and eighth graders who dissented were denigrated in front of peers. Nevertheless, the Seattle School Board got a strong show of support from parents—gay and straight—who allegedly applauded the district's teaching students about sexual minorities.

In a spirit of openness, Seattle's Public Network, KCTS, offered a forum to discuss use of *It's Elementary* in public schools. This video candidly undermines monogamous heterosexuality. In it, one semi-favorable mention of the "old way of thinking" was framed in sheepishly apologetic tones so as not to violate the straitjacket of politically correct, pro-gay thinking. Furthermore, no featured teacher, parent, or student dared explore traditional views to the contrary.

According to a federal judge in Texas, communities do not have the right to determine which books their tax-funded libraries offer. It comes as no surprise, then, that Seattle librarians may disregard parental complaints in purchasing a book about gay teens, *Two Teenagers in Twenty*. Despite protest, libraries may stock *Daddy's Roommate* and *Daddy's Wedding* [to Frank]. Other Alyson Wonderland books include *Heather has Two Mommies, Gloria Goes to Gay Pride*, and *How Would You Feel If Your Dad Was Gay?* Under guise of the First Amendment, the American Library Association stalwartly promotes children's access to pornography.

The Seattle-based Pride Foundation and at least one mainline church sponsor college scholarships for homosexuals. Scholarships also are available for gay students at California's Golden Gate University and Iowa's state universities. At major universities as Stanford, Brown, Duke, the Universities of Virginia and North Carolina, among others, no subject is taboo. God tells us it is shameful even to speak of such things, yet it is now possible to earn a college degree in gay/lesbian studies; and as many as twenty-eight gay characters are paraded before America's families on television. In February 2000, Fox's edgy *Ally McBeal* broke cultural ground by introducing "prime-time's first male-to-male kiss of passion in a regular series" (American Family Association; Eph. 5:12).

When talk-radio hostess, orthodox Jew Dr. Laura Schlessinger proposed good faith dissent, gay activists called her convictions "hate." The Gay and Lesbian Alliance against Defamation (GLADD) accused Dr. Laura of endangering children. Never mind that GLAAD participated in a radical transgender conference that gave lessons on sadistic sex and promoted breast removal to become "boyz." Incredibly, in 1998, the journal of the American Psychological Association (APA) published results of a study arguing that sex between adults and children, called "inter-generational intimacy," is not always harmful. If ratified, the *UN Convention on the Rights of the Child* allows children to engage in entertainment, sexual or religious activities of their own choosing—free from parental intrusion.

Conclusion

Orthodox Rabbi Daniel Lapin defines "America's real war" as a contest between modern secularism, on one hand, and traditionalism, on the other. His annual convention, *Toward Tradition* bids people of faith to return home to America's Judeo-Christian ethic. In so doing, they must discord empty deceptions of the wayward tradition of men.

CHAPTER 23

Hamartia Utopianism

> And when he is come, he will reprove the world of sin *[hamartia]* and of righteousness and of judgment. Of sin, because they believe not in me. Of righteousness, because I go to my Father, and ye see me no more. Of judgment, because the prince of this world is judged (John 16:8–11).

In the Greek, utopia means "no place." Representing an ideal state in literature, the term was named after a book, *Utopia*, written by English politician and author St. Thomas More in 1516 to picture an ideal commonwealth. Other versions include Plato's *Republic*, Bacon's *New Atlantis* (1626), and *City of the Sun* by the Italian Tommaso Campanella (1568–1639). Although most perceive utopia as an impractical idealistic goal or scheme, others anticipate it as an attainable condition, place, or situation of social and political perfection.

Utopian Science Fiction

Utopia is a common subject in science fiction, the works of which often deal with alternative realities, future histories, space/

time travel, and psychic powers. An early practitioner was English writer and globalist H.G. Wells (1866–1946). Wells was a Fabian Socialist who wrote *The Open Conspiracy* and *The New World Order*, not to mention scientific romances, as *The Time Machine* (1895) and *The War of the Worlds* (1898). In addition to these, and many short stories, Wells' later works were earmarked by an anti-establishment, anti-conventional humor remarkable in its day.

Wells' many other books include *Outline of History* (1920), *Blueprint for World Revolution* (1928), and *The Shape of Things to Come* (1933). While a number of his "prophecies" have seemingly been fulfilled, Wells in no way qualifies as a true prophet of God. Similarly, U.S. writer Gene Wolfe used science fiction for serious literary purposes, political and sexual radicalism. Among mainstream writers of science fiction include Aldous Huxley and George Orwell (Deut. 18:22; Isa. 9:15; Jer. 14:14 and 23:16).

Orwell was an English author and essayist whose works include the satire *Animal Farm* (1945), known for its provocative maxim: "All animals are equal, but some are more equal than others." Orwell's prophetic *Nineteen Eighty-Four* (1949) portrayed excessive state control over individuals. Aldous Huxley (1894–1963) was also an English writer and novelist whose *Brave New World* depicted an emotionless society of the future in which humans are laboratory mass-produced under the control of omnipotent "Big Brother."

Satirical disillusionment characterized Huxley's works. In his brave new world there is a pill for everyone. His later devotion to mysticism presumably led to experimentation with the hallucinogenic drug, mescaline, used also in religious rites by some North American Indians. At Huxley's deathbed, Harvard-trained Dr. Timothy Leary was said to have administered the psychodelic drug and hallucinogen, LSD, which often produces states resembling psychosis—e.g., schizophrenia. Leary was best known for his misguided *mantra*: "Turn on; tune in; drop out."

Aldous was the brother of Julian Huxley—English biologist, Fabian socialist, co-founder and first director-general of the United Nations Educational, Scientific, and Cultural Organization (UNESCO). Sir Julian was a member of Winston Churchill's so-called secret circle. He founded what is now called the Worldwide Fund for Nature. Given legal status by the *Biodiversity Treaty* (1992), this powerful non-governmental organization (NGO) boasts a global network of affiliates. Aldous was the grandson of English scientist Thomas Henry Huxley, who founded scientific humanism. Known as "Darwin's bulldog" for championing *On the Origin of Species* (1859), Thomas eventually admitted that evolution is no more than "tentative hypothesis."

Eerily, Wells' prophecies, Orwell's satire, and Huxley's futuristic disillusionment smack of twenty-first-century reality. Biblical signs of end times include one-world government (a New World Order), deceptively unjust egalitarianism (with some deemed "more equal" than others), and mandated submission to "Big Brother" (Rev. 13:1, 4–18).

Utopian Atlantis

Atlantis is a legendary ancient city (or island) existing at the helm of a world government based on ten geo-political regions. Said to contain elements of democracy, Atlantis is thought to represent the ideal, as envisioned by Nazism and Marxism. Hitler searched in vain not only for the Ark of the Covenant, the Holy Grail, and the sword that pierced Christ—but also for Atlantis. Nevertheless, his hapless future was no utopia. It included marrying his mistress, Eva Braun, and—on the following day, in April of 1945—committing suicide with her.

The ultimate rational system of Marxism is a sort of secular vision of the kingdom of God. Despite numerous Marxist-inspired revolutions worldwide, the empty promise of a classless utopian society has yet to actualize. Notwithstanding, Atlantis has been continuously reinvented dating back to the time of Plato and claiming locations as diverse as Guatemala, the Arctic North, and Santorini, Greece. Today, one organization is actively recruiting "freedom-loving citizens" with promise of a New Atlantis in the Caribbean—first of a new sovereign nation to be called *Oceania*.

Many believe the occult pyramid symbol on the one-dollar bill to be rooted in Atlantis. Despite hoopla, most authorities agree that Atlantis exists only in minds of those prone to imagine an ancient utopia as source for occult teachings. Born in Kentucky (1877), Edgar Cayce initiated the modern marriage of holistic health to the world of the occult. Although Cayce lacked medical training, he gave thousands of readings while in trances that involved medical diagnosis and advice. Furthermore, Cayce prophesied the come back of Atlantis.

What Plato, Hitler, and Cayce overlooked was this: "Except the Lord build the house, they labor in vain that build it" (Ps. 127:1).

Utopian *Novus Ordo Seclorum*

Novus Ordo Seclorum is Latin for "New World [without God] Order of the Ages," avowed aim of Illuminists and secular internationalists. Utopianism is about building a new society apart from God. It is likened to fashioning one's own Tower of Babel. Having personally scaled its counterpart, called the Spiral Minaret in desolate Iraq, I possess first hand knowledge of the pathetic, sun-baked brick residue of mankind's pitiful impertinence before the living God (Gen. 11).

Creation of a New Atlantis in North America is what Masonic authority Manly P. Hall identified as the unifying goal of secret societies. Hall further claimed that Freemasonry originated in Atlantis. It was Atlanteans, he added, who devised the Masonic "Great Plan" whereby the world would be directed toward global government. According to Hall, the U.S. is destined to restore the legacy of Lost Atlantis.

In his book, *The Secret Destiny of America,* Hall revealed that secret societies have worked for centuries to create an enlightened democracy, a *Novus Ordo Seclorum,* its roots planted in the American colonies. Hall claimed that, shortly after the Pilgrims, adepts arrived at Plymouth. An adept's assignment, said Hall, was to prepare our nation to become a secular state fated to reconstitute Atlantis and, thus, to rule the world. Adepts are highly evolved enlightened ones, allegedly qualified to lord over less accomplished esoterics in pursuit of similar goals.

Utopian Self-god

To be sustained, utopianism requires human perfection. Toward this end, New Age occultists hope to achieve the higher self.

They believe that multiple reincarnations with upward mobility provide needed opportunities to progress from embryo-god to ultimate oneness with the god-force, a human's highest destiny. By becoming god, these undertake the noble mission of producing balanced communities that boast group fusion and alignment.

"Triangles" is a meditation technique created by occultist and co-Masonic hierarch Alice Bailey. The idea is to line up energies of light and goodwill worldwide. For this phenomenon to be realized, one must discard individual thinking for group think—that is, collaborative consciousness sacrificing absolutes (e.g., the Ten Commandments) to ensure social harmony.

Repeated themes of the New Age movement are collaborative partnerships, global transformation, inter-religious cooperation, and earth stewardship mobilizing the planetary resource base toward ensuring a sustainable future—all in the name of world peace. In 1995, self-proclaimed demi-god the Dalai Lama, Aquarian conspiracist Marilyn Ferguson, global elitist Prince Bernhardt, and occultist Robert Muller gathered at the Spirit of Peace Conference sponsored by the UN University of Peace. The featured agenda called for an utopian New World Order.

The Bible prophesies that global allies, as these, will gather together in a unified mindset that controverts the pure doctrine of Christ. Ultimately, their utopian aspirations will require submission to Antichrist, whose mission is to undermine godliness by exalting man as the measure of all things. The Bible warns that these last days are characterized by self-love, even to the point of pantheistic self-deification by earning so-called egoic advancement. Though world peace is their claim, sudden destruction will be the unexpected reality (Rev. 17:13–14; 2 Tim. 3:2; 2 Thess. 2:4; 1 Thess. 5:3).

Utopian Commonism

Charles Darwin's historic optimism contends that, apart from God, and with the passing of time, human thinking, philosophy, and destiny are improving progressively toward a sort of utopia. This sentiment mirrors the Masonic pledge to "take good men and make them better." According to Masonic author, Charles Van Cott,

Masons need no faith in supernatural forces to fulfill this lofty charge. Not so according to Genesis 1:26 (Van Cott 1959).

Darwinian dogma took root in the late 1800s among intellectuals who promoted one-world Illuminist ideals in hopes of achieving global socialism by a succession of gradual reforms. Famous associates of the Fabian Socialist Movement included John Dewey, Dr. Annie Besant, H.G. Wells, and George Bernard Shaw whose impact on education, politics, literature, and the arts, respectively, dare not be underestimated.

The *Communist Manifesto* (1848) rehashes Illuminist Adam Weishaupt's writings and puts forward the theory that human society, having evolved through successive stages of slavery, feudalism, and capitalism, must then advance to communism. The jacket cover of *The Coming Century of Commonism* by Philip C. Born defines yesterday's "*-isms*" as communism and capitalism. The "*-ism*" of tomorrow, Born claims, is commonism. Four commissions laid the groundwork for commonism. International socialist David Multrany pioneered the path, followed by former West German Socialist Chancellor Willy Brandt and Gro Harlem Brundtland, Norwegian prime minister and vice-president of the World Socialist Party.

With the feigned fall of revolutionary communism, commonism was born. Its utopian ideology embraces the global commons and village, egalitarianism and interdependence, democracy and ecology, interconnectedness and global spirituality, disarmament and world peace. In the name of "the common heritage of mankind," commonism transforms private intellectual assets and nationally controlled natural resources into common property. Its dream takes form in urban clusters applauding an agrarian society designed to ease Big Brother control of human activities, reproduction, and wealth.

Tom DeWeese of the American Policy Center speaks of the dawn of this new era in which "national identities and individual religions appear to be morphing into nondescript and indistinguishable arrangements to some unidentified whole." Its would-be utopian hope is a spirit of cooperation resulting in global prosperity and increased standards of living worldwide (DeWeese 2000).

Utopian War-free Society

South African politician Cecil Rhodes favored world dominion under a ruling elite—this, by federating the English-speaking world under Anglo-Saxon rule. Professor John Ruskin mentored Rhodes. An occultist, Ruskin passed on to Rhodes and his subsequent scholars (Bill Clinton, for example) his dream for the "parliament of men" and "federation of the world" in the words of English poet laureate Alfred L. Tennyson. A member of the occult Society for Psychical Research, Tennyson popularized Rhodes' belief that Great Britain had a moral mandate to consolidate the world under British rule. Self-proclaimed "reddest of the red," Ruskin read Plato daily. Himself an advocate of Plato utopianism, Rhodes fabricated a plan including the founding of "so great a power as to hereafter render wars impossible." Nonetheless, his utopian ideal was to be achieved by means of chaos, or engineered crisis—e.g., environmental and energy crises, the AIDS crisis, global terrorism.

Utopian "Big Brother"

Utopianism is rooted in hollow belief that humanity's problems can be solved by human creation of a completely just society. A socialist is one who believes that the way to achieve good things is to have government do it. Denying personal responsibility, utopian myths foster increasing dependence on the all-powerful State. However, author-historian Dr. Stan Monteith warns that a government expected to provide everything one *needs* can also take away everything one *has*. Trinity Law Professor James Hirsen adds that "the origin of the grand experiment we call America was based upon divinely inspired and uniquely political perspective that individual rights do *not* come from government, but instead are endowed to mankind by the Creator."

Utopian "One World; One Species"

Myth of Overpopulation

According to the *Washington Times* (10 February 1999), overpopulation is not a problem in the U.S., nor is it in many other countries. All the while the UN is spreading overpopulation hysteria, another UN agency is releasing data which clearly demonstrate that the real population problem is too few children. According to the National Center on Health Statistics, only eleven states have replacement-level populations. The rest have below-replacement fertility rates. President of the Howard Center for Family, Religion, and Society in Rockford, Illinois, Allan Carlson agrees. He anticipates the population issue of the twenty-first century to be depopulation, not overpopulation.

International Population Reduction Plans

The ideal is to pinpoint, nurture, and place illumined, group conscious, politically eco-correct world citizens in the viable work force of the global community. To this end, international population reduction plans purpose to eliminate non-producers, as the elderly, and undesirables—those not so smart or beautiful, including the comatose, disabled, terminally ill, severely depressed, or mentally impaired.

Today's death culture is at the heart of international population reduction plans to ensure sustainability. Even as cleric Thomas Malthus advocated planned genocide, biologicals, famine, viruses, and diseases to do the job, the genocidal agenda of the environmental movement promotes elimination of people as the best way to protect earth. The idea is not new. In *The Impact of Science on Society*, Bertrand Russell (born 1872) encouraged population control by means of bacteriological warfare.

Dr. Stan Monteith calls Acquired Immune Deficiency Syndrome (AIDS) "the unnecessary epidemic." As a virus, AIDS is a medical concern, but instead has been treated as a civil-rights issue. It is the first politically protected disease, receiving the greatest number of tax dollars per death. Efforts to use standard public health measures to control the epidemic have been blocked consistently.

As a result, since the 1980s, over sixteen million have died of opportunistic complications on the heels of this dreaded syndrome.

PROACTIVE POPULATION CONTROL

Utopianism depends on the right kind of people. A professor at John Hopkins University, Simon Newcomb argued that "love of mankind at large should prompt us to take such measures as shall discourage or prevent the bringing forth of children by the pauper and criminal classes. No measure of repression would be too severe in the attainment of the latter objective."

A SUPERIOR RACE

When Darwinism was popularized in the 1870s and 1880s, William Graham Sumner applied survival of the fittest to understanding the poverty problem. He aligned with Newcomb in believing that nature rightly removes those who have "survived their usefulness"—for example, the drunkard in the gutter. Based on supremacy of the State over the individual, Nazism obsesses on a racist version of Darwin's survival of the fittest. In the 1930s and 1940s, Nazi Germany erroneously promulgated the notion of Aryans as a white-skinned, blue-eyed, fair-haired, super-master race.

Even today, humanists look for a superior race, their motto being, "one world; one species." Secular humanists hope to control evolution by means of genetic engineering—deliberately manipulating genetic material by biochemical techniques. Often achieved by introducing new DNA (deoxyribonucleic acid), genetic engineering is used to improve hereditary qualities. Accordingly, today's trend in e-commerce is to assist women in their aspirations to give birth to smart or beautiful babies—this, by artificial insemination.

Utopian Redistribution of the World's Wealth (Globalization)

Redistribution of the world's wealth, called globalization, actually expands poverty by taking away wealth and the incentive to produce it. A better idea is to share America's unparalleled freedom technology with the world. Nonetheless, the Global Resource Bank

Proposal *(Prospectus, 3)* suggests equally dividing assets of the entire world among all global citizens. In a 1974 report entitled the *New International Economic Order*, the UN General Assembly outlined a plan to redistribute the world's wealth.

Some might be surprised to learn that Karl Marx is quoted as having said this: "Free trade breaks up old nationalities. In a word, the free trade system hastens the social revolution. Gentlemen, I am in favor of free trade." Conversely, George Washington, Thomas Jefferson, Henry Clay, and Abraham Lincoln opposed the global theory of free trade that siphons off America's wealth, bringing her economy to the level of others (socialism). In Matthew 26:11, Jesus made it clear that we have the poor always with us. Better to teach them to fish for a lifetime of benefit than to provide fish for a single meal.

Utopian Culture of Peace

Rooted in the 1992 Rio Earth Summit, the *Earth Charter* is a type of planetary commandment—a Bill of Rights, if you will. Led by Maurice Strong, the Costa Rican Earth Council is in the process of drafting, refining, and implementing the *Earth Charter*. To enforce necessary environmental regulations worldwide, the charter will be imposed through global governance. Its utopian ideal follows: ". . . We are one human family and one Earth community with a common destiny. We must join together to bring forth a sustainable global society founded on respect for nature, universal human rights, economic justice, and a culture of peace."

God's True Utopia: The Millennium

God's *true* utopia is no sci-fi Atlantis consisting of a superior race of demi-gods sharing equally earth's ever-depleting resources. It is a New World Order of an entirely different sort. The Bible defines a thousand-year, post end-times period when Christ and His co-regents will take charge of earth. Then, every knee will bow to Jesus. All will confess Him to be Lord of the universe. At long last, Satan and his cohorts will be rendered ineffective (Phil. 2:9–11; Rev. 20:1–3; Isa. 24:21–22; Jude 6).

Not to be mistaken with "Y2K," the Millennium promises an altogether new dispensation on earth—that of deliverance, righteousness, liberty, peace, and restoration not unlike the Garden of Eden prior to the Fall. Throughout the Millennial rule and reign of Christ, the King of kings' subjects will be blessed with non-compromised spiritual revelation, righteous leadership, and a subdued animal kingdom. They will revel in unprecedented regeneration and renewal, great light and prosperity. None will suffer sickness. No longer a counterfeit, but God's true utopia one day will sweep earth with universal, experiential knowledge of the Lord. When the Prince of Peace returns, He will reprove the world of sin *(hamartia)*. At long last, the prince of this world (Satan) and his cadre will acquiesce to divine sanctions (Isa. 11:6–9, 30:18–20, 32:16–18, 33:24; Joel 2:25; Rom. 8:21–22; Ps. 77; Matt. 19:29; John 16:8–11).

Even so, come, Lord Jesus (Rev. 22:20).

CHAPTER 24

CONCLUSION
THE SIN FACTOR RESOLVED

> If we confess our sins [*hamartia*], He is faithful and righteous to forgive us our sins [*hamartia*] and to cleanse us from all unrighteousness. If we say that we have not sinned [*hamartanō*], we make Him a liar, and His word is not in us (1 John 1:8–10 NASB).

Born again or not, all grapple with sin. However quick we are to stumble into failings of the flesh, manifest carnality is not the enemy's lone trap. Subject to his wiles, many Christians remain ensnared in the crippling stranglehold of deceit. Deception, by definition, suggests subtlety and stealth. Deceived people are blinded to their own error. With their minds thus darkened, many brethren unknowingly serve as accomplices of the enemy.

God's Word

Be sure, any standard other than the "more sure word" misleads the gullible with the inevitable backlash of deception, which only Bible truth can expose and extricate. Sharper than any two-edged sword, God's Word alone surgically separates truth from error—be it intentional or unwitting, attitude or behavior, subtle or flagrant, an isolated incident or repeated pattern (2 Pet. 1:19; Heb. 4:12).

The plastic knife of feel-good psychobabble cannot begin to do the job of God's sharp and infinitely powerful sword of the living Word. Nonetheless, many ministers set aside the latter. Rather than study Scripture to show themselves approved, these load their bookshelves with self-help manuals and usher their callow flocks into gimmicky workshops—all in vain pursuit of personal fulfillment. Be assured that substituting Bartlett's quotations for scriptural passages, programs for Bible study, and entertainment for spiritual ministry fails to expose deception, rampant in the church these last days (2 Tim. 2:15; Matt. 24:24).

More often than not, America's Christians have come to feel at home with the world's latest fads, fashions, philosophies, politics, and entertainment all the while they mirror Saul's daughter, Michal, in being ill at ease with (and disdainful toward) unfamiliar manifestations of God's Spirit. Not to offend, many more broach tenets of their faith in timid whispers, if at all. Image all too often takes preeminence over holiness (James 4:4; 2 Sam. 6:16; 2 Tim. 1:8; 1 Sam. 16:7).

Those bereft of any clear time line for Bible eschatology recite flawlessly tonight's prime time television line up. While they stumble through verse two of the church's time-honored hymns, many youth rattle off from memory commercial jingles interjected incessantly throughout their favorite television or radio programs.

Conscience

While geo-political prowess, philosophical savvy, and a well-formed theological grid are not prerequisites for right standing with God, freedom from sin is. Simply put, sin separates us from God. This being the case, it stands to reason that we must separate sin from us (Rom. 1:18; Heb. 12:1).

Toward this end, God adds to the plumb line of His written Word a support mechanism that He graciously places within each of us. This we call "conscience." When healthy, our consciences discern between right and wrong regarding moral conduct. Whenever we miss the mark, God tweaks our consciences. Yielding to God's distress signal, we sigh deeply in repentance for having displeased Him. But be warned. Repeated refusal to pay attention cauterizes the conscience, rendering it unserviceable for godly purposes (1 Pet. 3:16; 1 Tim. 4:2).

Holy Spirit Empowerment

Without fail, it is truth that sets free and accomplishes God's bidding. Truth alone eradicates deception. Through His gift of the Holy Spirit, God guides us in all truth as expounded throughout His holy and unerring Word. Furthermore, He shows us of things to come. Given dogged advancement of Antichrist's great delusion, Christians need all the more to be fully armed with truth. Hence, added to Holy Writ, they require a limitless supply of Holy Spirit empowerment (John 8:32; 1 John 5:6; John 16:13; 2 Thess. 2:11; Eph. 6:13).

In the good fight resisting the so-called mystery of iniquity, we do well to ask (and keep on asking), to seek (and keep on seeking), and to knock (and keep on knocking) until we receive dynamite power from on high, as did the 120 in the upper room. Even then, we persist in praying for continuous refilling of the Spirit to overflowing levels (1 Tim. 6:12; 2 Thess. 2:7; Luke 11:9–13; Acts 1:8; Eph. 5:18).

A popular Breakthrough Series book by Dr. Bruce H. Wilkinson scrutinizes the most remarkable prayer of an honorable man. Jabez called upon the God of Israel with a four-fold request that God *bless* him, *expand* and then *empower* his ministry, and *preserve* him from evil. According to the first chapter of Acts, the Holy Spirit baptism fell on believers who demonstrated *homos* ("same") and *thumos* ("mind"), Greek for "one accord" (verse 14). No doubt the cry of their united heart mirrored that of Jabez. They, too, sought blessing, increase, empowerment, and safekeeping from evil (1 Chron. 4:10).

In cases of Jabez and upper-room seekers, God heard and freely granted their requests. And so it is with us today. Perceptive, sensitive mindfulness of one another, unity among brethren, and spiritual anointing combat complacency, infirmity, and weakness among our ranks (1 Cor. 11:29; 2 Cor. 13:11).

Unspoiled by prosperity, Job, as Jabez, was an upright man whom God allowed Satan to test. While Job's integrity remained intact throughout the season of his trial, God nonetheless spoke to him words of instruction, even reproof. Curiously, the name Jabez means "to grieve." Grieving for his sin, Job likewise sighed heavily, repenting in dust and ashes (Job 42:6).

Repentance (Dust and Ashes)

The lowest of all elements are dust and ashes, and biblical reference to them depicts the humiliation caused by sin. In the Old Testament, to throw dust or dirt at someone signals shame; moreover, mourning is expressed by various acts of self-abasement, which may include throwing dust or dirt on one's own head (2 Sam. 16:13; Josh. 7:6).

The expression, "dust and ashes," is a play on words, *aphar* and *epher*, signifying the body's being composed of ordinary chemical elements—and thus contrasting the lowliness of man with the grandeur of God. When Job covered himself with dust, he acknowledged before God that, minus imputed righteousness, he was nothing but dirt (Ps. 22:6).

Ultimately, the human body returns to dust. Recall that God cursed the serpent with dust as his perpetual food. As meat nourishes human bodies, the dust of humanity's fleshly sin nature sustains the Devil. Sobriety and vigilance are crucial in that the Devil, as a roaring lion, seeks whom he might devour (Eccles. 3:20; Isa. 65:25; 1 Pet. 5:8).

Sin is immeasurably destructive not only by virtue of its impact, but also because it invokes the anger and judgment of God. Repentance from sin recognizes that pursuing and, then, continuing in sin is utter folly. Most assuredly, God will bring down murderers and deceivers (Prov. 22:7–9; 2 Sam. 22:43; Ps. 55:23).

True repentance involves our putting away those things that the Devil can feed upon. Therefore, as believers, we must set aside every encumbrance and sin prone to entangle us. Doing so frees us to run with endurance the momentous race of life. By honing our consciences, yielding to the Spirit of God, and brandishing the sword of His Word, we avoid becoming tasty morsels to satisfy the voracious appetite of our enemy (Heb. 12:1).

As previously indicated, the Hebrew word translated "repentance" implies a sense of grief for sin; however, feeling bad in itself can invoke shame that, if unchecked, leads to condemnation, hopelessness, and spiritual defeat. In Christ, none of these are acceptable upshots. Paul rejoiced, not that the Corinthians were made sorrowful, but that they were made sorrowful to the point of repentance (Rom. 8:1).

In Psalm 72:9, to experience defeat is "to lick the dust"; and in Isaiah 52:2, to be restored from defeat is "to shake oneself from the dust." Repeatedly, the repentant sinner may cast his or her burden of sin upon the Lord, who will never allow the righteous to be utterly shaken (2 Cor. 7:8–11; Ps. 55:22).

Rather than succumb to the path of defeat, righteous Job allowed God to open his eyes in new ways. While a just man may indeed stumble and fall the proverbial seven times, he nonetheless picks up himself, dusts off, and carries on with fortified resolve (Prov. 24:16).

As is the case with "dust and ashes," Isaiah's lovely expression, "beauty from ashes," is likewise a play on words. Having humbled himself before God, and having endured his test with impeccable integrity, Job enjoyed restored prosperity and, more significantly, spiritual beauty from the ashes of defeat (Isa. 61:3).

A Change of Direction

True, we are commanded to "sin not"; but if in weakness or ignorance we do miss the mark, our heavenly defense attorney, Jesus Christ, is no further than a call away! When we freely confess to Him, He faithfully forgives and cleanses us. As one called alongside to help, Jesus not only covers our sins, but also comforts our distress over them (Titus 3:4–6; Phil. 2:12; Rom. 12:21; 2 Cor. 7:1; 1 John 1:9–10; 2:1–2).

God saves us according to His mercy, not our works. Once contrition arises from awareness of guilt, and we have contemplated sin's moral implications, we confess our failings to God and, then, repent. Simply put, to repent is to reverse a previous decision. As with due diligence we master a longhand, multi-digit division problem, we then work out our personal salvation with watchfulness, always in reverent submission to Him. Never are we overcome, for God faithfully leads the way to redemption, regeneration, a change of direction, vindication, and zeal (Phil. 2:12; 2 Cor. 7:11).

Moreover, God alone creates desire and provides capacity to extract sin and, in turn, to accomplish His own good pleasure in our lives. Once the choice is made to retain Spirit-empowered godliness in accordance with God's Word, we increasingly avoid the persistent tug of our lower nature and, all the more diligently, we aspire to moral excellence. With moral excellence comes knowledge and with knowledge, self-control. Scripture teaches that perseverance, godliness, brotherly kindness, and love, in turn, spring from self-control. Given these ever-increasing virtues and the boundless grace of God, we elude altogether the wasteland of sin and its inevitable consequences (2 Pet. 1:4–11; Gal. 5:16; Phil. 2:13).

The alternatives are plain: Will it be Bible truth, or grave consequences? With God's help, may we never fail to "buy the truth, and sell it not" (Prov. 23:23).

Select Bibliography

Chapter 1—*The Sin Factor*

Ashton, John F., Ph.D. 2000. *In Six Days*. Green Forest, AR: Master Books.

Breese, David. 1980. *7 Men Who Rule from the Grave*. Oklahoma City: SW Radio Church.

Rogers, Adrian. 2000. *Love Worth Finding* (February 6). Memphis: TBN.

Wright, Jack, Jr. 1994. *Freud's War with God: Psychoanalysis Versus Religion*. Lafayette, Louisiana: Huntington House Publishers.

Chapter 2—*Anti-Semitism*

Chilton, David. 1985. *Paradise Restored*. Tyler, Texas: Reconstruction Press: 224.

Levy, David M. 1992. *Malachi: Messenger of Rebuke and Renewal*. Bellmawr, New Jersey: The Friends of Israel Gospel Ministry, Inc.

Levy, David M. 1993. *The Tabernacle: Shadows of the Messiah—Its Sacrifices, Services, and Priesthood*. Bellmawr, New Jersey: The Friends of Israel Gospel Ministry, Inc.

McGregor, Jeff. 2000. *Slavery in Sudan: A Report on Slavery in the Context of Other Human Rights Abuses*. Seattle: Philosophy 338, University of Washington.

Rausch, David. 1988. *Building Bridges: Understanding Jews and Judaism*. Chicago: Moody Press: 87–171.

Rushdoony, Rousas John. 1970. *Thy Kingdom Come: Studies in Daniel and Revelation*. Fairfax, Virginia: Thoburn Press: 82.

Chapter 3—*Compassionless Conservatism*

Olasky, Marvin. 1999. *Compassionate Conservatism* and *The American Leadership Tradition*. New York: The Free Press, A Division of Simon & Schuster, Inc.

Chapter 4—*Cultism*

Breese, David. 1997. "The Marks of a Cult." *Midnight Call*. West Columbia, South Carolina: Midnight Call Ministries (November and December).

Martin, Stephen D., M. Div. 1997. "Hazardous Misconceptions about Cults." *Midnight Call*. West Columbia, South Carolina: Midnight Call Ministries (September).

Martin, Walter. 1977. *The Kingdom of the Cults*. Minneapolis: Bethany Fellowship, Inc., Publishers.

Chapter 5—*Darwinism*

Ashton, John F., Ph.D. 2000. *In Six Days: Why Fifty Scientists Choose to Believe in Creation*. Green Forest, Arkansas: Master Books.

Barnett, D. L. 1974. *A Startling Revelation on the Inspiration of the Bible*. Seattle: Community Chapel Publications.

Brown, Dr. Walter. 2001. *In the Beginning*. Phoenix: Center for Scientific Creation.

Duncan, Homer. 1980. *Evolution: The Incredible Hoax*. Lubbock: Missionary Crusader.

Hart, James L. 1997. *Eugenic Manifesto*. Washington, D.C.: Prometheus Press: 1, 32.

Chapter 6—*Democratic Transnationalism*

Allen, Gary. 1971. *None Dare Call It Conspiracy*. Rossmoor, California: Concord Press.

Allen, Gary. 1976. *The Rockefeller File*. Clackamas, Oregon: Emissary Publications.

Bluemel, Craig. 1996. *Announcing the Birth of the New World [Without God] Order*. Seattle: The Bible Answer Stand Ministry.

Bluemel, Craig. 1996. *The Jewish Cabala, Spiritual Inspiration for the New World Order*. Seattle: The Bible Answer Stand Ministry.

Bowen, William. 1984. *Globalism: America's Demise*. Lafayette, Louisiana: Huntington House Publishers.

Celebration of Sovereignty. 1996. Seattle: Hope for the Word (October).

Commission on Global Governance. 1995. *Our Global Neighborhood: The Report of the Commission on Global Governance.* New York: Oxford University Press.

Hansen, Carol Rae, ed. 1992. *The New World Order: Rethinking America's Global Role.* Flagstaff: Arizona Honors Academy Press.

Hirsen, James L., Ph.D. 1999. *Government by Decree: From President to Dictator Through Executive Orders* and *The Coming Collision: Global Law vs. U.S. Liberties.* Lafayette, Louisiana: Huntington House Publishers.

Kah, Gary H. 1992. *En Route to Global Occupation.* Lafayette, Louisiana: Huntington House Publishers.

Kah, Gary H. 1995. *The Demonic Roots of Globalism: En Route to Spiritual Deception.* Lafayette, Louisiana: Huntington House Publishers.

Kincaid, Cliff. 1995. *Global Bondage: The UN Plan to Rule the World.* Lafayette, Louisiana: Huntington House Publishers.

McAlvany, Don. 1993. *The Fourth Reich, Toward an American Police State.* Oklahoma City: Southwest Radio Church.

McManus, John F. 1996. "Conspiracy for Global Control." *The New American* (16 September): vol. 12 no. 19.

Rae, Debra. 1999. *ABCs of Globalism: A Vigilant Christian's Glossary.* Lafayette, Louisiana: Huntington House Publishers.

Still, William T. 1990. *New World Order: The Ancient Plan of Secret Societies.* Lafayette, Louisiana: Huntington House Publishers.

Tamedly, Elisabeth L. 1969. *Socialism and International Economic Order.* Cardwell, Idaho: The Caxton Printers, Ltd.

Teichrib, Carl. 2000. "The Most Trusted Man in America?" *Hope for the World Update.* Noblesville, Indiana: Hope for the World (Winter): 11.

Webster, Nesta H. 1924. *Secret Societies and Subversive Movements.* London: Boswell Printing & Publishing Co., Ltd.

Chapter 7—*Ecumenicism*

Carter, Jimmy. 1996. *Living Faith.* New York: Times Books, a division of Random House.

Colson, Charles and Anne Morse. 1997. *Burden of Truth: Defending Truth in an Age of Unbelief*. Wheaton: Tyndale House Publishers, Inc.

McCluney, Ross. 1994. "Sustainable Values." *Ethics & Agenda 21: Moral Implications of a Global Consensus*. New York: United Nations Environment Programme: 21.

Chapter 8—*Pseudo Egalitarianism*

Flynn, Ted. 2000. *Hope of the Wicked: The Master Plan to Rule the World*. Sterling, Virginia: MaxKol Communications, Inc.

Monteith, Dr. Stanley. 2000. *Brotherhood of Darkness*. Oklahoma City: Hearthstone Publishing.

Chapter 9—*Extreme Fundamentalism*

1983. "Exposé: Good Churches Slandered as Cults." *Balance Magazine*. Seattle: Community Chapel Publications (no. 2).

Blavatsky, Helena Petrovna. 1994. *The Secret Doctrine: The Synthesis of Science, Religion and Philosophy*. Wheaton: Theosophical Publishing House.

Chapter 10—*Globalism* (See **Chapter 6**—*Democratic Transnationalism*)

Chapter 11—*Jingoism*

Barton, David. 1999. *A Video Tour of the Spiritual Heritage of the United States Capitol*. Aledo, Texas: Wall Builders.

Christian Defense Fund Staff. 1997. *One Nation Under God, America's Christian Heritage*. Springfield, Virginia: Christian Defense Fund.

Hart, Benjamin. 1997. *Faith & Freedom: The Christian Roots of American Liberty*. Alexandria, Virginia: Christian Defense Fund.

Chapter 12—*Liberalism*

Borst, W.A., Ph.D. 1999. *Liberalism: Fatal Consequences*. Lafayette, Louisiana: Huntington House Publishers.

Bossie, David N. and Floyd G. Brown. 2000. *Prince Albert, The Life and Lies of Al Gore*. Bellevue, Washington: Merril Press.

Reardon, David C. and Amy Sobie. 1999. *Kate Michelman: A Case Study on Post-Abortion Trauma*. (January–March): vol. 7, no. 1.

Chapter 13—*Materialism*

Davis, June N. 1992. *Scripture Keys for Kingdom Living*. Denver: Scripture Keys Ministries.

Chapter 14—*New Age Mysticism*

1985. "Ecumenism, 'Global Spirituality' and Mother Teresa." *Christian Inquirer*. (April): 26.

Baer, Randall. 1989. *Inside the New Age Nightmare*. Lafayette, Louisiana: Huntington House Publishers.

Bluemel, Craig. 1996. *New Age Symbols and the Meanings—A Warning*. Seattle: The Bible Answer Stand Ministry.

Cumbey, Constance. 1985. *A Planned Deception: The Staging of a New Age "Messiah."* East Detroit, Michigan: Pointe Publishers, Inc.

Cumbey, Constance. 1985. *Hidden Dangers of the Rainbow: The New Age Movement and Our Coming Age of Barbarism*. Lafayette, Louisiana: Huntington House Publishers.

Doig, Desmond. 1990. *Mother Teresa: Her People and Her Work*:156, as quoted by Dave Hunt, *Global Peace and the Rise of Antichrist*:149.

1998. *Into the Sun*. Ramona, California: Lemurian Fellowship.

Rizzuti, James. 1997. "Diana, Teresa, and Deception." *Let's Talk Prophecy Newsletter*. Holly Springs, Georgia: Kathy Hooper Ministries.

Sanford, Agnes. 1972. *The Healing Light*. New York: Ballantine Books.

Scott, Brenda and Samantha Smith. 1993. *Trojan Horse: How the New Age Movement Infiltrates the Church*. Lafayette, Louisiana: Huntington House Publishers.

Tuoti, Frank X. 1995. *Why Not Be a Mystic?* New York: The Crossroad Publishing Company.

World Goodwill Quarterly Bulletin. 1992. "A Matter of Energy." *World Goodwill Newsletter.* New York: Lucis Trust: no. 1–2.

Chapter 15—*Occultism*

Dobson, Dr. James. 1992. "Satanism." *Information from Focus on the Family*. Colorado Springs: Focus on the Family: 1–12.

Kirban, Salem. 1980. *Satan's Angels Exposed*. Huntington Valley, Pennsylvania: Salem Kirban, Inc.

Pollard, Jeff. 1984. "Halloween: Whose Celebration Is It?" *The Evangelist* (October).

Spence, Lewis. 1960. *An Encyclopedia of Occultism.* Secaucus, New Jersey: The Citadel Press.

Warnke, Michael A. 1991. *Schemes of Satan.* Tulsa: Victory House, Inc.

Wright, Robin G. 1985. "Halloween: Satan's Celebration." *Christian Life* (October).

Chapter 16—*Postmodernism*

Baxter, Ern. et. al. 1980. *Secular Humanism: Man Striving to be God.* Milford, Michigan: A New Wine book co-published by Integrity Publications and Mott Media.

Duncan, Homer. 1980. *Secular Humanism: The Most Dangerous Religion in America.* Lubbock: Missionary Crusader.

Duncan, Homer. 1981. *Humanism in the Light of Holy Scriptures.* Lubbock: Missionary Crusader.

Kurtz, Paul. 1979. *Humanist Manifestos I and II.* Buffalo: Prometheus Books.

McIlhenny, Chuck and Donna. 1993. *When the Wicked Seize a City.* Lafayette, Louisiana: Huntington House Publishers.

Smith, Samantha. 1993. *Goddess Earth: Exposing the Pagan Agenda of the Environmental Movement.* Lafayette, Louisiana: Huntington House Publishers.

Thibodaux, David, Ph.D. 1994. *Beyond Political Correctness: Are There Limits to This Lunacy?* Lafayette, Louisiana: Huntington House Publishers.

Veith, Gene Edward. 2000. "Beasts are People, Too." *World Magazine* (27 May): 16.

Wyman, Hastings, Jr. 1994. "The Gay Agenda." *The Washington Blade.* Washington, D.C.: The Washington Blade (4 March): 35.

Chapter 17—*Progressivism*

Bernhoft, Robin, Ph.D. 1992. *Outcome-Based Education: Lobotomy by Robin Hood.* Seattle: PERC.

Blumenfeld, Samuel L. 1993. *NEA: Trojan Horse in American Education.* Phoenix: Research Publications.

Counts, G. S. 1934. *The Social Foundations of Education.* New York: Charles Scribner's Sons.

Fields, Melanie K., Sarah H. Leslie, and Anita B. Hoge. 1995. "When Johnny Takes the Test." *The Christian Conscience.* Des Moines: The Christian Conscience.

Gabler, Mel and Norma. 1987. *What Are They Teaching Our Children?* Wheaton: Victor Books, A Division of SP Publications, Inc.

Hefley, James C. 1979. *Are Textbooks Harming Your Children?* Milford, Michigan: Mott Media.

Huck, Susan L. M. 1980. "Your Children and America's Established Religion, Secular Humanism." *American Opinion.* Belmont, Massachusetts: American Opinion (January).

Hyles, Jack, Ph.D. 1973. *Satan's Bid for Your Child.* Hammond: Hyles-Anderson Publishers.

Kennedy, D. James, Ph.D. 1993. *A Godly Education* and *Education: Public Problems and Private Solutions.* Ft. Lauderdale: Coral Ridge Ministries.

Kjos, Berit. 1995. *Brave New Schools.* Eugene, Oregon: Harvest House Publishers.

LaHaye, Tim. 1980. *The Battle for the Mind.* Old Tappan, New Jersey: Fleming H. Revell Company Power Books.

Lapin, Rabbi Daniel. 1999. *America's Real War.* Sisters, Oregon: Multnomah Publishers.

Luksik, Peg, and Pamela Hobbs Hoffecker. 1995. *Outcome-Based Education: The State's Assault on Our Children's Values.* Lafayette, Louisiana: Huntington House Publishers.

McGraw, Onalee. 1976. "Secular Humanism and the Schools: The Issue Whose Time Has Come." *Family Choice in Education: The New Imperative (Critical Issues Series).* Washington, D.C.: The Heritage Foundation.

Morris, Barbara. 1961. *The Religion of Humanism in Public Schools.* Boston: Houghton Mifflin Company.

Tabor, Ron. 1996. *Outcome-Based Education.* Olympia, Washington: Parents and Taxpayers Across Washington State to Elect Ron Tabor State Superintendent of Public Instruction.

U.S. Department of Education. 1996. *Grant Award Notification.* Washington, D.C.: Office of Elementary and Secondary Education.

Wolf, Wayne. 1993. "The Myth of Local Control." *Des Moines, Iowa Report*. Des Moines: Des Moines, Iowa Report.

Chapter 18—*Racism* (See **Chapter 2**—*Anti-Semitism*)

Chapter 19—*Rationalism*

Burtt, E. A. 1925. *Metaphysical Foundations of Modern Physical Science*, ch. ii and ii. London and New York: Encyclopedia Britannica.

Eddington, A. 1939. *Philosophy of Physical Science*. Cambridge and New York: Encyclopedia Britannica.

Hurst, J. F 1865. *History of Rationalism*. New York: Encyclopedia Britannica.

Lecky, W. 1914. *History of the Rise and Influence of the Spirit of Rationalism in Europe*, 2 vol. New York: Encyclopedia Britannica.

McCabe, J. 1920. *Biographical Dictionary of Modern Rationalists*. London: Encyclopedia Britannica.

McCabe, J. 1948. *A Rationalist Encyclopedia*. London: Encyclopedia Britannica.

Milne, E. A. 1952. *Modern Cosmology and the Christian Idea of God*. New York and Oxford: Encyclopedia Britannica.

Ross, W. D. 1939. *Foundations of Ethics*. Oxford and Toronto: Encyclopedia Britannica.

Russell, B. 1937. *A Critical Exposition of the Philosophy of Leibniz*. London and New York: Encyclopedia Britannica.

Chapter 20—*Syncretism*

Advance Report. 1996. *Preliminary Estimates from the 1995 National Household Survey on Drug Abuse, Substance Abuse, and Mental Health Services Administration Office of Applied Studies*. Washington, D.C.: Drug Abuse, Substance Abuse, and Mental Health Services Administration Office of Applied Studies (August).

Bailey, Alice A. 1948. *The Reappearance of the Christ*. New York: Lucis [formerly Lucifer] Trust Publishing Company: 158.

Casper, Paul. 1980. *Eastern Paths and the Christian Way*. Maryknoll, New York: Orbis Books: 108.

Crismier, Charles. 1999. *Out of Egypt: A Prophetic Call to the End-Time Church*. Enumclaw, Washington: WinePress Publishing.

Hunt, Dave. 1990. *Global Peace and the Rise of Antichrist.* Eugene, Oregon: Harvest House Publishers.

Kennedy, Dr. D. James. 2000. *Truth Report.* Ft. Lauderdale: Coral Ridge Ministries.

Kinman, Dwight L. 1993. *The World's Last Dictator.* Woodburn, Oregon: Solid Rock Books, Inc.

Scholem, Gershom. 1978. *Kabbalah.* New York: A Meridian Book published by the Penguin Group, Penguin Books.

Snell, Merwin-Marie. 1993. "Future of Religion," *The Dawn of Religious Pluralism: Voices from the World's Parliament of Religions.* La Salle, Illinois: Open Court/Council for a Parliament of the World's Religions: 174.

Chapter 21—*Terrorism*

Morey, Dr. Robert. 2000. "Islamic Invasion of America." Radio Liberty (with Dr. Stan Monteith). Santa Cruz, California (28 August).

Morey, Dr. Robert. 2001. "When is it Right to Fight?" Radio Liberty (with Dr. Stan Monteith). Santa Cruz, California (16 January).

Chapter 22—*A-Traditionalism*

Concerned Women for America. 1994. *The Shocking Truth behind the Government's Safe-Sex Lie.* Atlanta, Georgia: Families First! Resource Center.

Danford, John W. 2000. *Roots of Freedom.* Wilmington, Delaware: ISI Books: 148–49.

Limbaugh, Rush. 1992. *The Way Things Ought to Be.* New York: Pocket Books, A Division of Simon & Schuster, Inc.

Reisman, Dr. Judith A. and Edward W. Eichel. 1990. *Kinsey, Sex and Fraud, the Indoctrination of a People.* Lafayette, Louisiana: Huntington House Publishers.

Reuters. 1997. "Abortion Rate Down." Seattle: *The Seattle Times* (3 January).

Chapter 23—*Utopianism*

DeWeese, Tom. 2000. "Dawn of the Era of Commonism." *The DeWeese Report.* Herndon, Virginia: A publication of the American Policy Center, vol. 6, no. 11 (November).

Hall, Manley P. 1978. *The Secret Destiny of America.* Los Angeles: Philosophical Research Society, Inc.

Van Cott, Charles, 32nd Degree. 1959. *Freemasonry, A Sleeping Giant: Amazing Truths and Facts about Freemasonry.* Minneapolis: T. S. Denison & Company, Inc.: 61, 87, 139, 235.

Chapter 24—*The Sin Factor Resolved*

Wilkinson, Dr. Bruce H. 2000. *The Prayer of Jabez: Breaking Through to the Blessed Life.* Sisters, Oregon: Multnomah Publishers.

Web Sites

American Policy Center/
Insiders Report
www.americanpolicy.org

Biography Channel
www.biography.com

Colson, Chuck
www.breakpoint.org

Concerned Women for America
www.cwfa.org

Conservative Caucus
www.conservativeusa.org
www.conservativenews.org

Crismier, Chuck
www.saveus.org

DeWeese, Tom
www.deweeseonline.com

Dobson, James
www.citizenlink.org

Earth Charter
www.earthcharter.org

Globalism
www.garykah.org

Hirsen, James and Alan Keyes
www.americanewsnet.com

History Channel
www.historychannel.com

Huntington House Publishers
www.huntingtonhousebooks.com

Kjos, Berit
www.crossroad.to

Klayman, Larry
www.judicialwatch.org

La Haye, Beverly
http://icm.com Beverly_LaHaye_Today/ archives.asp

Lamb, Henry
www.freedom.org

Lapin, Dr.
www.towardtradition.org

Media Bias
www.mediaresearch.org

Missler, Chuck
http://www.khouse.org

Oliver North
www.freedomalliance.org

Population Research Institute
www.pop.org

Rogers, Adrian
www.lwf.org

Schlafly, Phyllis
www.eagleforum.org

Solomon, Stan
www.stansolomon.com

Newsletters

Access to Energy. 1997. Cave Junction, Oregon: Oregon Institute of Science and Medicine (March): vol. 24, no. 7.

Action Gram. 1996–present. Puyallup, Washington: Facts for Freedom.

AIM Report. 1995–1996. Washington, D.C.: Accurancy in Media, Inc.

Citizen. 1994–present. Colorado Springs: Focus on the Family.

Christian Broadcasting Network (CBN). *News Facts* and *News Report*: 700 Club, 1996–present.

Countdown . . . The Christian Intelligence Journal. 1995–1997. Palos Verdes, California: Hal Lindsey Ministries.

DeWeese Report, The. 1995–present. Warrenton, Virginia: American Policy Center.

Ēco.Logic. 2001–present. Hollow Rock, Tennessee: Eco Environmental Comservation Organization.

Family News from Dr. James Dobson. 1994–present. Colorado Springs: Focus on the Family.

Family Voice. 1995–present. Washington, D.C.: Concerned Women for America.

Free American, The. 1995–present. Dulles, Virginia: Freedom Alliance.

God's News Behind the News. 1995–present. St. Petersburg, Florida: Cathedral Caravan, Inc.

Hope for the World Update. 1995–present. Noblesville, Indiana: Hope for the World.

Impact, Published for Friends Reclaiming America One Heart at a Time. 1995–present. Ft. Lauderdale, Florida: Coral Ridge Ministries.

Insiders Report. 1995–present. Chantilly, Virginia: American Policy Center.

Let's Talk Prophecy. 1996–present. Roswell, Georgia: Kathy Hooper Ministries.

Media Watch. 1995–1996. Alexandria, Virginia: Media Research Center.

Midnight Call. 1995–present. West Columbia, South Carolina: Midnight Call Ministries.

News Facts and *News Report*. 1996–present. Virginia Beach: Christian Broadcasting Network (CBN), 700 Club.

Personal Update, The Newsletter of Koinonia *House*, 1995–present.Coeur d'Alene, Idaho: *Koinonia* House.

Policy Institute Newsletter, Clare Boothe Luce. 1995–present. Herndon, Virginia: Dr. Ellicot and Darla Partridge Center.

Radio Liberty Newsletter. 2000–present. Soquel, California: Radio Liberty.

Report, The Phyllis Schlafly. 2000–present. Alton, Illinois: Eagle Forum.

Report, The Sekulow. 1995–present. Virginia Beach: The American Center for Law and Justice.

Viewpoint. 1999–present. Richmond, Virginia: Save America Ministries.

World Magazine, 1994–present. Asheville, North Carolina: World.

General References

1992. *American Heritage Dictionary of the English Language, Third Edition*. New York: Houghton Mifflin Company.

1987. *Amplified Bible*. Grand Rapids, Michigan: Zondervan Bible Publishers.

Baxter, J. Sidlow. 1998. *Explore the Book*. Grand Rapids, Michigan: Zondervan Publishing House.

Benton, William. 1959. "A New Survey of Universal Knowledge." *Encyclopedia Britannica, Volume 12*. Chicago: Encyclopedia Britannica: 981.

Bryant, T. Alton. 1967. *The New Compact Bible Dictionary, Special Crusade Edition*. Minneapolis: The Billy Graham Evangelistic Association.

1991. *Concise Columbia Encyclopedia*. New York: Columbia University Press.

Elliott, Stephen P., et. al. 1992. *Webster's New World Encyclopedia*. New York: Prentice Hall General Reference.

Gower, Ralph. 1993. *The New Manners and Customs of Bible Times*. Chicago: Moody Press.

Graham, Billy. 1992. *Storm Warning*. Dallas: Word Publishing.

Howard, Philip K. 1996. *The Death of Common Sense: How Law is Suffocating America*. New York: Warner Books, A Time Warner Company.

Keach, Benjamin. 1978. *Preaching from the Types and Metaphors of the Bible*. Grand Rapids: Kregel Publications.

MacKenzie, A. Russell. 1986. *Scriptures for Study and Witnessing: A Bible Insert Covering 50 Important Topics*. Seattle: Community Chapel Publications.

Meyer, F. B. 1997. *Devotional Commentary*. Wheaton: Tyndale House Publishers, Inc.

Monteith, Dr, Stanley. 1999 to 2001. *Tape of the Month Series*. Monterey Bay, California: Radio Liberty.

Nelson, Thomas. 1986. *Nelson's Illustrated Bible Dictionary*. Nashville: Thomas Nelson Publishers.

PC Study Bible for Windows. 1994. *Reference Library Edition*. Seattle: Biblesoft.

Rotherham, Joseph Bryant. 1981. *The Emphasized Bible*. Grand Rapids: Kregel Publication.

Ryrie, Charles C., Th. D. 1977. *The Starter Study Bible: New American Standard*. Iowa Falls, Iowa: Word Bible Publishers.

Schlessinger, Dr. Laura. 1996. *How Could You Do That? The Abdication of Character, Courage, and Conscience*. New York: Harper Collins Publishers.

Seiss, J. A. 1973. *The Apocalypse: Lectures on the Book of Revelation*. Grand Rapids: Zondervan Publishing House.

Smith, Huston. 1965. *The Religions of Man*. New York: Perennial Library, Harper & Row, Publishers.

Smith, Jerome H. 1992. *The New Treasury of Scripture Knowledge, Revised and Expanded*. Nashville: Thomas Nelson Publishers.

Strong, James, LL.D., S.T.D. and John R. Kohlenberger, III. 2001. *The Strong's Expanded Exhaustive Concordance of the Bible (Red-Letter Edition)*. Nashville: Thomas Nelson Publishers.

Thompson, Frank C., D.D., Ph. D. 1964. *The New Chain-Reference Bible, Fourth Improved Edition.* Indianapolis: B. B. Kirkbride Bible Co., Inc.

Wardner, James W. 1993. *The Planned Destruction of America.* Longwood, Florida: Longwood Communications.

Wright, Fred H. 1994. *Manners & Customs of Bible Lands.* Chicago: Moody Press.

Wuest, Kenneth S. 1961. *The New Testament, An Expanded Translation.* Iowa Falls, Iowa: Riverside Book and House.

Young, Robert. 1971. *Young's Analytical Concordance.* Grand Rapids: Associated Publishers and Authors, Inc.

Index

B

C

E

H

I

J

Q

R

S

T

U

V

W

Y

Z

To order additional copies of

ABCs *of* Cultural -*Isms*

Have your credit card ready and call

Toll free: (877) 421–READ (7323)

or send $15.99* each plus $5.95 S&H** to

WinePress Publishing
PO Box 428
Enumclaw, WA 98022

or order online at: www.winepresspub.com
see also: www.DebraRaeBooks.com

*WA residents, add 8.4% sales tax

**add $1.50 S&H for each additional book ordered